Jaroslav Mihálik, Jakub Bardovič (eds.)

MIGRATION—THE CHALLENGE OF EUROPEAN STATES

Bibliographic information published by the Deutsche Nationalbibliothek

Die Deutsche Nationalbibliothek lists this publication in the Deutsche Nationalbibliografie; detailed bibliographic data are available in the Internet at http://dnb.d-nb.de.

Bibliografische Information der Deutschen Nationalbibliothek
Die Deutsche Nationalbibliothek verzeichnet diese Publikation in der Deutschen Nationalbibliografie; detaillierte bibliografische Daten sind im Internet über http://dnb.d-nb.de abrufbar.

We gratefully acknowledge receipt of the grant Jean Monnet Chair in Migration "Migration: The Challenge of European States" under the Jean Monnet Chair scheme awarded in 2016 to the Faculty of Social Sciences, University of Ss. Cyril and Methodius in Trnava, Slovakia.

∞
Printed on acid-free paper
Gedruckt auf alterungsbeständigem, säurefreien Papier

ISBN-13: 978-3-8382-1344-6
© *ibidem*-Verlag / *ibidem*-Press, Stuttgart 2019
All rights reserved.

No part of this publication may be reproduced, stored in or introduced into a retrieval system, or transmitted, in any form, or by any means (electronic, mechanical, photocopying, recording or otherwise) without the prior written permission of the publisher. Any person who does any unauthorized act in relation to this publication may be liable to criminal prosecution and civil claims for damages.

Alle Rechte vorbehalten. Das Werk einschließlich aller seiner Teile ist urheberrechtlich geschützt. Jede Verwertung außerhalb der engen Grenzen des Urheberrechtsgesetzes ist ohne Zustimmung des Verlages unzulässig und strafbar. Dies gilt insbesondere für Vervielfältigungen, Übersetzungen, Mikroverfilmungen und elektronische Speicherformen sowie die Einspeicherung und Verarbeitung in elektronischen Systemen.

Printed in the United States of America

CONTENT

FOREWORD 5

PART I: MIGRATION: THE EUROPEAN DISCOURSES

1   Politicization, Securitization, and Migration 7
2   Critical Views on the Current Migration Policy of the European Union 29
3   Immigration and Free Movement: Migration Discourses in the UK and the Visegrad Four 47

PART II: MIGRATION: SOUTHERN EUROPE

1   Foreign Policy Analysis and Migration: Case Study of Slovenia and Western Balkans 61
2   Armenian Return Migration from EU States 81
3   Moldovan Labour Migrants in EU Countries: Status and Prospects (Based on Sociological Research in Germany, Italy, Portugal, UK) 97

PART III: MIGRATION: CZECHIA AND SLOVAKIA

1   The Theory and Practice of Migration with a Focus on Czechoslovakia in the 20th Century 117
2   The Czech Extreme Right of the 21st Century at the Time of the Migration Crisis 133
3   Migration as an Issue in the 2017 General Elections in the Czech Republic 149
4   Impacts of Migration on Public Administration 171

PART IV: MIGRATION: BEYOND EUROPE

1   Immigration Policy in Australia, Canada, New Zealand and the United States 187

REFERENCES 203

ABOUT THE AUTHORS 231

FOREWORD

Dear readers,

This book is a collection of chapters by distinguished authors from academic institutions throughout Europe addressing the growing importance of migration policy making and the refugee crisis that European Union member states and other countries are currently facing.

By focusing on the most important effects that the new age of migration from third world countries has brought to the European Union we introduce analytical studies dedicated to a critical overview of the politicization, securitization and social discourse of migration. The authors critically analyze the impacts of such processes on public administration and governance and present critical views of the current migration policy of the European Union. Similarly, we discuss the rise of the radical right in EU member states, the rise of populism and the alienation of citizens from formal politics which is also caused by the growing interest in security and public safety.

The pan-European character of the publication's scope is vested in its narration; we cover the situation in Western Europe, the critical positions of the Visegrad countries as well as foreign policy making in Slovenia and the Western Balkans. Moreover, the authors address case studies from states such as Armenia and Moldova, including their labour migrants in the Western world. The authors go even further afield and cover the immigration policies of countries that are well-known for their open and liberal immigration activities such as Australia, Canada, New Zealand and the United States.

This book is one of the main outputs from the Jean Monnet Chair in Migration: The Challenge of European States, a project that the Faculty of Social Sciences at University of Saints Cyril and Methodius in Trnava, Slovakia has been granted for the period 2016-2019. The Jean Monnet Chair in Migration is a teaching and research post with a specialization in European Union studies for university professors or senior lecturers.

More specifically, the Jean Monnet Chair in Migration: The Challenge of European States carries out following activities:

1. deepens teaching in European integration studies embodied in an official curriculum of a higher education institution;
2. conducts, monitors and supervises research on EU subjects, also for other educational levels such as teacher training and compulsory education;
3. provides in-depth teaching on European integration matters for future professionals in fields which are in increasing demand on the labour market;
4. encourages, advises and mentors the young generation of teachers and researchers in European integration subject areas.

We believe the following chapters significantly contribute to the current state of academic and research discussion related to the post-modern migration and refugee crisis, involving a wide range of authors to critically rethink the current human capital and provisions guaranteeing the future of European integration and cohesion policies.

Jaroslav MIHÁLIK
Managing editor

PART I:
MIGRATION: THE EUROPEAN DISCOURSES

1 POLITICIZATION, SECURITIZATION, AND MIGRATION[1]

Jarmila Androvičová and Martina Bolečeková

During the so-called "European migration and refugee crisis", the territory of the Slovak Republic experienced less intensive migration flows of migrants and refugees compared to other Member States of the European Union (EU). Despite this, due to the intensity of immigration flows heading for the EU and the media coverage of the whole situation, and due to the fact that Slovakia has been part of the EU since 2004 and also the part of the Schengen zone since 2007, the "migration issue" became more discussed in Slovakia than ever before. Nevertheless, in our opinion, there is still lack of objective information on migration in Slovakia. That might be one of the reasons why immigration is nowadays often perceived and presented as a threat.

Currently, migration is the subject of so-called politicization and securitization. Migration and security were linked together since the moment when migration topics started to be politicized. Political representatives who actively use (and misuse) the migration issue mostly fuel the fear of immigrants. In the beginning, public order and criminality of migrants were in the centre of their attention. Immigrants were seen as provoking conflict, or susceptible to criminality. Later on, especially after the 11 September 2001 attacks, the focus was shifted on to the migration-terrorism nexus, but also to the "Islamization issue", i.e.

---

[1] This chapter is published within a research project VEGA n. 1/0949/17 "Concept of the soft power in the context of the transforming international environment and its potential for the small states strategies".

the perception of migration as threat to culture. Both areas are interlinked by the fact that the Muslim community is perceived as the most threatening community, at least in Europe.

The main aim of the following chapter is to contribute to the discussion on the "character" of migration. We will argue that simplistic labelling of migration as a security threat is not correct. To introduce broader context and prevailing attitudes towards migration processes, we will firstly explain the meaning of the terms "politicization" and "securitization" of migration. Following that, to substantiate our statement with arguments, we attempt to present a more objective and systematised view of the benefits and risks directly or indirectly linked to migration processes. The last part of the chapter offers one of the possible solutions how to address the problem of the politicization and securitization of migration.

1.1 Politicization of migration

The growing importance of migration as a political issue, and the clash of different opinions and ideologies concerning immigration, is referred to as the politicization of migration (see e.g. Castles, 2000; Bade, 2005). Historically, we can connect it to post-war migration in Western Europe. After World War II the most rapidly developing European countries (at that time it was mainly Great Britain, France, Belgium, Germany, Switzerland) recruited foreign workers from less developed European countries (at that time Spain, Italy, Greece), as well as from non-European countries (mainly culturally related countries, e.g. former colonies). These foreign workers helped to create and maintain the economic boom of the 50s and 60s. However, problems arose in the 70s. The oil crisis and economic recession meant that part of the foreign work force started to be made redundant. Furthermore, the original assumption that foreign workers would only stay temporarily proved incorrect. It was just not so easy to send people back home and to close the borders. Immigrants had slowly formed communities and lives in new countries and social networks which connected their new countries with their homelands. When the governments of Western Europe's immigration countries decided to close the borders and to stop active recruitment of foreign workers, immigrants tried to find new ways to come. They started to use family reunification rules, or they applied for asylum. It is exactly this period when the term "bogus refugee" started being used. This behaviour on the part of immigrants was perceived as "abusing" the legislation as international asylum law was designed primarily for politically persecuted persons, and this was one of the reasons why part of the domestic public and politicians started to focus their attention on the immigration problem. The second reason for growing negative attitudes towards immigrants was connected with the fact that the original assumption that workers would only stay temporarily meant that social investment into their integration had been neglected. The urban areas where immigrants were settled started to change, and enclaves of decline appeared. The clear outcome was that immigrants were still there but placed at the margins of society with poor chances for development, even for their children.

Immigration started to be problematized and politicized. Many right-wing and extremist parties and politicians adopted nationalist rhetoric and built their agenda on criticising and rejecting immigration. Despite this, the situation of immigrants did not change in the sense that they left or ceased coming. Later, when the economic and political situation in Western Europe stabilized, ethnic minorities gradually formed and stabilized their communities and also improved their social and economic situation and their civil and political rights. They also had their advocates—anti-racist movements were emerging, and new ideas of pluralism and multiculturalism advocated equality regardless of ethnic, cultural, religious origins— and their supporters saw diversity as a value with the potential for social growth and development.

The politicization of migration can thus be observed at different levels and in different social areas. In public discussion, the most apparent is immigration as a topic of political parties' campaigns. With the risk of simplifying we can say that conservative right-wing parties have been the most cautious and restrictive towards immigration. Liberal parties have been more open, as far as the economic situation permits, i.e. if immigrants are economically beneficial. Left-wing and social democratic parties have traditionally been the ones who have defended the rights of immigrants most and have highlighted their contribution to the host country, not only on the economic level, but also on the cultural level, and have insisted on respect for their human rights. This, however, differs considerably from country by country. For example, in the case of France, Sitek (2011, p. 45) states that in French political thinking there is a strong belief about the difference between right-wing and left-wing approaches to the solution of various problems, and this bipolarization became, in the second half of the 20th century, the driving force of French politics. In the 70s, according to Sitek, immigration became the main point of the disagreement between left- and right-wing political representatives. On the other hand, more recently a gradual blurring of differences between left and right can be observed even in France. For example, in the case of parties building their programmes on anti-immigration rhetoric, the shift from open neo-fascism to national populism can be observed, which paradoxically means an increase in racism, although in its diffuse and subtle form with the denial of open racism (Krzyzanowsky, Wodak, 2009, p. 1).

Apart from party conflict, other forms of conflict and struggle over immigration can be identified on different levels, for example between pro-immigration actors, such as social movements, non-governmental and international organizations and politicians, and representatives of public administrations and employers, between employers and politicians etc. Immigration policy and practice are in fact constructed by many other actors. Apart from politicians, professional and interest groups have aims that often diverge from general public opinion. Due to this, according to Freeman (In: Kostlán, 2014, p. 395) the character of immigration policy is rather open-ended. The proclamations of politicians based on anti-immigration rhetoric are accompanied by political pragmatism based on the consideration of concrete economic interests (the need for a foreign work force). The requirements of an open global economy are thus in conflict with the politicians' interest to use enemy-building rhetorical strategies[2].

Other important axes of politicization are formed around non-economic questions based on values, principles and identities. So-called new social movements often succeeded in their fight for immigrants' rights and race equality. Since in liberal democracies the violation of individual rights is forbidden and secured by higher norms (international human rights treaties) anchored in constitutions and national laws, many regulations and decisions that were in a conflict with these norms had to be annulled. Still, the prevailing tendency, closely linked with the politicization of migration, is its securitization.

1.2 Securitization of migration

We do not contest the fact that migration processes, and their consequences, can pose security risks for different subjects. However, there are few scientific studies which have verified or deny the claim that migrants in general, or specifically irregular migrants, pose a threat to the receiving state (Olejárová, 2016). On the other hand, these phenomena quite often become the object of securitization.

Recently, the circumstances mentioned above triggered the formation of a neologism—securitization. Securitization is commonly defined as the presentation[3] of a certain topic by the securitization actor[4] as a societal or existential threat for a particular reference object which requires the immediate adoption of measures (legislative or financial

---

[2] This has been recognized by Hollifield (2004) as a "liberal paradox". The liberal paradox stems from the different logic of the economic and political rationality of modern states. While economically, the state is following the ideology of the free market, politically it is defined by its territory and national sovereignty. At the same time, the state is in ambiguous situation due to the fact that it may lay down rules for entry into its territory, but cannot significantly influence the character of migration flows depending on global economics.

[3] Presentation by means of a speech act, language, interpretation or perception.

[4] The securitization actor can be an individual, organization, state, media, political parties etc.

measures) and emergency solutions for the removal of these threats (Lasicová, Ušiak, 2012).

The term securitization is closely connected to the Copenhagen school of thought and the formation of the new security agenda, which widened and deepened the understanding of security[5] and security threats[6]. For the analysis of the migration-security nexus, the importance of the Copenhagen school lies within the horizontal division of security between the narrow—mostly military—conception of security, and the wider concept that perceives security as a phenomenon involving not only military but also political, economic, environmental and societal sectors of security. The vertical division of security elaborated by the Copenhagen school develops the area of referential objects of security studies: it is not only the state itself, but also an individual, society, supranational entities or humankind as a whole who can be treated as objects of security studies (Lasicová, 2006; Ušiak, Nečas, 2011). Academics therefore reflect the migration-security nexus in correlation with state sovereignty as well as human security[7]. Also, this concept

---

[5] Security, in its broader sense, can be understood as "The state of social, natural, technical, technological system or other system that—under certain internal and external circumstances—enables fulfilling of given functions and their development on behalf of the man and society." (Šimák, 2006, p. 8)

[6] The researchers in the field of security studies (i.e. Hofreiter, Lasicová, Nečas, Ušiak) treat risk as a potential jeopardy of the subject's security, as a potential security threat.
The explanation of the term security threat is therefore based upon the definition of risk: whereas the risk represents a potential danger which can occur at acertain point in the future, the threat effects immediately, i.e. the threat can be defined as an activated risk (Šimák, 2006).

[7] The first definition of human security appeared in 1994 in the Human Development Report of the United Nations Development Programme, defining human security by using seven components: 1. economic security (i.e. reduction of poverty), 2. food security (access to basic food), 3. health security (access to health care and protection from illnesses), 4. environmental security (healthy physical environment), 5. personal security (protection from war, physical torture, domestic violence, drug use), 6. community security (survival of the traditional cultural and ethnic groups), and 7. political security (protection of the basic human rights, prevention from political oppression). This definition of human security is considered to be too vague and some researchers propose to narrow its content.

reflects objective and subjective perceptions of security based upon the evaluation and review of security risks and threats by particular subjects.

According to Didier Bigo (2002), the popularity of the securitization view cannot be explained as a response to a real threat. "*Securitization of the immigrant as a risk is based on our conception of the state as a body or a container for the polity. It is anchored in the fears of politicians about losing their symbolic control over the territorial boundaries. It is structured by the habitus of the security professionals and their new interests not only in the foreigner but in the 'immigrant'. These interests are correlated with the globalization of technologies of surveillance and control going beyond the national borders. It is based, finally, on the 'unease' that some citizens who feel discarded suffer because they cannot cope with the uncertainty of everyday life. This worry, or unease, is not psychological. It is a structural unease in a 'risk society' framed by neoliberal discourses in which freedom is always associated at its limits with danger and (in) security.*" (Bigo, 2002, p. 65)

Bigo basically points to two levels of securitization. One is the institutional level: this is related to the prioritization of security optics in the established practices of security professionals and the state administration, and is enshrined in the laws and official documents of the state. An example of such practice is e.g. the possibility for the state administration to refuse different kinds of stays with reference to the fact that the immigrant poses a security risk to society. Didier Bigo thus emphasizes everyday securitization even without significant politicization of the problem. On the other hand, Bigo also emphasizes the political level of securitization with the active engagement of politicians, media and the public. On the one hand, the discursive securitization is needed in order to legitimize institutional securitization, e.g. increased expenditure for guarding the borders. On the other hand, engaging in securitization speech acts can be politicians' strategy how to distract attention from more serious problems they do not wish to be confronted with. Finally, politicians like to stylize themselves into the position of defenders of the nation, which means they seek possible enemies.

Various authors try to explain why this topic is becoming more and more popular with the public and why support for xenophobic, populist or even extremist forces in Europe is growing. Finally, in the case of the politicization and securitization of migration, it is not always easy to answer the question of whether the initiators are primary politicians who subsequently influence public opinion, or whether the politicians are just reacting to a certain public mood that is well known to them e.g. from various opinion polls.[8]

The question of why the public is more willing to respond to policy securitization strategies is however very difficult. Zygmunt Bauman (2016) is not the only one who associates it with the widening of social inequalities within European societies. This is not only about the real and quantifiable dimension of these inequalities, but also about their symbolic level. Groups of people who feel marginalized and experience various types of disadvantage (especially in the labour market) seek people who are responsible for their bad situation (migrants). They feel satisfaction when there is someone who is even more marginalized and in comparison with whom they can suddenly feel part of the core of the society. Bauman (2016, p. 19) literally writes that migrants represent the desirable bottom that can make their own way of life a little less humiliating, and therefore a little less unbearable.

---

[8] This is not quite clear even in Slovakia, as it is true that the willingness of politicians to use anti-immigration rhetoric as part of the election campaign for the 2016 parliamentary elections was based on certain assumptions that such a strategy would probably be successful. These took into account data from past opinion polls, the fact that politicians had experience with successfully using securitization strategies against autochthonous minorities, and an increase in the popularity of the extremist Kotleba—LSNS party. However, the fact remains that in Slovakia, the main responsibility for the negative effects of the securitization campaign, which shows some of features of the so-called moral panic (see: Androvičová, 2016), lies with politicians. In a situation where there were no frames for public discussion about migration since it was a new topic for many, it is possible to say that such a one-sided portrayal of the topic (as was typical, for example, for the then prime minister Robert Fico, who in addition had most of the media space) can be considered an abuse of the topic in the pre-election struggle.

At the same time, it is important to say that these groups of people are really the most vulnerable and can potentially be negatively affected by immigration (whether this is an objective or subjective view) as they do not have the tools to deal with these negative impacts individually. Therefore, it is necessary to say that the kind of "moralizing" discourse of the middle class that addresses xenophobic attitudes (through raising awareness, education, various campaigns) may not be successful unless the structural causes that lead to such attitudes persist. At the same time, the groups in society who are often engaged in raising awareness about migration benefits are not considered legitimate by the addressees. Consequently, there is not only a barrier between the domestic population and immigrants or foreigners, but also some intra-society cleavages, e.g. between "we ordinary working people" vs. "those from NGOs" or "human rights sanctifiers" etc. The debate between such alienated sides is then very difficult.

As already mentioned above, the securitization of migration has had a rising tendency over the last few years. According Monika Wohlfeld (2014, pp. 72-73), the reasons for this can be identified as follows:

- the security agenda has become interconnected with various aspects of politics (widening of the concept of security);
- numbers of migrants and especially irregular migrants have increased;
- migration, mostly irregular migration, has started to be connected with the "war against terrorism" and other transnational threats.

The Slovak migration expert Boris Divinský (2016) points to the fact that security concerns are mainly connected to illegal[9] migration; the factor of illegality brings about many features, activities and processes

---

[9] Although we would prefer the usage of the adjective "irregular" in this context, we respect the terminology used in the original source.

unfavourable for the transit/host countries and their population as well as for the migrants themselves.

In the following overview table, the most serious migration-related problems are presented: in the first column the problems related to the transit/host countries, and in the second column the security-related problems of migrants themselves, their families and communities (stemming from their illegal entry, movement, stay and employment), as listed by Boris Divinský (2016, pp. 6-7).

Table 1: Illegal migration risks

Illegal migration risks	
Transit/host countries	Migrants/their families or communities
uncontrollable crossing of the state borders by migrants and their unauthorized entry to the states' sovereign territories	various complications and risks on the migration route (medical, security, climate-related)
activities of the organized (criminal) groups of smugglers—human smuggling	increased risk due to the activities of human smugglers and traffickers
other attendant forms of cross-border criminality	financial and professional undervaluation or even abuse of illegal migrants on the labour market by the employers in the host country
unauthorized and unregistered stay and movement of migrants on the state's territory	excessive mental load stemming from the worries over disclosure, detention or expulsion
illegal labour activities of migrants, including their illegal employment, tax evasion and involvement in the shadow economy	limited access to basic rights and services which are normally available to legal migrants
forgery or illegal manipulation with travel and identification documents, residence or work-related documents and permits	minimal opportunities to participate in programmes for the protection of vulnerable and disadvantaged groups of people in

	the state
different security threats, hinderance of the fight against terrorism and the protection of the state	higher incidence of xenophobic behaviour, prejudice and intolerance in the majority population
deepening social, ethnic, religious and political tensions in society, radicalization of society and potential violent clashes	more difficult integration of illegal migrants into the new society
rising economic, technical, personnel and administrative demands on illegal migration management, border protection and the labour market	Lack of awareness of possibilities for legalization of their stay and employment in the host country

In our opinion, the uncritical perception of migration as a security threat is not the correct approach to this phenomenon. As noted by Koser (2011), migration is a global process that can have an uncountable number of forms and thus, it is important to distinguish which particular form of migration might cause potential security concerns. Although most experts agree that it is not possible to prove a direct connection between migration and terrorism, organized crime and threats to human life or health, assumptions and prejudice often prevail over reality. This results in the establishment of new policies and diverse restrictive measures targeted against the supposed threat, which can finally negatively influence the human security of the migrants themselves. The balance between freedom and safety has been significantly shifted in favour of safety during the so-called migratory and refugee crisis in Europe. Part of this process could be considered a reaction to the real threat (terrorist attacks in France and Belgium), while on the other hand, a very important part of this process is a discursive construction of the enemy mainly designed to gain popularity in political competition.

To evaluate the impacts of migration correctly, we need to bear in mind the complexity of migration processes. In the following part we point to the multiple impacts of migration, not only the risks but its benefits as well.

1.3 Benefits and risks of migration

The most commonly cited risks connected to migration movements include the violation of borders, burdens on the health care, education and social security systems and on the housing supply; health hazards; criminality; increase in the unemployment rate of the receiving country's citizens due to more workers available on the labour market; deflation of salaries; endangerment of the native language, culture and values of the host countries; as well as cross-border problems, especially human trafficking and terrorism (Thomson, 2013). However, there are not only risks connected to migration flows. The migration processes, just like other processes involving human beings and their social interactions, bring about many positives and negatives, benefits and risks to all subjects involved. Therefore, in the following part we will focus on the diverse impacts of migration.

First of all, we need to identify who are "the subjects involved" in the migration processes. Often, when discussing migration processes and migration policies, we first think about countries and we tend to forget about the migrants themselves. When analysing benefits and risks of migration, it is necessary to distinguish at least two basic levels: the macro and the micro level of the analysis. Additionally, when analysing the impacts of migration processes on states, not only destination countries but also countries of origin and transit countries need to be taken into account.

The impacts of migration processes can be observed in all spheres of societies and lives of migrants—social and cultural, economic, political, safety etc. The following table attempts, by means of a few selected examples, to illustrate the diversity of benefits and risks which can be linked to migration processes.

Table 2: Migration processes

Migration processes			
Countries of origin		Countries of destination	
positives	negatives	positives	negatives
Remittances Employment Demography (Repatriation)	Brain drain Employment Demography	Labour force (qualified/cheap) Demography Diversity	Labour force (cheap) Demography Diversity
Migrants / families / communities			
positives		negatives	
(Decent) work Financial benefit Security Skills/Education Rights		Work conditions Separation Security Brain waste Discrimination	

When talking about countries, we could find the impacts of migration in the same area on both sides—the countries of destination, as well as the countries of origin. Sometimes, the same migration process causes a negative impact in the country of origin and a positive impact in the country of destination (for example, the emigration of a qualified labour force is a loss for the country of origin, while a gain for the receiving country); and vice versa, the same migration process can cause a negative impact in the country of destination, and a positive impact in the country of origin (for example, when an unemployed labour force leaves the home country for a country with a high unemployment rate).

On the other hand, we can also identify situations when the same migration process brings negative impacts on both sides, but there are also win-win situations. As an example of the former, situations of forced migration can be mentioned, when flows of migrants leave their home countries because of armed conflicts, and they enter neighbouring countries which have no capacity to deal with migration flows of large numbers of people.

Ideally, migration processes can, and sometimes really do, bring benefits for all. For example, overpopulated areas can benefit from emigration, and on the other hand, countries suffering from demographic decline can benefit from the immigration of a productive labour force from the overpopulated areas. (We deal with this from the other point of view in the next part.) Yet it is hardly ever that simple. Migration processes are very complex, and it is not possible to separate particular impacts from others. Moreover, some of the impacts of migration are not visible directly and it can take years till they appear in their full strength.

On the level of individual migrants (and their families and communities), the perception of benefits, but also of risks, often reflects the causes and motives for migration. In the case of voluntary migration (labour or study migration, family reunification etc.), the financial benefits, or other social benefits, would probably be perceived as the most important pull factors. In the case of forced migration, it would be probably be the security situation in the receiving country, the guarantees of basic rights or a healthy environment. Concerning risks, in our opinion both categories mentioned, i.e. voluntary and forced migrants, can face the same types of problems in the host country.

Similarly, by evaluating different combinations of impacts of migration processes in the countries of origin and destination, the same migration processes can be beneficial or risky, or beneficial and risky, to both subjects when considering the macro and the micro level. Moreover, most migration processes bring positives and negatives at the same time to all subjects involved[10].

---

[10] As an example, we model a situation of the qualified migrant who leaves his home country and his family to find better paid work in the host country. For the country of origin and his family the positive could be that the migrant will probably send his savings back to his family in the home country. The negative impact of migration for the country of origin is the loss of qualified labour; the negative impact for his family in this particular situation would be the split of the family. On the contrary, for the receiving country the qualified labour force would be a benefit, while the need to invest in integration could be perceived as a problem. For the migrant, apart from financial benefits as a positive and separation from his family as a negative, another positive could be acquiring new skills, and another negative possible discrimination in the workplace or in the receiving society.

Nevertheless, we were easily able to identify several benefits and risks of migration processes for everyone involved. It is not a general rule that if the migration process brings benefits to one subject, it necessarily has to be a risk for others. Therefore, the aim of any migration policy should be striving for a multiplication of the positive effects of migration, and, at the same time, prevention of potential risks related to this phenomenon. Such an approach assumes, above all, an ability to analyse objectively the course of migration processes, and to reveal their consequences and impacts in their whole diversity.

1.4 De-politicization of migration: the role of migration policy

The rational discussion about the positives and negatives of migration is very important in contemporary societies where migration and cultural differences are becoming an everyday reality for more and more people. Since part of the political elites, non-governmental and international organizations, social movements and the EU itself has been aware of that fact, many activities have been developed in order to prevent the undesirable problematization of migration. Policies which attempt to foster an "objective" approach to migration, based on a calculation of risks and benefits and opportunities and obstacles, have started to be called *migration management*[11]. As the policies of migration management are enhanced mostly on the international and supranational level we can say that migration management represents a globally relevant discourse (see: Geiger, Pécoud, 2010).

The main aim of the policies of migration management is to overcome the negative politicization of migration. Nowadays, the need for experts who are not part of the state apparatus, but who are more apolitical or neutral, is increasing. They can be members of the staff of international organizations like the International Organization for Migration (IOM) or domestic non-governmental organizations, or they

---

[11] The term migration management started to be used frequently in the late 90s.

can work in the private sector. Their role is to enter the legislative process: to comment on legislation that is being prepared, to submit documents and studies before important political decisions are made, and, in such a way, even to set immigration policy frameworks.

In the policies of migration management, the emphasis is put on introducing migration as a "normal" everyday part of our societies. As an example we can cite various official documents, campaigns and expert reports. In the Hague Declaration it is stated: "*It is essential to understand migration as a normal fact of life for individuals, families, communities and states*" (UN, 2002). The 2009 Human Development Report regards movement as "*a natural expression of people's desire to choose how and where to lead their lives*" (UNDP, 2009, In: Kalm, 2010, p. 32). Often, this idea is reinforced by emphasising the universality of the migration process and by setting it into historical context: "*Since human beings first emerged from the African continent many thousands of years ago, every part of the world has been subject to overlapping waves of immigration. It has thus been a central part of human history—shaping and reshaping societies, cultures and economies. The twenty-first century is no exception. The millions of migrants who circulate around Asia or Africa, or who travel from developing to developed countries today, are just the latest bearers of an age-old tradition.*" (ILO, 2004b, In: Kalm, 2010, p. 32). This view on migration is intended to introduce it as a natural activity to which people have a natural predisposition. At the same time, many documents emphasize its specificity under the current conditions of a globalized society.

Defining migration as a natural, everyday part of people's lives over the course of history is closely related to the next central feature of the global discourse on migration: migration is described as a (potentially) positive phenomenon (Kalm, 2010, p. 34). In the summary of the first Global Forum on Migration and Development (GFMD), it was stated that the Forum had "*established a new approach to migration by promoting legal migration as an opportunity for development of both origin and destination countries, rather than as a threat*" (GFMD, 2007, p.

16). The Hague Declaration states that *"we believe that migration is a normal phenomenon which can contribute positively to economic and social development, cultural richness and diversity"* (UN, 2002, p. 4). The migrants themselves are often presented positively, according to Sara Kalm (2010, p. 34), sometimes even in "heroic terms": *"Throughout human history, migration has been a courageous expression of the individual's will to overcome adversity and to live a better life"* (UN, 2006a, In: Kalm, 2010, p. 34). Migrants are often seen as having *"entrepreneurial spirit and are motivated by a determination to succeed in life"* (GCIM, 2005, p. 48).

In migration policies, the discourse of benefits for all is often applied. Migration can therefore be a mutually beneficial solution. For example, the International Organization for Migration (IOM) refers to the so-called win-win migration potential: *"Legal labour migration can thus be a so-called "win-win" solution"* (IOM, 2018a); or even the win-win-win potentials—migration can be beneficial to countries of origin and destination countries and to the migrants themselves (IOM, 2008). Of course, the precondition for the effective use of this win-win potential is effective migration management.

A similar "migration-friendly" language can also be found in some European Union documents. For example, in the 2011 Global Approach to Migration and Mobility, it is stressed that cooperation in the area of migration must be "mutually beneficial" or beneficial to all stakeholders. Mobility partnership *"provides the comprehensive framework to ensure that movements of persons between the EU and a partner country are well-governed"* (EC, 2011, p. 10). The main instruments of Mobility partnerships are visa policy and readmission agreements. The document highlights the so-called "More for more" approach: *"More for more approach, implying an element of conditionality...an appropriately sized support package geared to capacity-building, exchanges of information and cooperation on all areas of shared interest should be offered by the EU and by Member States on a voluntary basis"* (EC, 2011, p. 11).

However, it has to be said that migration management and global discourse on migration have recently become the subject of systematic criticism. This criticism on one hand focuses on the concrete practices that come out of these policies; and on the other hand, it questions some general principles. Regarding the concrete practices it is, for example, stressed that readmission agreements, which are one of the tools of mobility partnerships, are in fact the kind of pressure that the EU and its Member States can develop on non-EU countries through diplomacy. This, however, often implies the use of power: if countries do not accept the returnees, they risk losing development aid or other forms of cooperation with the EU and naturally, many countries cannot afford it. Several IOM activities have also been the subject of systematic criticism (see: e.g. Georgi, 2010). For example, the so-called Assisted Voluntary Returns and Reintegration programme (AVRR) is called by Andrijasevic and Walters (2010) "neoliberal deportations"; they question the willingness of these returnees, and the effectiveness of the reintegration help provided (e.g. Coakley, 2011).

More general criticism emphasize that the whole of migration management is, in fact, a way of de-politicizing migration. Geiger and Pécoud (2010, p. 11) emphasize that *"the very notion of 'migration management' is characterized by its apolitical and technocratic nature, and its popularity (to the detriment of other notions such as 'the politics of migration') is in itself a way of de-politicizing migration. Policies would not result from political choices, but from "technical" considerations and informal decision-making processes on the most appropriate and successful way of addressing migration."* This de-politicization is further evident in the "triple-win" objective, which negates the existence of divergent interests and of asymmetries of power and of conflicts (both between and within countries). It is also perceptible in the managerial/technical language used by migration management actors. In their view, there are policies that work and policies that don't work—hence the popularity of notions such as "good" (or even "best") practices. For whom and from which point of view they are good or best is often blurred.

The goal of such criticism is to point to the fact that migration management policies, however hard they try to be seen as benefiting all, simply represent the interests of the more powerful states and actors (for example, the IOM as an international organization is funded mainly by the governments of the developed countries, which means countries of destination whose interests are often different from those of the countries of origin). The existence of divergent interests is thus denied, which critics consider to be less fair than to admit them and fight them. At the same time, what, on the one side, seems to be the democratization of migration policies, can in fact be the delegation of decision-making to experts who are not subject of democratic control.

Rodrigues (2001) points to the paradox of taking measures and standards aimed to increase the transparency of decision making in the area of immigration and subjecting them to public scrutiny. The inclusion of private sector players into these processes is liable to cause an overestimation of their capacity to determine such complex sensitive issues as migration. At the same time, providing various indicators measuring the success of adopted measures provokes a technical debate, which gives the impression that it is possible to solve these complex socio-economic problems by simple technological solutions. Politicians and governments are making their decisions based on the materials and arguments of external experts and organizations and by can thus escape a political debate about immigration policy. An important element of de-politicization is also "hyperlegalism" in relation to higher standards and regulations (such as international law or EU legislation). Their strict interpretation and fulfilling the minimum standards often prevents value-based and ideological debate on immigration policy. Politicians declare that their actions are standard and comply with EU legislation and international instruments but in fact they close the debate about whether they are correct and necessary.

At the same time, policies of migration management are often costly, which contrasts with the officially declared goal of effectiveness. Preventing undesirable forms of mobility has gone hand in hand with statistical planning and building up the extensive systems of expertise dedicated to the bureaucratic calculation, assessment and dispersal of risk information. Governing through risk management requires the constant monitoring, adaptation and correction of processes of communication. It requires substantial personnel and technical capacities. Moreover, it presupposes the reconfiguration of power and authority in regulating migration by involving additional institutions and actors in the process. In fact, the real power over migration policies and processes is in the hands of institutions that are not the subject of democratic control: they are led by managers, and not by elected representatives of the people.

Conclusion

In this chapter, we pointed to the signs and sources of the politicization and securitization of migration; and we also focused on benefits and risks that are directly or indirectly linked to migration processes. We used this approach to validate our statement that migration, in general, should not be labelled as security threat without critical evaluation of respective migration flows and the impacts they cause. Migration processes are too complex to be easily and definitively evaluated with regard to whether they bring more positives or negatives. We tried to underline the fact that when evaluating benefits and risks, we need clearly to identify the level of the analysis, and also whose security we are referring to.

In our view, migration can bring many benefits to all subjects involved. Nevertheless, migration as a political topic is being significantly securitized. Within political debates on migration, as well as in the media, the security view prevails over all other aspects. At the same time, we have to admit that this approach seems to be very successful as a political strategy. We do not contest the security perception of migration in general, as long as the argumentation which is being used is objective. But we consider it a problem when the information which is being presented is incorrect or false; and when it is misused as a tool to gain political capital.

In the final part, we presented one of the possibilities which could help to de-politicize and de-securitize migration: to entrust decision making on questions concerning migration to experts (whether on the national level, the supranational EU level or on the global level). The problem of decisions that are taken outside standard democratic procedures lies in the fact that it is not necessary to explain these decision to the public (which is of course very demanding and often unrealistic in the context of the negative politicization mentioned above). In the long run, however, this might mean that people will not identify with such policies. When they are not able to express their disagreement in the standard election process, it can be easier to manipulate and mobilize them against these policies.

In addition, migration is a very specific topic. In some cases, expert decision making can be accepted or even perceived as desirable (e.g. in areas where most people respect the fact that they do not understand the problem and do not want to engage in its solution). However, migration is about belonging—it is about the question: "Who will be part of our country, who will be our neighbour or the classmate of our children?" And that is a topic which can easily mobilize the interest of the broader public, and which is perceived as very sensitive. Therefore, in our opinion, migration is, and must remain, a topic of public debate and a political problem, although it is certainly very harmful when politicians understand it only as a tool for obtaining political points—in any way possible, regardless of the consequences.

2 CRITICAL VIEWS ON THE CURRENT MIGRATION POLICY OF THE EUROPEAN UNION

Milan Čáky

Migration as a phenomenon, whether individual or mass, has always been present in the history of mankind. History shows that if migrants arriving *en masse* in the receiving country do not adapt to the culture and civilization of the domestic population but dominate it this can lead to the demise of indigenous peoples. The current migration crisis faced by Europe is caused not only by environmental problems but also by the security policy of the Western powers. The European Union's institutions, especially the European Commission, were not prepared for this humanitarian crisis, linked to the uncontrolled mass arrival of numerous migrants from Africa and the Islamic world. Mass migration was mainly of an economic nature, with the Brussels administration approaching it as a migration covered by UN resolutions on the protection of (and especially individual) refugees and the respect for their rights. The political consequences of the failure of the European Union institutions to tackle the consequences of illegal mass migration was a threat to the security of the citizens of the Member States of the European Union. The migration crisis, to which the institutions of the European Union reacted late and slowly, has created a general crisis in the Union. It has broken with Member States to tackle this crisis and ultimately has begun to touch upon the crisis of values on which the European Union is created.

2.1 Migration as a historical phenomenon

Migration as a historical phenomenon has always been linked to human history and has been natural part of it. Looking at the history of ancient times, evidence has been found in constantly moving tribes and ethnics, for example, during the period of the Roman Empire, where the Roman incursions stimulated the migration process. As an example, we can mention the migration of many members of the Jewish tribe not only to the territory of Greece and to ancient Italy, but also to other parts of Europe.

In the process of their migration, the Jews also brought the ideology of Christianity and made a significant contribution to the extinction of the original civilization values of paganism, an important ideological value of the Roman Empire, which resulted in the migration of the Germanic tribes. The expansion of Christianity into the space of Europe and the world and its institutionalization in a steady form has become one of the important elements of Western civilization.

Western education has also greatly enriched, for example, the tribes of Arabs, temporarily living on the Pyrenean Peninsula—on the territory of today's Spain. Colonization of both parts of the Americas—North and South can be regarded as part of the migration of Europeans to the new territories. It is possible to make an important historical conclusion from the processes of colonization of both parts of America—since Europeans were civilized at a considerably higher level, they destroyed not only the culture of the original civilizations on the American continent (for example the Aztecs, Mayans, Incas and all the tribes in North America), they have taken on their territory, creating a new civilization at a qualitatively higher level, with little or no regard for the indigenous population.

For example, in the process of long-term formation of the American national identity, the opposition between the emerging nation from the ranks of the original immigrants—the settlers, i.e. the American nation—and the endogenous peoples of Europe that existed on an ethnic basis. As stated by Baršová and Barša (2005) this contradiction reflects the fundamental difference between the New and Old World countries, so the creation of the new American nation was overlapping with the immigration and settlement of the new country. New exogenous nations have emerged that have universalist character with the particular features of one or another ethnic group. However, multiculturalism including religious ideologies that were present in the process of creating a new universal nation did not become a state ideology.

Historically, migration processes were also taking place in Central Europe. They were mostly the result of significant changes in power and stimulated by the emergence of new ideologies By placing them on the territory of Slovakia, we can talk about the migration of Czech exiles— connected with the cultural influence, because they brought about the use of the Czech liturgical language and encouraged the reflection on the liturgical understandable language but also on its written form. The German colonization of towns in Slovakia, the arrival of the German Saxons, and the emergence of the German bourgeois state significantly contributed not only to the growth of towns in Slovakia but also to the development of crafts and trade, as the German colonists came from an economically and civilizationally developed environment and secured the development of trade with more advanced cities in Germany. There was no civilization contradiction between the civilization of the native— domestic population and the colonists because they all professed Christian values, and on these principles created a secular and sacral culture.

The civilization benefit of the strangers in our territory is indisputable from today's point of view. There were practically no problems between the indigenous population and the descendants of immigrants until the World War II. Under the influence of the Nazi ideology on the theory of German superiority the political representatives of the descendants of the strangers formulated the ideology of ethnic superiority that the original inhabitants understood as endangering their existence on their own historical territory. This was politically pronounced, for example, in the attitude of the Sudeten Germans to Bohemia during the Protectorate period (1939—1945) and the subsequent decision on the deportation of the Sudeten Germans, but also in solving the issue of the Carpathian Germans in Slovakia—their voluntary or forced departure from the territory of Slovakia.

After World War II, the largest political migration wave in Europe was recorded by changes in the pre-war frontiers, especially in Germany, and the removal of Sudeten Germans from Czechoslovakia and Germans from Silesia. Responding to war conflicts that affected the civilian population, the emergence of a bipolar world and dictatorial regimes, disrespecting human rights, it was the universal will of the UN member states to accept basic agreements to secure the rights of politically persecuted refugees. That is why, on July 28, 1951, the Geneva Convention was adopted dealing with their status and rights, confirmed by the United Nations in 1967.

It is clear from the text that the right to asylum and the benefits thereon have a person who has left its country primarily for political persecution and persecution as a result of the violation of fundamental human rights not because of an escape from a fair punishment for committing a crime. The Convention does not recognize the right of asylum for migrants who have left their country for economic reasons—economic migrants. What is important and is not currently being ignored is that the right of economic migrants, migrants who migrate for economic reasons, is not considered to be a human right.

2.2 Civilizational migration from the beginning of integration processes in Europe

Legal migration has not only had economic reasons but has gained a civilization character. Its growth especially since the beginning of integration processes in Europe, has been linked to the need of a new labour force in the countries of the European Economic Community—for example the rise of a large Turkish enclave in Germany or the arrival of a large number of inhabitants from the original colonies to European countries. It was a largely controlled migration of former colonial countries to European metropolises: the arrival of numerous migrants to France from the Maghreb countries (mainly from Tunisia, Morocco and Algeria) and sub-Saharan African countries, the spread of enclaves of migrants by coming from the original colonies in Great Britain, Netherlands, Belgium and others. Such migrants often had the citizenship of the European country concerned when they arrived at

European metropolises, and most were involved in the labour process to make economic gains for the recipient country. At the same time, they brought their culture to the new countries, which they tried to preserve. Therefore, West European officials have long viewed this process as a new and positive phenomenon that they considered *"multiculturalism"* enriching the original culture of European nations with the culture that migrants brought from their countries. It can be said that a significant proportion of migrants of this period after initial problems are basically accepting European values, civil, social (labour) and party cultural as well as integrating into the existing society. Official institutions have pointed to their economic benefits, although it may be a fact that they mostly occupied undemanding jobs that the domestic population was not interested in. Legitimate migrants constituted a large workforce that was missing mainly in industrialized Western European countries (Germany, France, Great Britain, Sweden, etc.).

A large proportion of legal and illegal migrants after arriving in the European Union grouped themselves into ethnic communities that did not show an effort to integrate into the majority population. In France they expanded the ethnic communities that existed during the French colonial politics (Annamites, North Africans, Africans from Sub-Saharan African countries, French Caribbean residents), or created new ethnic enclaves. In Germany, a large Turkish ethnic community was formed, the Indians, Pakistani, Anglo-African Africans, and so on.

Most resonated problem has been associated with the strengthening of influence of those communities that professed Islamic faith. The rise in the influence of Islamic religion was particularly noticeable in France, where the arrival of new migrants increased the number of Muslims and the influence of the Islamic community, which saw the realization of their religious rights—including the emergence of new mosques as their natural law and the beginning of social exclusion. Comprehensive Islamic communities have expanded their influence in the UK, Germany, Sweden, and later in Italy, Austria, the Netherlands and other Western European countries.

The import of Islam into the Christian environment in Europe and unwillingness or inability to resolve its social status have increased social exclusion, leading to the radicalization of these communities and their opposition to the majority population. One outcome of this process which was already evident in the early 1990s was a growing hatred of the majority society leading to organized terrorist attacks that had social causes but also a religious background. In France, these terrorist attacks were performed by domestic Islamists in connection with Islamic radicals abroad. The European Union administration in Brussels has not evaluated these expressions of growing Islamic terrorism as a systemic problem associated with Islamic ideology but only as a problem that arose as a result of the social exclusion of individuals or groups. It did not consider the growing influence of radical Islam as a problem associated with expanding the influence of Islamic radicals in the countries of the European Union and their connection to the emerging Islamic state in the territory of Iraq and Syria.

Security risks in the countries of Western Europe have increased with the arrival of a large wave of migrants since 2015 as a result of the worsening living conditions in Sub-Saharan African countries and the irresponsible intervention of Western countries in the Middle East and North Africa. The protracted military conflict in Afghanistan, the economic breakdown in Iraq caused by the US military invasion, the aid to civil war in Syria and Libya did not lead to the establishment of democratic regimes but to the economic devastation of these countries, the creation of the Islamic state and power division that caused an unprecedented wave mass migration not only to neighbouring countries (Turkey, Jordan, Lebanon) but also to Europe. The Arab Spring, the declared goal of which was to create democratic regimes (for example, in Tunisia, Libya, Egypt, Syria), has missed its effects because, as it seems, has been a catalyst for the rise of political Islam. But its real goal could have also included the control of oil extraction and the attempt not to impose other powers on these sources of oil—such as China which was evident, for example, in Libya. The military intervention of the Western powers has resulted in an expansion of the influence of radical Islam and, as a result, led to Arab tragedy, which can be clearly seen in the devastating multi-year civil war in Syria, in destroyed Iraq or Libya. It opened the way for the emergence of the Islamic state, the civil war and the subsequent mass migration of the people of these countries to Europe.

Both legal and illegal migration to Europe, although in limited numbers has existed as a social or political phenomenon over the long term, and from a historical point of view we can see it as a natural phenomenon that accompanied European history. However, since 2014, the number of illegal migrants to the European Union has started to grow unusually which we consider to be a new phenomenon which has not previously existed. The European Union's administration, in particular the European Commission and its leaders, was slow in addressing this migration problem. Frontex, which was set up in 2004 as the European Border and Coast Guard Agency, based in Warsaw, but with insufficient staff (about 315) and insufficient budget (€ 250 million), could not face this problem because its missions and roles include, inter alia, the sole responsibility for controlling the external borders of the country on whose territory these borders are located.

On 13 May 2015, the European Commission adopted an important document—Action Plan against migrant smuggling for 2015-2020, published on 27 May 2015 (European Commission, 2015). It identified the European Migration Agenda for that period in which one of the priorities of the fight against migrant smuggling has been an effort to prevent criminal networks from gaining profit from the migration crisis. At the same time, in specific steps, it aimed to deter refugees from migrating to Europe.

The document has already stated that illegally created networks carry a huge number of migrants, making huge amounts of money for this activity endangering the lives of migrants. Moreover, the document states that smugglers get the most money, they often push hundreds of people to vessels that are not suitable for sailing or use trucks. It is clear from the report that illegal migration by sea, especially on the eastern and Mediterranean routes, is growing radically. While there were 225,000 migrants coming through this route in 2014, the Western Balkan route has significantly increased the number of migrants coming to the European Union. The report also demonstrates that migrant smuggling profits are worth millions of Euros (European Commission, 2015).

Interestingly, none of the measures proposed by this Action Plan for the European Institutions has been fully implemented.[12] The European Union institutions could not take the necessary decisions to protect the borders of the Member States of the European Union.

For example, only in 2015 around 800,000 illegal migrants came to Europe. In the following year, the migration wave to the European Union culminated especially in Germany. The number of incoming migrants has increased as a result of the German chancellor *"Flüchtlinge Willkommen"* policy, as well as direct political and financial support from the European Union, in particular the European Commission and European Commissioner Dimitris Avramopoulos, responsible for the EU migration policy. Migrants created the so-called Balkan migration route, which began in Turkey and Egypt, passed through Greece, Macedonia, Serbia, Hungary, Austria into the target country—Germany and Sweden. This migration wave has been uncontrolled and had a mass character.

The number of illegal migrants exceeded one million in 2016. The German government placed them in accommodation facilities where they were subjected to documents check (if any) and to an official hearing to determine the eligibility of asylum. The Balkan route has caused considerable difficulties for the governments of the transit states that have tried to prevent this mass transit migration. The massive and uncontrolled influx of migrants meant a serious security risk not only for transit countries but also for the Member States of the European Union, as Islamic radicals and militants of the Islamic state were also among the migrants. The uncontrolled crossing of the borders of the Member States of the European Union also meant violation of the agreement on the

---

[12] For example, the revision of the EU rules on the transfer of migrants by 2016, the drawing up and monitoring of the list of suspicious vessels, the financial support of the EU Member States affected by the mass migratory wave.

protection of the Schengen area. Therefore, the Hungarian government has decided to prevent this massive and uncontrolled migration. In order to comply with the rules on the protection of the Schengen area, the existing Dublin agreement has built a barrier at its southern border—a fence intended to stop massive uncontrolled migration and to allow crossing of state borders to persons of foreign countries only under the common Schengen border agreement. The Hungarian government has in fact concluded the Balkan migration route with this measure.

Uncontrolled illegal mass migration into European Union countries was primarily due to economic reasons. Such uncontrolled migration has become both an economic and security risk for Europe. It has increasingly been shown that the arrival of such a large mass of migrants, especially from the Muslim world, can lead to problematic relations with the domestic population.

After the Balkan route a new route was created—Mediterranean route to Italy and Spain. This route was mainly due to migrants from Sub-Saharan Africa, who crossed the Mediterranean Sea and the Saharan Desert on their way, as well as numerous migrants from the Maghreb countries.

The *welcome* policy, which was also announced in some Arabian mass media, greatly encouraged illegal mass migration into Europe, leading to an enormous increase in the number of illegal migrants who decided to go to Europe, especially to Germany. The bureaucracy of the European Union in Brussels and the institutions of the European Union, in particular the European Commission, did not manage the migration situation. The European Commission and its President Jean Claude Juncker, and European Commissioner for Migration Dimitris Avramopoulos, unilaterally interpreted the EU treaties, and despite the disagreement of the Visegrad countries forced the system of compulsory reallocation of migrants, although it was already apparent that such a system would not work.

Thus, it encouraged not only another massive illegal migration to Europe, but ultimately allowed the smugglers to obtain illegal financial gain from this activity. The Brussels bureaucracy of the European Union believed that the aging population of Europe needs to be tackled by migration from the third world.

This has weakened general security in the Member States of the EU and the security of its citizens. The activities of some European Union institutions dominantly by the European Commission contributed to the process of political destabilization within the European Union. The cohesion between the EU Member States and EU institutions has significantly weakened. Representatives of the European Commission (in particular its President and some Eurocommissioners) have exercised competences that have affected the sovereignty of the Member States.

European Commission President Jean Claude Juncker, in charge of the European Commission's management, found it impossible to name, formulate and implement appropriate solutions to the problems that had arisen. The European Commission reacted slowly, which was politically destabilizing. European Commissioner for Migration Policy Dimitris Avramopoulos and European Commission President Jean Claude Juncker insisted on the adoption of a permanent mechanism for redistributing migrants (mandatory quotas) although it was obvious that this mechanism would be unsuccessful with the Member States rejecting it. They have not respected the will of some Member States of the Union, which created a crisis of trust between the institutions of the European Union and some Member States. Federica Mogherini, EU foreign policy representative, has been unable to communicate effectively with Turkey and Libya and to ensure that these countries protect their borders more effectively and prevent the uncontrolled and illegal mass movement of migrants in the Mediterranean. The European Commission has failed to take effective measures to protect the external borders of the Member States of the Union in this area. The treaty with Turkey on the detention of refugees in Turkey was negotiated by German chancellor.

Robert Schuman who came from Luxembourg has made a significant contribution at that time to the creation and development of the integration of Europe by creating the first transnational community that has become the basis of a unifying Europe and has worked for united and pro-European manner. Jean Claude Juncker, also from Luxembourg, as the President of the European Commission failed to face the current new European challenges and undertake the necessary measures to protect the cohesion of the Member States of the Union, to find a new form of European identity, because at the time of its operation, the European Union is undergoing a serious political crisis.

The protection of the borders of the Mediterranean countries, in particular the border with Libya and the strengthening of Frontex's competences, has been a good move on the part of the European Commission, but this move has come late. Frontex has not yet been able to effectively protect the Mediterranean border of Italy, Greece, Malta or Spain. In this area, it was a passive spectator of organized illegal mass migration. The organization could not effectively prevent the arrival of large numbers of illegal migrants across the Mediterranean Sea.

Although it was clear that the vast majority of illegal migrants do not come for political but economic reasons, the Euro Bureaucrats criticized the Prime Minister of Hungary Viktor Orbán—and this is a paradox—for complying with the Schengen Agreement by building a fence. The proposals and approaches of the V4 countries to address the emerging migration crisis of the Euro-bureaucracy were rejected, even though their rational meaning had already been shown.

2.3 The political consequences of the migration crisis

These consequences were most evident in the receiving countries—Germany, Austria, France. The development has soon shown that German welcome policy has not been sufficiently reconsidered by its formulation to the public with the words "We can do it!" There has been increasing social and security risk of uncontrolled reception of such a large number of migrants who often refused to return to their home country after asylum rejection. Security risk in Europe has been manifested not only in the increase in crime but also in the serious assaults committed by migrants (let´s mention Charlie Hebdo and Bataclan in Paris, the assassinations in Nice, Cologne, Berlin and others).

As a result of rising social tensions, rising crime rates and a deteriorated security situation, also political tensions have increased. In Germany, it was not only the emergence of the Pegida movement and the anti-immigration party Alternative für Deutschland, but also the critique of Merkel's policy by the Bavarian CSU coalition partner, headed by the party chairman, and also by the Bavarian government chairman Horst Seehofer who demanded effective protection of German borders, especially Bavaria, through which the largest number of illegal migrants have arrived. Political tensions and changes in the attitudes of the Germans and their official immigration policy were strongly reflected in the results of the 2017 Federal Assembly elections. The political party Alternative für Deutschland won 12.6% of the vote in the polls acquiring seats in Federal Parliament (Bundestag) and becoming part of the German political scene. The fact that migration policy had a significant impact on internal policy is evidenced by serious internal political changes. For example, the unusually long and complicated way of negotiating among coalition political parties in setting up the federal government after the Bundestag elections in 2017.

Although the chancellor, after several months of interviews, managed to form a government cabinet, Horst Seehofer a major critique of the immigration policy has become the Minister of the Interior, whose competencies included the issue of border protection. Parliamentary elections showed a significant shift in German internal politics: Merkel's political position was significantly weaker than in previous years. The differences in political attitudes of Seehofer as a new interior minister and German chancellor became increasingly apparent and took the form of open political misgivings, perhaps even a political crisis, which was reflected in the possibility of the resignation of the Interior Minister. While Merkel, in relation to the V4 countries, sought to bring them together with the Brussels bureaucracy into a system of permanent reallocation of migrants, Seehofer expressed a different stance and defended the V4 countries.

For example, in an interview for Die Welt am Sonntag, he stressed that the countries of Eastern Central Europe are not willing to show solidarity with the reception of migrants, according to the idea of European bureaucrats from Brussels, "*because they have their historical experience of the struggle for freedom*", "*they want to decide who to receive*" which according to him has its origin in their history, culture, literature, in their liberal thinking (ČTK, 2018). He recalled that these countries are rejecting a common redistribution system enforced at European Union level because for hundreds of years they have been dominated by foreign states and therefore now insist on the principle of self-determination and national identity.

The German office, together with French President Emmanuel Macron, has for a long time been privileged to decide not only on the important personnel issues of the European Union, but under the general and inconclusive term of the European values they also want to decide on a further common EU migration policy based on the European asylum system. This should aim to show the solidarity of the European Union member states with the European solutions to the migration crisis, e.g. an agreement on the redistribution of legal or illegal migrants to all EU Member States. Merkel's statement, which was echoed at the other European Council meeting in June 2018, when it stated that Europe needs a robust asylum system that resists crises, is well known.

The countries rejecting the joint migration policy—especially the V4 countries—have been reminded that European solidarity (apparently the European funds) is not a one way route. This approach has long been underlined by the former President of the European Parliament and, until recently, the President of the German SPD, Martin Schulz, who declared that German Social Democrats continue to bind distribution of European funds with the re-allocation of migrants, in line with the principle of accepting migrants.

This policy was joined by French President Emmanuel Macron, speaking at the European Parliament in April 2018, emphasizing the common internal solidarity of the Member States of the European Union, declared the need to adopt a system of quotas governing the reallocation of migrants between the Member States of the European Union, to ensure the geopolitical and economic recovery of the European Union.

Macron (by the way, a former employee of Banque Privee de Rothschild in Paris, formerly a pro-activist of the Socialist Party) has spoken out for a multi-racial Europe and open door policy, and hence for the further transfer of the African population to Europe because he believes not only in helping the economy but in European tradition and honour.

At a meeting of the European Council on 29 June 2018, which sought to find a way out of the current migration crisis in Europe, he expressed—in a similar vein to Merkel's office—the need to adopt the European solution to the migration crisis. He strengthened the adoption of a common agreement on the establishment of contact centres in Europe, which would serve for the rapid adoption and redistribution of political migrants and the rejection of illegal migrants not meeting the set criteria, in cooperation with the UN to implement the regional disembarkation and admission of migrants to centres established outside Europe, expanding the European Union's influence in cooperation with Turkey and African states and adjusting the Dublin Treaty. Adopting these measures would not mean to stop illegal mass migration into Europe nor would they be viable, as Turkey, Libya and other African states have refused to set up additional camps for migrants in their territory.

The irresponsible and almost anti-European policy of the Brussels bureaucracy and some European politicians on migration policy has led to an increase in the impact of anti-immigration political parties that have been politically classified as right-wing extremist. It turns out that the increase in the impact of AfD in Germany is not a random or exceptional phenomenon, but that it is the political response of dissatisfied citizens to the policy of the government and the European Union. In Germany, for example, these policy changes seem to be longer and may lead to a rethink of political attitudes to migration policy in other countries of the European Union as well. Notwithstanding the political positions of the V4 countries which were clearly defined on the issue of the migration policy of the Brussels bureaucracy the change in the political forces in Germany has influenced the growth of critical attitudes in Italy to the migration as well as economic policy of the Brussels bureaucracy.

An anti-systemic anti-migration Lega Nord was set up in Italy, with Matteo Salvini, a Member of the European Parliament, and an anti-system Movement of Five Stars headed by Beppe Grillo and Luigi Di Maio.

The issue of illegal immigration was triggered not only by the criticism of Brussels' economic policy, which according to the parties has deprived Italian economy, but primarily illegal migration policy, was triggered before the parliamentary elections in early March 2018. Matteo Salvini has already proposed in the election program that the European Union should help tackle the causes of mass illegal migration from those areas that are more disadvantaged.

Italy would support such projects directly in their countries of implementation because Africa is not in Italy and Italy cannot accept all migrants. Already in the La Lega Nord electoral program in the parliamentary elections held on 4 March 2018, the Salvini Party demanded, inter alia, blocking the landing of migrants on the Italian coast, repatriating all immigrants who have come to Italy illegally, resuming border controls in order to stop inflows of migrants by using the rejection policy and the control of public funds used for the receiving of migrants. In relation to the Brussels policy, the Salvini party's program called for a revival of Italy's national sovereignty, a lesser restriction on the part of the European Union to Italy, the political and monetary sovereignty of Italy, a revision of treaties aimed at restoring the sovereignty of the Member States, greater legislative powers for the regions, and a shift in relations of EU and the Russian Federation (Lega Nord electoral program, 2017).

The criticism of the Brussels migration policy was a central theme in parliamentary elections. Lega Nord gained 17.63% of votes, which meant that together with the Five Stars Movement, they formed the basis of today's coalition government in which Matteo Salvini received the post of Interior Minister and Vice-President of the Italian Government. The Lega Nord (similarly the Five Stars Movement) in its electoral program declared that its political goal is not to leave the European Union or exit the Eurozone and abandon the common European currency but remain a member of the European Union, assuming that all the treaties which restrict the exercise of full and legislative sovereignty and return to the European Economic Community before the Maastricht Treaty. Lega Nord declared that Italy would require changes to the basic treaties of the European Union not only on access to migration policy but also on the question of Italy's position in the EU. Salvini pointed to the unacceptability of the EU's migration policy—a policy of organized labour and labour import into Italy and other countries of the Union, linked to illegal and organized smuggling of migrants under the pretext of rescuing migrants, benefiting not only African immigrants and misguided NGOs in the Mediterranean but also the Italian mafia.

Conclusion

The EU's migration policy has revealed serious contradictions between the Brussels administration, in particular the European Commission and the many Member States of the Union. The European Commission is striving to take on more and more competences at the expense of the Member States and to decide on them also on matters that are of major concern to the Member States. Some Member States consider this to be a threat to their independence, which gives them dissatisfaction with the Brussels administration's policy, in particular the European Commission. The refusal of decisions by the Brussels administration is justified by reference to the principle of sovereignty of the people. The dissatisfaction with the Brussels policy has not only the effect of non-systemic political parties, but also the weakening of the political cohesion of the European Union's Member States, based on their defense of national interests and the rejection of Brussels migration policy.

The definition of European values and European solutions, as the Brussels bureaucracy understands in substance, is fundamentally contrary to the European traditional values (especially Christianity) in which Robert Schuman created European integration. Instead of

Christianity as a common European value, European bureaucracy actually supports the creation of parallel communities, refusing to accept European culture. They stand in opposition to national culture (as part of a common European culture) and gender ideology. This weakens and changes the original European moral values (family, country, nation, etc.), which are the essence of European civilization.

The current Brussels administration is unable to protect the real European values on which European cohesion is based. It creates a line of conflict between the EU institutions and the Member States of the Union, thereby jeopardizing the further existence of the European Union and the values on which it is based, the European Commission has not managed the challenges that have emerged from the migration crisis. With its indecision, it was unable to protect the borders of the European Union and exposed the long-standing European unity to the danger of disintegration.

The current Brussels administration has failed to grasp the fundamental differences between Western democracy, as it has been forming for centuries in Europe, and political Islam. Political Islam is a source of Islamic radicalism. Compatibility between political Islam and Western democracy is questioned.

3 IMMIGRATION AND FREE MOVEMENT: MIGRATION DISCOURSES IN THE UK AND THE VISEGRAD FOUR

Karen Henderson

At first sight, comparing migration discourses in the United Kingdom (UK) and the Visegrad Four states (Czech Republic, Hungary, Poland and Slovakia) may appear a rather difficult task. As Valerie Bunce once put it when discussing democratisation in different parts of the world, 'Are we comparing apples with apples, apples with oranges (which are at least varieties of fruit), or apples with, say, kangaroos (Bunce, 1995, pp. 112-3)? In other words, are the cases perhaps too different to compare as there are too many contrasting variables to reach any valid conclusion about causation?

To name but a few divergences between case studies, the countries have very different histories, both in terms of processes of modernisation and of state-building and also, crucially, different experiences of democracy, with all four Visegrad states subjected to Soviet-style communist rule for over 40 years after 1948. In contemporary times, they have also had radically different rates of immigration, as will be discussed below, with the UK having far more experience of dealing with immigration than the other states. In addition, to touch upon the variable most interesting to control, governments have pursued very different attitudes to immigration and the integration of foreigners. In the case of both the UK and the Visegrad Four, however, recent discourses have been influenced by sovereignty considerations relating to European Union (EU) powers over the movement of persons.

Yet taking unlike case studies is often useful in highlighting broad issues that can sometimes be overlooked in more detailed studies. This brief chapter looks in particular at three areas: the differences in patterns of immigration and experience of immigration; the central arguments about immigration in popular and political discourse; and the portrayal of 'us' and 'them'. Analysis focuses primarily on the UK and the Slovak case studies, but because Visegrad Four collabouration has been central to many official Slovak initiatives regarding migration in recent years, examples from other Visegrad states—in particular Hungary—are also mentioned. In the last section the paper looks at possible reasons for the current rather hostile Slovak reactions to immigration.

A final reflection will be introduced at this early stage in the paper, although it might normally be found in a conclusion contemplating future research directions. While the British and Slovak case studies appear so different that systematic comparison is hard, there are also 'in between' countries that throw up interesting reflections on both. Ireland, in particular, has much in common with both of the very different case studies under discussion here. Like Slovakia, Ireland is a small state on the periphery of Europe with a history of suppression by larger neighbours, and both have long histories of emigration, with family stories of relatives settled in the USA. Yet when Ireland rather suddenly became a country of immigration after the EU's eastern enlargement in 2004, it reacted far more hospitably than when Slovakia was faced with accepting Syrian refugees in 2015. A Special Eurobarometer survey in October 2017 shows that the Irish are second only to the Swedes when it comes to regarding immigration from outside the EU as an opportunity, rather than a problem, whereas Slovakia, as well as Hungary and the Czech Republic, were among the least welcoming states (European Commission, 2018a, p. 58). The regular Standard Eurobarometer surveys also indicate that Slovaks (and Czechs) are among the least positive EU member states regarding immigration of people from other EU member states, whereas the Irish had the most positive views of all EU member states towards immigrants from both third countries and EU member states (European Commission, 2018b, T119-T120).

At the same time, Ireland also has much in common with the UK. It faced a sharp increase in immigration after the 2004 EU eastern enlargement, having joined the UK and Sweden as the only EU member states to introduce free movement of labour immediately, rather than delaying by up to seven years. Like the UK, it was a particularly attractive destination because the English language enables more immigrants to function easily in the labour market. It also, like the UK, lacks some of the more restrictive continental European bureaucracy. There are no identity cards for Irish citizens, so EU citizens do not have to register either, and it also has a public health care system, rather than an insurance-based one Prior to the economic crisis of 2008, it also had a strong economy, although it was then affected by the recession far worse than the UK. Indeed, Irish research based on the European Social Survey shows that that the recession led to the Irish having rather negative views, by west European standards, of immigration (McGinnity, Kingston, 2017; McGinnity et al., 2018). Yet, unlike the UK, Ireland did not turn against the EU because of the sharp increase in immigration by EU citizens. It is notable that whereas Standard Eurobarometer surveys show that UK citizens are nearly as tolerant as the Irish to third country immigrants, the British—unlike most EU nations—are not much more favourable towards immigrants from other EU member states than to non-EU citizens.

Consequently, it appears that causation is not simplistic, and when discussing attitudes to immigration Europe does not divide neatly into two halves.

3.1 What is the experience of migration?

Although it is easy to look at Slovakia as a traditional country of emigration, locating precise figures can be challenging, not least because in the major period of emigration from Slovakia to the USA from the late nineteenth century to the beginning of the first world war Slovaks did not have their own state and were living in part of Hungary. While it is generally accepted that Ireland lost the highest proportion of its population to America in this period, assertions that Slovakia follows in second place are contested (Bahna, 2011). While emigration was reduced in the interwar period, further waves occurred in the wake of the Second World War and the Soviet invasion of 1968.

Slovakia has also been a major country of emigration since the fall of communism in 1989 and EU accession in 2004. Eurostat figures show that while nearly 4 per cent of EU citizens of working age live in another EU member state, the proportion is higher for Poland, Slovakia and Hungary (though not the Czech Republic), although Ireland has a higher proportion than all four Visegrad states, and Romania—with 19.1 per cent of citizens working elsewhere in the EU—appears to have a population over twice as mobile as that in Poland. The UK, on the other hand, has the second lowest per centage of citizens working elsewhere in the EU (1.1 per cent, compared to 1.0 per cent for Germany) (Eurostat, 2018a). It should be noted, however, that migration of pensioners is also significant in the case of high-wage and high-cost member states.

Yet EU statistics do not tell the full story. United Nations data shows that the UK has a larger number of citizens living abroad worldwide than any other member state, 4.9 million, followed by Poland with 4.7 million (United Nations, 2017, p. 13).

When it comes to immigration, however, the differences are more clear-cut. The Visegrad Four states have relatively little experience of accepting immigrants. In 2016, Slovakia—as in previous years—received the lowest number of immigrants as a proportion of its population of all member states, and the actual number of immigrants, 7.7 thousand, was the lowest in the EU, although Slovakia is of median size among the post-communist member states. Allowing for returning nationals—over half the total number of 'immigrants' in the Slovak case—we find that Latvia had a slightly smaller number of foreign immigrants, but it is a smaller country. The proportion of immigrants annually is slightly higher in Hungary, Poland and the Czech Republic, but still far lower than in the UK or Ireland (Eurostat, 2018b).

The origins of the foreign and foreign-born population in the Visegrad states also do little to prepare citizens for coping with otherness. (N.B. In every country, many of the resident who were born abroad have at some subsequent point acquired the passport of the state where they reside, so that the number of foreign-born residents normally exceeds the number of foreign citizens.) On 1 January 2017, only 3.4 per cent of

Slovakia's population was foreign-born, but a large majority of these people—2.8 per cent of the total compared to 0.6 per cent—were born in another EU member state. Such a high proportion of foreign-born residents born in the EU was otherwise only found in Ireland, but here the 4.1 per cent of citizens born outside the EU (as opposed to 12.6 per cent born in the EU) exceeds the total per centage of foreign-born residents in Slovakia.

A look at the main countries of birth of foreign-born residents is also revealing: in Slovakia, 47.2 per cent of them were born in the Czech Republic, so many of them would have had the common Czechoslovak citizenship at birth. Likewise, in Hungary, where 5.2 per cent of the population is foreign born, 40.2 per cent of foreign-born residents (though only 15.9 per cent of residents without Hungarian citizenship) are from Romania (Eurostat, 2018b), so a majority are likely to be ethnic Hungarians, who under Hungarian law find it easy to acquire citizenship. In the Czech Republic, over 50 per cent of foreign-born or foreign residents come from three Slav countries: Ukraine, Slovakia and Russia.

In the case of the UK and Ireland, however, the most common country of origin of foreign residents is Poland. In the UK, this is followed by India, though it should be noted that since immigration to the UK from former colonies has been widespread for over half a century, many British-born British citizens also have a south Asian cultural heritage.

Finally, since the hosting of refugees and asylum-seekers has become a highly controversial topic in the EU since 2015, it is worth looking at the relevant statistics. Although the number of asylum applications in the EU as a whole doubled to around 1.3 million in 2015 and 2016 (compared to 2014 and 2017), Hungary was the only Visegrad state affected by this influx, receiving 174,434 first-time asylum applications in 2015. However, in 2017 this number had reduced to 3,113, while Slovakia, for the second year in a row, received the smallest number of asylum applications of any EU member state: 148. By comparison, Ireland, a similarly sized country to Slovakia but much further from the main migration routes, received 2,912 applications in 2017 (Eurostat, 2018c).

Consequently, it may seem strange that immigration and refugees has become a political issue at all in the Visegrad states, and Slovakia in particular. What will be suggested below is that whereas in states such as the UK and Ireland, where immigration has been substantial, it has had an effect on the everyday lives of ordinary people, in Slovakia and the Visegrad Four, arguments against immigration have been created top-down, from political elites. In countries where residents are genuinely affected by immigration, political pressure is bottom-up, with voters pressurising politicians who may or may not choose to exploit the issue for electoral gain.

3.2 The arguments on immigration

Although the objective situation regarding migration is very different in the case studies under discussion, a number of common themes can be identified, and they tend to be negative. These are: cultural threats; economic threats; security threats; and arguments regarding sovereignty.

The first argument is that society will be 'flooded' by immigrants and that this will somehow undermine indigenous culture. Although specialist reports in Slovakia have highlighted the need for Slovakia to take in immigrants for economic reasons (Domonkos et al., 2010; INEKO, 2016), in early discussions politicians suggested that they could accept people from countries with similar cultures, such as Serbia and Ukraine (Slovak Spectator, 2010), which was essentially in denial of general western experience that most immigrants would come from further afield. This idea crept into the official Interior Ministry Concept of a Migration Policy for the Slovak Republic (Androvičová, 2015).

The first internationally high-profile Slovak statement of cultural exclusiveness was the comment of an Interior Ministry spokesperson amid the refugee crisis in August 2015 that Slovakia could only accept Christians and atheists, arguing rather disingenuously that 'we don't have any mosques so how can Muslims be integrated if they are not going to like it here?' (BBC, 2015). It is notable, however, that Islam is not a registered religion in Slovakia since it does not have the requisite 20,000 adherents among Slovak citizens. Rather than assisting the registration of Islam, in November 2016 the Slovak parliament amended the law so that 50,000 adherents are required to register a religion.

Despite a presidential veto, 103 of Slovakia's 150 parliamentary deputies voted to override the presidential veto. This is a further example of the 'top-down' nature of anti-immigrant sentiment in Slovakia. The Slovak prime minister, Robert Fico, in 2015-2016 also promoted the idea of Muslims as a threat to Slovak culture by suggesting (with no evidence) that they could not be integrated (Úrad vlády Slovenskej republiky, 2015). He repeatedly emphasised that Slovakia would reject having 'compact' Muslim communities, ignoring the possibility that effective policies for integrating immigrants might be the best way to prevent such a scenario (Sme, 2018; DennikN, 2016). The most recent (2014) Migration Policy Index (MIPEX), which measures policies to integrate foreigners in 38 states, including all EU countries, ranked Slovakia four from bottom, with only Latvia, Cyprus and Turkey scoring worse. It was the only Visegrad state that had not improved its score since the previous 2010 index (MIPEX, 2015).

The most extreme arguments of cultural threat from immigrants suggest that an alien culture could become predominant and subordinate the indigenous population. These suggestions are strongest in Hungary, where during the 2018 parliamentary election campaign it was suggested that if the opposition won, Hungarian women would be forced to wear burqas. This was slightly reminiscent of a passage in the famous 'Rivers of Blood' speech about immigration to the UK, which contained the phrase 'In this country in 15 or 20 years' time the black man will have the whip hand over the white man.' (Daily Telegraph, 2007) The cases differ, however, in three crucial points. Firstly, Enoch Powell's speech was delivered in April 1968, fifty years earlier (Crine et al., 2016). Secondly, although he was a politician in the right-of-centre Conservative Party, while the left-wing Labour Party took the lead in fighting racism, the speech was so widely condemned by his own party that he was dismissed as a shadow government minister. Thirdly, when Powell talked of immigrants dominating over the indigenous population, he was not—allegedly—promoting his own ideas, but rather giving a direct quotation of what he had been told by one of his constituents. In other words, his argument was that pressure against immigration was coming from the bottom up, from the ordinary working people who were living with immigrants.

The second major argument used against immigration is the economic threat. This tends to be more potent for lower-earning residents who could be 'undercut' by immigrants sending remittances to countries with a lower cost of living. The argument was powerful in some areas of the UK in the run-up to the 2016 referendum on leaving the EU as people felt that 'East Europeans' were stealing 'their' jobs. Given the small number of immigrants in Slovakia, the argument is less powerful, but has been used regarding Serbs coming to work there. Interestingly, the discussion in Slovakia makes no mention of the fact that Serbia is a leading candidate for EU membership, and that were it to join, Slovaks would ultimately have to accept Serbian workers under EU freedom of movement rules, just as the UK had to accept Slovaks.

The third argument relates to security. This has dominated much of the discussion of the refugee crisis in the Visegrad Four, with the concepts of Muslims/refugees/terrorists being conflated. Since the region has virtually no experience of terrorism, it is unclear why the argument is so powerful, and this provides us with another example of 'top-down' xenophobia in Slovakia and its neighbouring countries. At the time of the terrorist attacks in Paris in 2015, the Slovak prime minister immediately jumped to the conclusion that they supported his arguments against accepting Muslim refugees, even though there was no evidence that refugees were involved (Úrad vlády Slovenskej republiky, 2015). It is a classic example of 'securitisation'. A public issue becomes securitised, rather than merely politicised, when it is presented and widely accepted as an existential threat requiring emergency measures (Buzan et al., 1998).

Security arguments have been less prominent in UK discourses on immigration. This may to some extent stem from the fact that most terrorist attacks committed in the UK over the last 50 years were related to the 'Troubles' in Northern Ireland, part of the UK, and while the perpetrators were sometimes referred to as 'Catholics', the idea of assigning responsibility for attacks to anyone who happens to be of the same religion is clearly absurd in a society where most people come into daily contact with neighbours of that faith. Where politicians have used security arguments in the UK, it has often been linked to EU-related sovereignty issues, with criticisms that it is too hard to deport criminals from other member states.

This brings us on to the fourth common argument in anti-immigration discourse. This is not an argument for or against immigration *per se* but rather an objection to foreigners (in this case EU institutions) deciding whether or not a given country should have to accept immigrants. This was central to the British campaign to leave the EU, which emphasised the uncontrollable nature of immigration from other member states, including erroneous arguments which suggested that Turkish accession was imminent and could not be vetoed by the UK.

Because of the relatively low number of immigrants in the Visegrad Four, free movement within the EU has yet to be politicised, and sovereignty arguments relate to the introduction of 'quotas' for the redistribution of refugees in autumn 2015 (Visegrad Group, 2015). It was an issue that led to a revival of Visegrad Four collabouration, with first Slovakia and then Hungary taking action against the EU at the European Court of Justice. Although they ultimately lost the case, (Court of Justice of the European Union, 2017) the new EU member states made the contentious nature of the issue so very clear that implementation of refugee quotas has been limited. While Slovakia politicised the issue heavily in the run-up to the March 2016 parliamentary elections, and later put up billboards stating that 'quotas do not apply for Slovakia', this was not in fact true: it was the UK for whom quotas did not apply, since the country had negotiated opt-outs on many EU justice and home affairs issues.

What is striking, however, is the similarity of the arguments used by Slovakia and Hungary when discussing refugee quotas and those used by the UK 'Brexiteers' to attack free movement. The 'Vote Leave' campaign stated that 'In a world with so many new threats, it's safer to control our own borders and decide for ourselves who can come into this country, not to be overruled by EU judges' (VoteLeave, 2016). Likewise, after the Bratislava Summit in September 2016, the Slovak prime minister stated that only Slovaks could decide who crossed their border (a comment later echoed by his successor) and after the Hungarian 2018 election, the prime minister stated that 'Hungarians have decided that only they can decide with whom they want to live in Hungary, and the government will stick to this position'. This was not of course true: under EU law, all Muslims (as well as non-Muslims) with EU passports are entitled to enter and work in both Slovakia and Hungary. Likewise, when the Slovak prime minister stated in late 2015 that 'We are monitoring every Muslim in Slovakia, and most of them are here legally', (TA3, 2015) he was effectively announcing the intention to discriminate against them in contravention of basic EU principles.

3.3 Us and them

Underlying the various arguments to explain hostility to immigration are numerous assumptions about 'us' and 'them'. It is easy to criticise Slovaks for contradictory views on free movement, whereby—as shown by numerous Standard Eurobarometers—they support free movement in principle, while not favouring EU citizens coming to their own country. However, the British abroad have been criticised for similar double standards for refusing to regard themselves as immigrants, preferring instead the term 'expatriates'. The term has a slightly colonial feel, being used primarily to discuss the movement of more affluent professionals to other countries. Interestingly, however, EU figures show that 'mobile citizens' (those living in another member state) are more likely to have higher education than those who stay behind. This applies not only to

UK citizens living elsewhere in the EU, but also to mobile citizens from the Visegrad Four countries (Eurostat, 2018a).

Slovak discourse, on the other hand, tends to differentiate on the grounds of race, with religion in particular being emphasised. It is notable that, despite Slovakian experience of producing refugees, which is shared by the other Visegrad states, there is very little tendency to identify with the plight of contemporary Muslim refugees, who are generally presented negatively (Kissová, 2017). The same applies to economic migrants. In September 2015, the Slovak President Kiska made a speech which was generally praised by the liberal press in Slovakia for demonstrating a more humane attitude towards refugees than the government. However, he was keen to emphasise that 'I am not talking about economic migrants, who should be speedily returned to their safe home countries' (Kiska, 2015). This appears a reasonable comment, but no-one in Slovakia linked it to the highly relevant fact that President Kiska had himself gone to the USA as an economic migrant in the early 1990s. As with the refugees, the 'us' and 'them' remained separate.

Some of the reasons for Slovaks not identifying their own experiences with those of incoming migrants may result from lack of familiarity with immigrants. This leads to a tendency to generalise about whole ethnic groups, as when the former Slovak prime minister referred to Muslims as people who did not want to be integrated. Generalisation may also stem from another aspect of the communist period: Communist ideology placed an emphasis on collective rather than individual rights. Furthermore, unlike the British and the Americans, Central Europeans have never had to confront the historic guilt of dealing with a multiracial society formed as a consequence of empire and slavery.

3.4 Why are Slovakia and the other Visegrad states so hostile to immigrants?

As the EU struggles to cope with still increasing numbers of asylum seekers in some of the southern states, negative attitudes to immigration and otherness in new member states present a challenge. A number of explanations can be suggested for these attitudes.

First of all, research repeatedly shows that familiarity and everyday contact with immigrants leads to more positive attitudes towards them (Heath and Richards, 2016). In the Visegrad Four, the unfamiliarity with immigration is in part a communist legacy. Soviet-style Communist states had firmly closed borders, and just as it was hard for citizens their own citizens to leave, so too was it hard for anyone to enter illegally. Overstaying—another source of illegal immigration—was also hard to accomplish in a closely-monitored community. On top of this, Communist ideology sought simplistic rather than complex solutions to problems, and some of this thinking can be seen in Visegrad responses that want the EU to close its borders more effectively, rather than pursuing this aim as part of a multi-faceted strategy that also includes redistribution of refugees.

Secondly, it is possible that the incoherence of twentieth-century history in East Central Europe affects the ability of some citizens to identify the experiences of refugees and economic migrants from other parts of the world with their own past travails. Irish history is relatively simple, with one major powerful enemy (the British) from whom they gained their independence in the twentieth century. The Visegrad Four countries, on the other hand, experienced multiple border changes and generally five separate political regimes within a single century. In the same period, Slovaks have regarded both Hungarians, Russians and Czechs as oppressors. Oversensitivity to the powers of EU institutions is perhaps not that surprising.

Thirdly, there is little understanding that EU membership in a globalised world requires accepting into society people from other races, religions and cultures. Leaders in East Central Europe present their xenophobic views as a return to traditional, national and (mostly) Catholic values without questioning whether, compared to the very Catholic Ireland, they are not perhaps returning to the roots of a closed communist society. Even academic research still routinely refers to 'citizens' rather than 'inhabitants' when discussing social developments.

The idea that in the EU as a whole 7.5 per cent of residents are not citizens of the country where they live, and that meaningful social research must necessarily take this into account in order to make valid conclusions and recommendations, is overlooked.

Fourthly, it is possible genuinely to learn from the mistakes of others. Although some Slovaks make rather simplistic, sweeping statements that 'multiculturalism has failed' in western Europe (often citing right-of-centre politicians who never supported multiculturalism in the first place), with hindsight integration of immigrant communities could have been handled better in some parts of some EU member states. Unfortunately, the negative generalisations heard from contemporary Visegrad politicians suggest that exclusion of the other rather than successful integration is their goal.

Conclusion

Comparing apples and oranges is of limited value, yet the discussion presented here is not intended as a rigorous comparative study, but rather as a reflection on similarities and differences worthy of investigation.

However, when comparing the reactions to immigration in Slovakia (and to a lesser extent the Visegrad Four) and in the UK (with some references to Ireland), what is most striking is the failure of political leadership in the new EU member states. It has been suggested elsewhere (Henderson, 2017) that some of the difficulties faced by the EU in dealing with new member states derives from the 'missing left': that is, that post-communist parties with left-wing economic policies rarely have tolerant, liberal, left-wing social agendas. Xenophobia is an easy emotion to exploit, and the problem is not just that illiberal politicians in Visegrad states have chosen to do so, but also that they have not faced concerted opposition from parties prepared to promote anti-discrimination policies.

It is easy for politicians to claim that they are responding to public moods when opposing immigration, and it is notable that illiberalism in the Visegrad states was on the rise, with an extremist elected regional governor in Slovakia in 2014 as well as the Orbán government gaining a second successive term in office, before the eruption of the refugee crisis (Kazharski, 2017). However, a choice has clearly been made by political elites to exploit rather manage tendencies towards xenophobia. Pressure from below has been limited: there has been little immigration and controversial negative everyday consequences from it, and the willingness of citizens to move abroad suggests that many are well able to cope with otherness. A more responsible attitude on the part of the rather inexperienced and unstable political elites, which would be more appropriate for a member state of the EU, could do much to relieve the tension around refugee and immigration policy in East Central Europe.

PART II:
MIGRATION: SOUTHERN EUROPE

1 FOREIGN POLICY ANALYSIS AND MIGRATION: CASE STUDY OF SLOVENIA AND WESTERN BALKANS[13]

Hana Hlaváčková

This paper focuses on the time of the migration crisis as a specific period influencing political discourse. I am interested in discourse formulated by Slovene politicians towards the western Balkan countries. For several reasons it is important to study Slovenia: (1) Slovenia is a non-Balkan country, but with Balkan roots and connections; (2) Slovenia is a member of the EU, so relations between Slovenia and the western Balkans are interesting for study; (3) Slovenia was part of the Balkan route since changes happened during the 2015 migration crisis. The main aim is to show how a long-term role can or cannot change under the influence of the migration crisis and period following it. In my research I use a constructivist framework for foreign policy. Role theory is a specific approach to the study of the foreign policy of a state which can be used to study its long-term role and compare it in the time of crisis, when a change of role is possible. The role of small states is determined by the relationship to the external environment. The conception of role consists of internal shared expectations, external expectations and national role conception and then also role performance. I will use this pattern to

---

[13] This chapter is the outcome of research project no. 57-02 "Territorial studies, economy and international relations" implemented by the Metropolitan University Prague and funded by the Institutional Support for Long-term Strategic Development of Research Organisations in 2018.

observe the role change during the migration crisis. The main research question is to observe whether role change has taken place or not.

The background of relations between Slovenia and the countries of the western Balkan region (in this context Croatia, Macedonia, Bosnia and Herzegovina, Serbia, Montenegro and Kosovo) must be seen from the historical perspective. Slovenia was part of Yugoslavia, as were all other countries of region. Since 1991 Slovenia has experienced the fight for independence, as have the other countries. The Slovene fight against the Yugoslav National Army was the shortest (and most peaceful). Since then Slovenia has tried to get as far as possible from the whole Balkan region.

Politicians have repeated that they are not a Balkan country and have nothing in common with them. The reasons are obvious—the Balkan region was involved in a war, all European countries thought the Balkans is the poorest region, and maybe in some way lost (because the EU did nothing to moderate the conflict). Such a brand was undesirable for Slovenia. That is why they moved mentally closer to Europe (western, central, south-eastern). These efforts to become part of Europe are still continuing, although by the end of the 1990s Slovene politicians found their identity a little bit closer to the Balkans. They wanted to become a bridge between the Balkan and the EU, for example to mediate meetings.

This can be interpreted as meaning that Slovene politicians finally got self-confidence and found a way how to be useful and indispensable for other European states (EU). There are several reasons for this—close ties with the region (economic, social, cultural, linguistic) and a prestigious sort of work for their diplomats and politicians.

Relations with the states of region are marked by a common history and the very fast proclamation of independence. There are still unsolved problems at the borders with Croatia and unsolved property issues with other states. Slovenes call it the heritage of Yugoslavia. Slovenia helped other countries to get independence, like Croatia and Bosnia and Herzegovina and Macedonia. Later Slovene politicians also supported Montenegro and in 2008 also Kosovo (which slightly problematizes relations with Serbia).

1.1 Theoretical and methodological framework

At a time of change in the international system, we need to focus on foreign policy analysis. With the migration phenomenon, we can observe some changes in a state behaviour. To observe role construction, there are more actors than is visible at first sight. In this part I would like to introduce how the role of a state defines its behaviour.

Firstly, we need to define how the role is determined. According to Elgström and Smith (2006) a role is constructed by power in the international system or by the status of the actor. Small states are predetermined to different roles, mostly without high goals or leadership. For example, typical roles for small states are mentor, model, intermediary, bearer of values (Elgström, Smith, 2006; Waisová, Cabada, 2009). The role of small states is determined by their relationship to the external environment, which is the international organization or group of states to which the state belongs (Beneš, Harnisch, 2014). We can define the role according to specific relations towards other actors. There is a connection between the process of role conception and external expectations. The role is then influenced by norms and values which the state accepts.

Role conception is also connected with the concept of identity. Identity has influence in forming political discourse. The creation of a role is part of social reality and is formed by external and internal actors. These actors have some expectations which can form the role itself. In some cases, the role can be changed over time. Change is connected with norm and ideational changes. This is called process of socialization which is for constructivists very important (Breuning, 2007; 2011).

Role conception consists of frameworks of behaviours, decisions, functions and commitments to community. Political decision makers take on a particular role with their own definitions, decisions, commitments, rules and activities. In this context it is clear that the role has to be studied in a social context and is formed by intersubjective meanings (Harnisch, 2011).

Role theory is a reflection of international context. Role conception has to be seen in the broader context of how foreign policy is created (Holsti, 1970, p. 246). The whole process has several important parts. First is the conception of role that consists of internal shared expectations, external expectations and national role conception, and then comes the role performance. There is also the possibility of change; however, change itself is not an easy or quick process.

According to Lisbeth Aggestam (1999, 2006) these conceptions have the following meaning:

- **Role expectations**—can be external and internal. Internal expectations are formed by political culture, society, politicians themselves. External expectations are formed by the institutional structure where the actor belongs.
- **National role conception**—is a normative interpretation of the actor. The conception is long-term and shows what possibilities and strategies the actor can play. It is formed by history, culture and societal characteristics.
- **Role performance**—is the actual behaviour of the actor. It can be influenced by specific situations. The actor plays their role.
- **Role change**—role is a stable figure; it has to be consistent so politicians can fulfil it. The role can be changed according to the context. The situation must be one of severe conditions—political instability, a change of norms and speculation about the role.

The process starts with defining role expectations. These expectations are made on the institutional level and second from external actors such as the EU or NATO. Internal and external expectations, influenced by identity, form a role conception which is somehow interpreted by politicians. It leads to role performance. The role is a construct, so performance leads to determination of whether the expectations were fulfilled. If not, the role can be changed by politicians. This means that there is the possibility of change, which can be seen in the time of crisis or political instability (Aggestam, 1999).

K. Holsti (1973, 1987) showed 17 roles that states can play. Among these 17 are some types which are not suitable for the current time period (he created his typology during the Cold War) and some of types are not suitable for small states. Here in the table they are all presented. I will only work with some of them, divided into two groups for easier determination. In this table the types of roles are divided according to responsibility: whether such a state needs to play a role with responsibility or not.

Table 1: Holsti's and Aggestam's roles

Role with responsibility	Role without responsibility
regional leader, regional protector, ideational protector, mediator-integrator, leader, promoter of security	independent state, regional subsystem cooperator, developer, bridge, role as an example, independent actor, role of internal development, isolated state, protected state, ally

I work with these roles in the context of the long-term roles which are created by the above-mentioned processes. Firstly, there is need to understand how such roles are created by the era in which they occur. The observation of long-term roles comes from research conducted during my PhD studies. It is also an output of my dissertation thesis (Hlaváčková, 2017). Below I will introduce the long-term roles and then compare them with Slovene behaviour to show whether the roles performed were changed at the time of the migration crisis.

1.2 Slovene long-term roles towards western Balkan countries

In this part of the article I would like to briefly introduce findings from my PhD thesis. I have focused on Slovenia's long-term roles towards western Balkan countries. Based on the process introduced, I have conducted discourse analysis of policymakers (president, prime minister,

minister of foreign affairs). This discourse analysis was divided according to Fairclough (1992, 1995) into three levels of analysis—discourse production, discourse praxes and sociocultural praxes. From analysis in this framework, I have created a role set. It was impossible to find a single role because Slovenia behaves differently towards each country of the western Balkans. There are groups of roles based on mutual history and mutual relations.

Table 2: Long-term roles

Roles of Slovenia	developer, supporter	role as an example	developer, supporter, mediator	example, developer, independent actor
Countries of western Balkans	Macedonia Bosnia and Herzegovina Montenegro	Montenegro	Serbia Kosovo	Croatia

All of the roles are performed without responsibility. Slovene politicians sometimes spoke to the public about their responsibility rooted in common history, but this was not frequent and this responsibility was not proven in discourse praxes. I will briefly introduce each role so you can visualize Slovenia's performance of roles.

The role of developer means that the state focuses on help to other states which are less developed. It means that the developer behaves as a superior. The developer has material opportunities so it can help. Not every state that helps with development is a developer; such help needs to be structured and long-term.

The role of supporter means that a state speaks (only) supportively. I have constructed this role in additional to those already mentioned. This role is typical for Slovenia. It was not on the list but it was observed in the discourse. The supporter does not have any responsibility. But it always says that it supports the other country. It does not mean that it has to do so. Support can be a kind of mask for a state when it wants to demonstrate good relations with states or international organizations.

The role of being an example shows that this state, Slovenia, assigns importance to its image. It is prestigious to be first post-Yugoslav country in the EU. Example means that Slovene politicians usually point out how successful Slovenia is and so everyone should follow it. This role is long-term and it shall not be violated. It is based on trust in the surrounding area.

The mediator/integrator is an actor who focuses on mediation between states or organizations. This role is long-term and one condition is that a state has to be mediator always, not only once. Integration is the main topic. This is most important for Slovenia. Western Balkan countries need to be integrated into the EU. It can help to stabilize them to be good partners. An independent actor behaves on their own, unbounded, freely. They can cooperate, but there is a conflict of interests, they follow their own interests. No one would expect more.

Below I would like to describe briefly the relationship of Slovenia towards each country of the western Balkans.

Macedonia[14] has a special relationship with Slovenia; it is one of the two countries in Slovenia's development aid programme. Cooperation is based on long-term programmes. Slovene politicians always emphasize that Macedonia should follow the Slovene example and become a member of the EU and NATO. In practice Slovene institutions provide financial sources and technical help to get closer to the EU. Slovenia is active through political dialogue, political visits and the exchange of know how. During the turmoil in Macedonia in 2015, the Slovene government criticized Macedonian politicians and tried to push them towards political dialogue. The Slovene government has the feeling that it can help Macedonia with its integration and also with the stabilization of its political and security situation. Beyond this there are of course economic objectives. Economic exchange between Slovenia and Macedonia will be easier after Macedonia's accession to the EU. From the

---

[14] Macedonia is not the official name of the country, but Slovene governmental documents only use the name Macedonia, not FYROM. For this reason I also only use this name.

political discourse it is obvious that Slovene politicians show their superiority insofar as Slovenia has successfully joined EU, so it has experience to share.

Bosnia and Herzegovina is a country with less economic importance but more importance when it comes to security issues. Bosnia is far from success in the European integration process; however, in the Slovene discourse it was obvious that politicians connect security stabilization with integration into the EU. Large-scale cooperation on its path to the EU could help to stabilize the country. Slovenia implements large scale of programmes with technical help and activities to fight corruption and organized crime. Assistance with security stabilization is supported through activities in EUFOR, the EU mission in Bosnia. We cannot speak about responsibility, but Slovenia is part of a group of states (the EU) who are responsible according to the discourse analysed. In Slovene discourse, we can observe that Bosnia is presented as a weak country that needs help, not a partner for economic cooperation. It is obvious that politicians show their superiority in every meeting and proclamation. The interests of the Slovenian government in Bosnia are more ideational than material.

Serbia is an economic partner country. In the discourse it is possible to see claims that Serbia is a strong country and closest to integration into the EU of all countries in the western Balkan region. The economic exchange between Slovenia and Serbia is massive. However, in the discourse politicians highlight their superiority, they show their power. This has its roots in history. With Croatia, Slovenia did not solve problems during the EU accession process very successfully, and Slovene politicians do not want to repeat this failure in diplomatic negotiations with Serbia, because there are still some unsolved problems between Slovenia and Serbia from the Yugoslav era. A condition for Serbia and other western Balkan countries to join the EU is that they should first solve all problems coming from the past. So Slovenia again wants to show that Serbia needs to cooperate. Slovenia only provides a small amount of development aid to Serbia. Only Albania receives less money for development assistance. Slovenia supports reforms and changes on

Serbia's road to the EU. Slovenia also played a special role in 2008, when Kosovo claimed its independence. At the beginning of 2008, Slovene diplomats promised that they would support Serbia in the Serbian-Kosovar question, but in February, when Slovenia had the presidency of the EU Council, they were among the first group of countries to accept Kosovar independence. In its documents Slovenia says that it tries to help and normalize relations between Serbia and Kosovo. However, it does not promise responsibility for doing this. Slovenia also has security concerns so it helps with the reform of the Serbian army so that it gets closer to European standards.

Kosovo is defined in Slovene documents as a country that needs to stabilize and that needs help with government reforms and the fight with organized crime, corruption and terrorism. In the discourse analysed, politicians say that Kosovo has to be stabilized through integration and that Slovenia helps with it. Again, Slovenia does not take any responsibility for this. Slovenia also has an eminent interest on the calming of Kosovar-Serbian relations and their integration into the EU and NATO because of economic exchange and security stabilization in the region. Slovene politicians argue that they have experience to share. Again, we can observe the feeling of superiority.

Montenegro is the second country in Slovenia's development assistance programme. Slovenia also acts as an example with the rhetoric in the discourse that it successfully joined the EU, and Montenegro, with the same experience of achieving independence democratically, needs to follow Slovenia and become a responsible EU member state. Slovenia allocated huge amount of money to reforms in Montenegro, mainly for institutional changes. Slovenia shares know how, helps with administration and gives technical support. The reasons are ideational, because Slovenia wants to integrate the whole region in order to stabilize its neighbourhood and spread ideas, norms and values. There are also material reasons, for economic exchange. From the security point of view, Slovenia supports the fight with organized crime and corruption that destabilizes country. To sum up the relationship, it can be said that

Slovene politicians show their superiority and the asymmetric relation behind their efforts.

Croatia is already an EU member but plays a huge role in the refugee crisis and has been a key player in the western Balkan region for a long time. Slovene-Croatian relations are very complicated and have suffered from an argument about Piran Bay which again intensified in 2017 after unsuccessful international arbitration. There are other diplomatic problems, but economic exchange works without all these problems being resolved.

All western Balkan countries are at some stage of the EU integration process (more detailed in: Bauerová, Hlaváčková, Cabada, 2014; Cici, 2011). Slovenia plays various roles in the context of European integration and pursues its internal interests. These interests also influence its behaviour in the refugee crisis analyzed below.

1.3 Slovene behaviour in the refugee crisis

We can observe a long-term migrant flow from countries south of Europe. The reasons why people migrate are examined in many works and analyses. In our context the so-called Balkan route is important, and this is not a new trend. The EU's European Border and Coast Guard Agency (Frontex) and the International Organization for Migration (IOM) have been observing organized crime coming through this route for years, or indeed decades. After the 2014 Arab Spring, when many countries became fragile and failed states, the Balkan route has also been used by migrants searching shelter, security or new home in Europe. The Balkan route leads through the western Balkan countries to Slovenia. As was mentioned above, Slovenia has a special relationship with the Balkan countries.

In 2015 the borders between Serbia and Hungary were most affected. Slovenia was a country at the sidelines. However, when Hungary closed its borders, migrants changed their route towards Croatia and

Slovenia[15]. Slovenia was and still is a transit country[16]. However, the country has never before had experiences like those in 2015. Hundreds of thousands of people were crossing the borders to reach the EU.

Western Balkan countries were also part of this flow. Each had its specific reaction. Not all of them were affected by the same amount of refugees. However, the EU expected the western Balkan countries to behave like all EU countries and to protect the Schengen area. The reality was different. No-one was prepared for such a situation. During the crisis there were rumours that the behaviour of the western Balkan countries could influence the speed of their integration into the EU. The situation was serious. Macedonia faced a big flow of refugees coming through its territory illegally. It declared a state of emergency, closed the borders and built a fence. The problem was located on the border with Greece. Macedonia hsent in the army and this step was subject to enormous criticism from the EU. It also caused unrest among the refugees (Migrant crisis: Macedonia shuts Balkans route, 2016).

Bosnia and Herzegovina was also in the path of the new Balkan route and became part of the migration flow. Bosnian politicians also said that they are only a transit country, so they can only help with transport and let the refugees go. They had prepared some crisis scenarios but did not have enough capacity to act as an EU/Schengen country (Milekic, Toe, 2015). Serbia, the country which is closest to European integration and EU accession, behaved in a way which also faced massive criticism. A large number of refugees were coming to Serbia and through it. Politicians in Serbia called for help from the EU and set an ultimatum

---

[15] In July 2013 the Slovene and Croatian governments signed an agreement about a new regime on their borders. It made normal traffic easier so travellers did not wait for a long time at border checks. This is the period since Croatia entered the EU. Croatia is still not a member of Schengen area, so this border is also a Schengen border. When Croatia enters Schengen the responsibility will be on their shoulders, but until now it has been with the Slovene government. In the medium-term perspective, the Western Balkan countries will not become of EU or Schengen area members very quickly (for more see: Bauerová, Hlaváčková, Cabada, 2014).

[16] Until July 2015 Police counted illegal migrants in units: in 2007 it was 2479 migrants, which was actually a 38% decrease from the previous year.

that they would just push refugees into EU when the EU did not send any help. However, after negotiations Serbia started to cooperate with the EU (Randjelovic, 2015).

Alongside the migrant flows, illegal practices such as smuggling and illegal transport by unlicenced taxi services, buses, etc. also blossomed. These practices still continue and there is a need for interstate cooperation, especially between the police and custom services.

Croatia was also part of the changed migrant route and was criticized in particular by Slovenia. Slovene politicians criticized the Croatian government for not sharing information about the numbers, groupings or even the existence of migrants approaching the Slovenian-Croatian borders. This situation was influenced by their mutual argument about borders, because at some points there is still no formal delineation of borders. Croatia is not a member of the Schengen area, so the Croatian government argued that they have no duty towards the EU in such a situation (AlJazeera, 2015).

The Slovene government, at the time of the refugee crisis (they always call it a refugee crisis, not a migration crisis as is more common in other EU countries) prepared crisis management plans, but all the crisis scenarios dealt with hundreds of people, not thousands (Žurnal 24, 2015). In February 2016 a total of 442,000 refugees arrived. At first Slovenia tried to stop them at the border to check up on them, but as the numbers grew, they also only helped with transit (Policija Republike Slovenije, 2016). Slovenia asked for financial, material and personnel help and got it from the EU and individual countries. In 2016 Slovenia and other states took crisis measures, such as building a fence to help stop migrants. The Slovene government hsent army troops to the border to help secure it and prevent anyone crossing illegally. This encountered substantial criticism from across the whole of Europe.

As was mentioned in the section on long-term roles, Slovenia cooperates with Balkan countries, specifically in a Brdo Process, which is a platform for discussion. Since the crisis began, Slovenia used the Brdo Process to arrange several meetings where common policies towards refugees were discussed. At one meeting it was stated that there was a need to organize a regional approach that could help dealing with migrants in a unified way. Other arguments called for more cooperation was regarding citizens from western Balkan countries who were exploiting the asylum system at the time of refugee crisis, especially Kosovars. It was also mentioned that the EU should be the coordinator who could help to fight the people smuggling which has its roots in western Balkan countries, and that a common approach should also be taken on issues such as the returns policy (Ministrstvo za notranje zadeve Republike Slovenije, 2015).

1.3.1 Political discourse

The Slovene decision makers whom I observed were the president, prime minister, minister of foreign affairs and minister of the interior. Other actors follow the direction which these actors prepared. By focusing on the topics in their discourse, I would like to show how political actors speak about the refugee crisis and western Balkan countries.

Slovene politicians speak about protecting the borders of the EU because this is their obligation (Ministrstvo za notranje zadeve, 2015). President Borut Pahor argued that the crisis is a refugee crisis and people crossing the border needed help. He called the situation a humanitarian crisis. He criticized Hungarian president Orbán for closing borders (which happened from 16. 10. 2015) and ignoring people's needs. He also criticized Serbia (RTV Slovenija, 2015). What is important is that Pahor point out that that it is the EU that holds responsibility, not Slovenia or the western Balkan countries. He called for joint action by the EU. He did not mention that western Balkan countries were behaving incorrectly or inadequately. We could not observe any change in the long-term discourse towards western Balkan countries in his speeches and interviews.

Minister of Foreign Affairs Karl Erjavec claimed that it is obvious that migrants will not stay in Slovenia; however, Slovenia has to be prepared. His plan was that Slovenia should accept quotas due to the need to divide migrants equally. Minister of the Interior Vesna Györkös

Žnidar was always more critical and argued that it is a humanitarian crisis, but Slovene security needs to be put first. There are security rules that need to be adhered to. Slovenia is the smallest country on the Balkan route so no-one should think that it has any responsibility for the whole region.

In December 2015 Slovene Prime Minister Miro Cerar said that if the situation worsened, then Slovenia would build a fence, what it actually later did. On 11th November 2015 Slovenia started building a razor-wire fence along its border with Croatia to control the flow of migrants. He also called for coordination with Turkey, but he did not mention or criticize western Balkan countries. Responsibility, according to Cerar, lay with the EU. His argument for using the army was that Slovenia is a really small country with limited capacity. He defended the idea of building a fence to help coordinate the refugee flow. For him, this was the last resort; because it is not good to build walls in Europe, but in this situation it was necessary. And, last but not least, Slovenia is merely "fulfilling its obligations towards the EU."

We can observe that politicians very often mentioned the topic of security topic. Some of them linked security with refugees who need help. However, after counting the migrant flow, all politicians argued that there was a need to organize border crossings.

1.3.2 Roles towards western Balkan countries during the refugee crisis

In this part I will focus on role construction. Through the discourse of Slovene politicians I will show how discourse was constructed at the time of refugee crisis. I will also show commonalities with the long-term roles mentioned earlier and answer the question of whether or not the roles changed during the refugee crisis.

President Borut Pahor did not emphasize any security threats and argued that Slovenia could handle anything to do with migration. He spoke about security challenges for the EU and NATO, not for the Balkan countries that are on the Balkan route. He does not consider Balkan countries to be responsible. This approach responded to Slovenia's long-term role. Slovenia, through his words, is trying to play a leading role, but not as a responsible actor. He claimed that the behaviour of western Balkan countries should not prevent their integration process. On the contrary, their stability could be provided only by their integration into the EU and NATO. Balkan countries cannot become another conflict area.

In the president's words, Slovenia assists the stabilization of the western Balkan countries in the long-term perspective. Slovenia promised to help with (1) their future in the EU, (2) their future in NATO, (3) solving mutual problems, (4) the fight against terrorism and (5) dealing with refugees. This obviously shows a general Slovene role, but it can also involve more specific support. He has even mentioned regional responsibility. However, responsibility was limited to these words. Pahor sees migration flows as an intermezzo in ensuring security. He believes that Slovenia has a leading role in solving the humanitarian crisis. He criticized borders where there were disputes— Croatian/Serbian, Serbian/Macedonian, Macedonian/Greek. This was the only criticism of western Balkan countries on his part.

Prime Minister Cerar argued similarly that Slovenia should be active in securing Europe and in mediating cooperation between the EU and the western Balkans. Slovenia should focus on integration without a pause during the migration crisis. It is the key to stability in region. He admits selfish interests, but he is very open about Slovenia's role. The president understands the region as a single unit, while the prime minister sees each country individually. Cerar pointed to the relationship between Slovenia and Kosovo. He promised cooperation with Belgium on the stabilization of the whole region. During the humanitarian crisis he criticized the behaviour of Croatia and Serbia in particular. He also claimed that they do not cooperate and because of this Croatia and Serbia create tensions on their borders.

Minister of Foreign affairs Erjavec was undoubtedly part of the migration discourse in Slovenia. He is not only the creator of Slovenia's role, but also a provider of its roles. He claimed that the region is unstable, but steps towards integration are important even during the time of crisis. He said that Slovenia will not stop until the region is stable.

Minister of the Interior Žnidar criticized Croatia most often, because they did not cooperate in dealing with refugees[17]. Other criticism pointed out that Slovenia and the European Commission organized meetings with the western Balkan countries but Croatia did not attend. She also claimed that it is hard to coordinate return policies with Croatia. Žnidar said that each state should cooperate whether it is member or not.

To sum up the roles towards western Balkan countries we need to come back to the beginning of the whole process of role creation. Let us focus on the concept from national role conception to role performance. During the refugee crisis Slovenia created a national role conception based on several factors that can be observed in political discourse. (1) Slovenia is not a Balkan country, but it can play a major role between the EU and western Balkan countries. (2) Western Balkan countries need help, even Serbia (the closest country to EU accession). (3) Slovenia can be a developer, who helps with integration and stabilization. (4) Even during the migration crisis, there is a need to focus on cooperation in the region, but all responsibility lies with the international community, EU and NATO. (5) Slovenia has its interests in Balkan countries (not only political, but economic). (6) Slovenia can mediate discussion and action in solving problems during the refugee crisis. (7) Western Balkan countries cannot be blamed for their behaviour during refugee crisis.

Now we come to the answer to the question about possible role change. No change in the role set was observed. No change in responsibility was observed except for a small mention by the president. So the same role set was observed.

---

[17] The Ministry of the Interior criticized Croatia, who wanted to demolish the fence that the Slovene government had built. The Croatian government claimed that it is not on Slovene territory. Here we can see interference from their mutual problems.

Table 3: Roles during refugee crisis

Roles of Slovenia	developer, supporter	role as an example	developer, supporter, mediator	independent actor
Countries of western Balkans	Macedonia Bosnia and Herzegovina Montenegro	Montenegro	Serbia Kosovo	Croatia

1.3.3 Quantitative results of discourse analysis

In this part I would like to show some quantitative results. The interesting ones come from use of the Voyant tool. The purpose of this tool is that in a tag cloud we can see most the visible topics that are in the data corpus. It was interesting to observe how politicians speak about the migration crisis or if they mention Balkan countries together with the crisis. Let us look at some examples.

The tag cloud below introduces the whole political discourse. All the politicians I studied are included: President Borut Pahor, Prime Minister Miro Cerar, Minister of Foreign Affairs Karl Erjavec and Minister of the Interior Vesna Gyorkos Žnidar.

Picture 1: Tag cloud—political discourse

Note: (translation: eu—European Union; beguncev—refugees; ljudi—people; pomoč—help; sodelovanje—cooperation; meje—borders; zaščito—secure; hrvaško—Croatia; mednarodno—international; policija—police; unije—EU)

It is possible to see the main topics that I have mentioned above. Here is another tag cloud created from the documents of RTV Slovenia about the migration crisis. It is always interesting to compare whether society—as reflected in the media—has the same opinion or discourse.

Picture 2: Tag cloud—RTV Slovenija

Note: (translation: meje—borders; ljudi—people; hrvaška—Croatia; pomoč—help; begunce—refugees; prebežnike—migrants; poti—route; krize—crisis; nadzor—surveillance; policija—police; zaščita—protection; vlada—government; srbija—Serbia; migrant—migrant; evropske—European)

It is interesting that the two tag clouds are not so very different. In the media tag cloud we can see similar interpretations of the Balkan route, Croatia creating problems or other Balkan states as Serbia. Looking at it we do not see any criticism of the western Balkan countries.

To conclude, it can be said that Slovenia did not make any criticism that could change its long-term role. Tag clouds changed when the refugee crisis appeared and some countries became more prominent, but it did not change its behaviour.

Conclusion

Slovenia was for a long time part of the Balkan region. Slovene politicians who are now in post remember Yugoslav times and the period since the declaration of independence. During the 1990s the Balkan region was at war. The so-called Balkan wars in Bosnia and Herzegovina, Croatia and

Serbia were a painful experience for thousands of citizens who lost their homes and became refugees. At that time, at the end of the 1990s, no one had a problem with refugees (or migrants). In Slovenia a lot of organizations helped. This experience influences Slovene politics nowadays. This is the reason why the Slovene government calls this situation a refugee crisis, not a migrant crisis. This is also a reason why they try to behave humanely towards refugees. However, criticism also appeared, more from Slovene citizens. There was criticism about government practices during crisis.

I have focused on the roles performed by Slovenia towards western Balkan countries during migration crisis. I have compared the situation before the crisis and after summer 2015. It has to be said that there was no visible change. Politicians did not speak about western Balkan countries in a negative way. I could not observe any idea that western Balkan countries behaved incorrectly during the crisis. Only one state was massively criticized, and that was Croatia, which did not cooperate in the organization of the flow of migrants.

Slovenian politicians did not change their discourse so their role has not been changed. All western Balkan countries were invited to adhere to European standards of dealing with such a crisis. Some of them were not able to follow the standards, but they were only criticized gently, and the politics of Slovenia has not been changed.

In the discourse it was obvious, that western Balkan countries are still on their way towards the EU and nothing, especially not such a crisis, should stop them. On the contrary, the integration process should be accelerated because it is their future and the only way to stabilize the whole region.

2 ARMENIAN RETURN MIGRATION FROM EU STATES

Lucie Macková

Return migration has not received a lot of attention despite its significance both for the EU states and for the countries of origin of the returnees. What we often see is not a clear-cut migration trajectory starting with a decision to migrate and ending with the integration into the country of settlement but a situation where in fact only some migrants follow these stages. There can be several short visits before the decision to migrate, periods of return of various lengths and finally, some migrants decide to re-migrate to a different country. The notion of an open-ended return is increasingly prevalent (Porobić, 2017) Throughout history, the rate of return was fairly high and it is estimated that between 1880 and 1930, one quarter to one third of all immigrants to America repatriated back to Europe (Wyman, 1993 in Levitt, 2001). Discussing return migration is especially important in the context of large-scale emigration or displacement, whether the causes are related to conflict situations, economic, social or political reasons.

In the Armenian case, with high levels of emigration and low levels of immigration, return migrants who come from the 8 million large Armenian diaspora are likely to fill the gap in the labour market and influence the development of the country of origin, mainly by through social remittances (Levitt, Lamba-Nieves, 2011). Some Armenian returnees can also come from the Syrian diaspora who have been expelled by the conflict (Al Jazeera, 2017). The Armenian state draws on the discourses of return migration and development, for example, in its Strategy for Migration Policy for the years 2017-2021 and in the Strategic Programme of Prospective Development for 2014-2025 (State Migration Services, 2017). However, the return is also important because of EU policy and its directive on returns (European Parliament, 2008) and the budget that is spent on assistance to various groups of returnees. In fact, we can see an entire industry being developed around the process of returns from the EU and we have to inquire whether this assistance is well-spent and what can be done to enhance the experience of the returnees. That is why we have to discuss return migration on the micro level to understand the lived experience of the returnees.

This paper uses semi-structured qualitative interviews with returnees and key informants in Armenia. The returnees in my sample have spent at least one year abroad prior to returning to Armenia. The period of fieldwork in Armenia took place between 2016 and 2018 with various visits amounting to 4 months. This paper will proceed as follows. It will discuss the specifics of the Armenian return migration from the EU states with the focus on two returnee groups: (i) those assisted by the AVRR (assisted voluntary return and reintegration) programmes or other types of programmes facilitating returnee reintegration, (ii) returnees who decided to return on their own (spontaneous returnees). The return motivations connected to the type of return will also be discussed as well as the role of organizations assisting the returnees from EU states. After that, the paper will focus on the role of the returnees and different issues connected to their return, i.e. (i) return preparedness, (ii) social capital and (iii) human capital. This paper will conclude by giving some policy recommendations for the organizations assisting the returnees and the receiving states.

2.1 Armenian returnees from EU States

There are various categories of Armenian returnees from EU states. We can distinguish on the temporal scale: whether the returnees migrated themselves or whether they are the second or third generation of the so-called classical diaspora. In those cases, it might be questionable whether they should be classified as returnees or migrants if they had never lived in Armenia before their decision to migrate. There are also the returnees who decided to return of their own accord, without the assistance of any organization (but with possible assistance of non-governmental organizations within Armenia). These returnees can be skilled, and often they had increased their levels of human capital while living in the EU countries. Another category of migrants is those assisted by the AVRR programmes. In Armenia, these programmes are mainly run by the International Organization for Migration (IOM) and OFII (French Office of Immigration and Integration), which deals with the returnees from France. The local non-governmental organizations often work as implementing partners for these programmes or are directly commissioned by various EU member states to deal with the returns from that specific state (such as Belgium or Austria). At this point, it is important to say that very few organizations work with both groups of returnees because they might have different needs.

The motivation to return is important for subsequent reintegration in the country of origin. However, it is crucial to distinguish between return on the scale from voluntary to forced. IOM distinguishes between three types of return: (i) "Voluntary without compulsion, when migrants decide at any time during their sojourn to return home at their own volition and cost"; (ii) "voluntary under compulsion, when persons are at the end of their temporary protected status, rejected for asylum, or are unable to stay, and choose to return at their own volition"; and (iii) "involuntary, as a result of the authorities of the host state ordering deportation" (IOM, 2012). The widest definition that can be used for voluntary return is the absence of force in return (Black et. al, 2004, p. 6). However, people are often forced by external circumstances (such as visa expiration) to return.

If the return is forced or semi-voluntary (Sinatti, Horst, 2015), it is more difficult for the returnees to integrate fully because some of their objectives might not have been accomplished. Moreover, it is questionable to what extent these return schemes are voluntary as many returnees report different levels of coercion to take part in these programmes. This has been reported even in the Armenian case (Lietaert et al., 2016). It has been argued that IOM employees are aware of this tension between the stated objective of these programmes and the reality for the returnees (Koch, 2014). Moreover, returnees might not have enough time to plan and prepare for their return if they take part in the

AVRR programmes, which can lead to problems with reintegration back into the society in their country of origin. Therefore, the extended timeframe and the degree of voluntariness of the return are important for a sustainable return experience.

2.1.1 Returns assisted by the AVRR programmes

The AVRR programmes represent an important factor in successful returnee reintegration. For example, Black et al. (2004) argued that one factor that affects the sustainability of return is the availability of programmes for returnees. According to Van Houte and Davids (2008), returnees can become disappointed with the support that they receive from non-governmental and international organizations because of the unrealistic expectations they create. Another factor is that the support is short-term, often only extending to several months. There are various components of return assistance, including the transport to Armenia, social assistance and training or small loans to start their own business. Usually, the returnees are given an in-kind support and money is rarely involved. In 2015, there were 499 returnees from the EU assisted by AVRR programmes run by IOM and 433 in 2016. The numbers for the EEA (European Economic Area) are 511 in 2015 and 436 in 2016 (IOM, 2017).

Graph 1: AVRR from the EU/EEA to Armenia

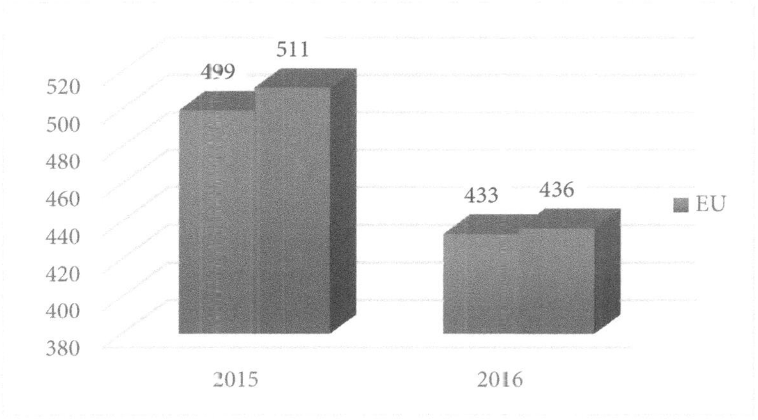

Year	EU
2015	499, 511
2016	433, 436

Source: IOM (2017)

According to a member of staff at OFII (French Office of Immigration and Integration), they assist around 250 persons per year (22 July 2016, personal communication). Together with the assistance provided by other organizations, it can be assumed that there are more than 1,000 returns to Armenia per year (excluding the returns from Russia which are of a higher scale). Many of these returnees go through some assistance in the post-return phase. However, the key informants warn that the return programmes might not be a panacea to solve the returnee situation:

> The economic growth cannot come from reintegration programmes. This type of assistance is not really sustainable, it is a temporary measure (member of staff at OFII, personal communication, 25 July 2016).

Many Armenian returnees who returned from the EU within AVRR programmes had had their asylum claims rejected. These returnees did not have a lot of say in whether they actually wanted to return but were forced to do so by the external circumstances. According to the literature, the availability of assistance upon return is not a key factor in determining whether migrants will return voluntarily. Therefore, these programmes do not usually represent a pull factor in return migration. The threat of deportation can represent a far more important factor (Collyer et al., 2009). Koser and Kushminder (2015) also argued that a negative decision on asylum is a strong determinant for return, but also a strong indicator of a lack of reintegration after return. Furthermore, they argue that the programmes in themselves do not generally motivate return (regardless of the size or content of the programmes) but the threat of removal is important for the decision to avail themselves of the AVRR programmes, which can enable them to "safeguard dignity and rights" while returning (IOM, 2018b). There are different types of programmes with a largely similar content which can offer the returnees post-return assistance and various organizations are already working in this field (see Table 1).

2.1.2 Spontaneous returns

When discussing the role of return migration from the EU to Armenia it is also important to discuss the voluntary returns from the EU countries during which the returnees were given the chance to use their own agency and plan for their return. The spontaneous returns include returnees from the group of skilled migrants or the "repats". Returnees to Armenia come from many different EU countries. Some of these returnees need to renegotiate their identity upon return and may face disillusionment or internal tensions (Pawlowska, 2017). It is difficult to establish the precise number of returnees in many different contexts and even more so when the state does not record the numbers of returnees. Armenia is one of the few countries in the world that has a Ministry of the Diaspora and according to their records, "there were around 65,000 returnees who have returned to Armenia since the early 1990s but only 35,000 of them ultimately remained" (July 6, 2016, personal communication). These numbers include all returnees, not only those returning from the EU states.

When discussing this category of returnees, it is important to inquire about the Armenian diaspora in the EU countries to understand the historical context. The 1915 Armenian genocide contributed to the dispersal of Armenian communities across the world (Brubaker, 2005). However, Armenians migrated even earlier and had a reputation as skilled businessmen and craftsmen (Panossian, 2006). Some scholars have argued that Armenians have always been a diasporic nation, even before the genocide (Adalian, 1989 in Pawlowska, 2017). While historical Armenia included both Eastern (today's Armenia) and Western Armenia (nowadays in Turkey), many of the Armenians in the classical diaspora comprise people originally from Western Armenia and not the South Caucasus (Bakalian, 1994).

The term diaspora has been used by many different authors to denote a large group of members of one nation who reside outside their country of origin. In Greek, diaspora means scattering or dispersion. This term was first used with "classical diasporas" such as the Jewish or Armenian diaspora. The concept of the diaspora is understood not only as a physical entity including certain characteristics (Sheffer, 1986; Safran, 1991) but diaspora can also mean having this label ascribed by others. Diasporas can be real or imagined communities (Anderson, 1983). In addition, diaspora members may have skills and resources that they can use to promote changes in their countries of origin, which may or may not contribute to actual development (Castles, 2010). Some diasporas have influence over the political situation in their countries of origin.

An important group among the spontaneous returnees are former students who have decided to come back after the end of their studies. According to Collier (2013), this type of migration is the most beneficial for the country of origin. This group has reported an increase in skills, especially if they also have an experience with part-time work or internships. According to a survey carried out by the CRRC (Caucasus Research Resource Centre), many Armenian returnees agreed that they gained new skills while working abroad. According to the CRRC, "of those who had worked upon return (42% of the respondents), 32% said that their experience abroad opened the door to better work opportunities in Armenia after their return" (CRRC, 2012, p. 62). Many of them used their experience from abroad in their daily work. They mentioned professional skills (such as technical skills) and language skills as the ones most commonly used. There are various organizations that work with the spontaneous returnees (see Table 1). Only some of them (IOM, UNHCR, and State Migration Service) focus on both of these groups as both groups of the returnees might have different needs. Table 1 summarizes the main organizations in Armenia that work with people availing themselves of the AVRR programmes and with the spontaneous returnees.

Table 1: Main organizations working with the returnees in Armenia (2016)

Name of the organization	Assisted voluntary return	Spontaneous return
International Organization for Migration (IOM)	YES	YES
United Nations High Commissioner for Refugees (UNHCR)	YES	YES
State Migration Service of the RA Ministry of Territorial Administration and Development	YES	YES
Caritas Armenia	YES	NO
French Office for Immigration and Integration (OFII)	YES	NO
French Armenian Development Foundation (FADF)	YES	NO
People in Need	YES	NO
Mission Armenia	YES	NO
German Agency for International Cooperation (GIZ)	NO	YES
Repat Armenia	NO	YES
Birthright Armenia	NO	YES

Source: IOM (2016), author

2.2 Returnee experiences

This chapter will discuss different returnee experiences to illustrate the reality of return migration to Armenia. It will highlight the differences between the groups of returnees and the status of their return (on the scale from voluntary to forced). It will start with discussing the role of return preparedness for the returnees and it will be argued that return preparedness is necessary for the subsequent returnee reintegration. Next, it will assess the importance of social networks (social capital) in return migration. For many migrants, networks represent the most important resource when returning back to their country of origin. However, their networks might not be working very well after a longer period of absence. Finally, this chapter will inquire about the role of skills (human capital) for the returnees. It will show that the education and skills of the returnees matter for their successful engagement upon return. However, it might be problematic for some skilled returnees to find a job that matches their levels of skills.

2.2.1 The role of return preparedness

Cassarino (2004) cites returnee's preparedness and resource mobilisation as two important factors for returnee reintegration. Return preparedness means the willingness to return home and the readiness to return. The circumstances in the host and home countries are important for a sustainable return (Black, Gent, 2006). As Bimal Ghosh (2000, p. 185) points out, return "is largely influenced by the initial motivations for migration as well as by the duration of the stay abroad and particularly by the conditions under which the return takes place". Spontaneous returnees are aware that there is a need to prepare before going back to the country of origin. Many of them have arranged jobs before returning to Armenia. However, the same might not be true for the returnees assisted by the AVRR programmes, which often have a limited timeframe and ask returnees to return in a short period of time, usually days.

One returnee assisted by the AVRR programme was allegedly confronted with the following choice before leaving her host country.

The woman was told, "If you don't go to Armenia, you will be put in handcuffs and sent to Armenia like your son" (woman, 52, returned from Germany). Therefore, the degree of voluntariness during the return process has to be questioned for AVRR returnees and sometimes these programmes are seen as a softer alternative to deportation (Leerkes, Os, Boersema, 2017). Some returnees face the dilemma whether to go back without adequate preparation. The support that is given to them takes place mostly post-return but even then, they might not have enough resources to be able to start a sustainable return project. Therefore, the level of willingness to return is connected to the subsequent return experience. The returnees taking part in the AVRR programmes need to have some time to think about their future in Armenia and they need to be prepared for their return.

Some spontaneous returnees also face issues with their return and despite careful planning and preparation, they might face some disillusionment when it comes to work-related opportunities.

> This is the age when you can try but opportunities here [in Armenia] are slim. I do not exclude going back to Europe (man, 31, returned from Germany).

Therefore, the returnees try to engage in strategies such as gradual return when they first come to "see how things are" in Armenia and only decide later if they are going to stay permanently in the country or not. There are some organizations such as Repat Armenia or Birthright Armenia that try to engage skilled returnees and offer them some initial support that can help them with adjustment to the Armenian environment. Another example of these projects is the UNDP TOKTEN (Transfer of Knowledge Through Expatriate Nationals) programme. This programme was created in 1977 and connects migrant professionals who can be called upon to volunteer their services on a short-term basis to specific programmes in their countries of origin (Mahroum, Eldridge, Daar, 2006). The rationale for this programme is that some of the migrants might decide to come back on a more permanent basis.

Some key informants have also shared their opinions about the return to Armenia and thought that there are opportunities to come but own effort or initiative by the returnees is needed.

> I think opportunities in Armenia are increasing for others to come and share skills. I think this creates more opportunities. Many people are just living their lives and to go to a new country to share skills is an effort, it takes planning. It takes some investment. And the practical side of life is what sometimes gets in the way (staff member at Birthright Armenia, 12 June 2016, personal communication).

Others pointed out the barriers that are inherent in the decision to return to the country of origin and some organizations are working with the returnees to inform them about the challenges.

> Of course, moving back to Armenia is not a one-day decision, they should come round to this idea gradually. Of course, there can be a lot of barriers they need to think about. Therefore our idea was also to present cases showing how these difficulties can be overcome. If a person wants to return, it is their decision and they should know beforehand that there will be problems (staff member at GIZ, 13 June 2016, personal communication).

Return preparedness is a key component for a successful return experience. Many returnees who face a return that happens in a short period of time struggle with subsequent reintegration. For the returnees who planned their return in advance, it can be much easier to reintegrate and social and human capital also play a role in this.

2.2.2 The role of social capital

Social capital and personal networks are important for returnee reintegration. Diaspora practices used by the returnees, such as building their own institutions and networks of support, can help them but it can also be problematic because they create divisions between them and mainstream society (Pawlowska, 2017). If the returnees' networks are not sufficient, they try to use the next available option, which is the support offered by reintegration programmes. However, these might not offer the same outputs as genuine personal networks. The return experience differs for different groups of returnees and is dependent on the motivation to return. If the return is seen as forced, the returnees might be struggling with creating new networks in Armenia. That is not to say that the returnees who return voluntarily do not struggle with their day to day lives but they have social networks which they can capitalize on. The return for some categories of returnees can be extremely difficult as is illustrated by the following quote:

> I am alone here. It is a torture for me. If I had a safe chance to go back I would go (man, 61, returned from Belgium).

This person had his family members in Belgium and he struggled with the return to Armenia, which was semi-voluntary (Sinatti, Horst, 2015). After the return, he was assisted by a non-governmental organization but its level of support was not the same as could have been expected from his social networks. However, many of the members of his social network were in Europe and this person could not engage with them except for occasional calls.

On the other hand, some spontaneous returnees reported that the help received from their networks was crucial for their decision to return and to stay in Armenia. Many people noted that their families and friends were supportive of their decisions to move. For some returnees, the migration experience was so life-changing that they had to create new social networks. One returnee had the following experience:

> I have been in Yerevan for two years now and I have already built new friendship networks (woman, 27, returned from France).

Other returnees mentioned their neighbours and local communities and how they were able to reintegrate with their help. Therefore, social capital is important for returnees and they can avail of it, for example, when looking for a job or in their day to day lives. However, the returnees who lack their own social networks often struggle with reintegration and the organizations which offer the AVRR programmes might not be able to replace the returnees' personal networks.

2.2.3 The role of human capital

Human capital (or the levels of skills and education) can be obtained before leaving the country of origin, after migration and after return. For some of the returnees the skills they have learnt during their stay abroad may be an important factor for obtaining a job in Armenia. The skills can include professional or language skills but also soft skills. For example, some research found that highly-skilled migrants to the Netherlands are in a better position to contribute to the development in their countries of origin by the way of economic and social remittances (Sturge, Bilgili, Siegel, 2016). However, increasing the skill level while a migrant is not a guarantee that returnees will obtain a job after their return to Armenia. Some returnees were also unhappy with the comparatively low-paced working conditions in Armenia. One returnee mentioned the difference in the work environment and emphasized the skills that she learnt while living abroad.

> I also learnt about working relations. You have to be effective and create some value. You know how the Armenians work. They say another day has passed at work, I got my salary... During my studies, I learnt things about business but that was secondary. The most important thing was how I started to perceive reality (woman, 27, returned from France).

It was quite common for the returnees to develop their skills and competencies while living abroad as is shown in the following quote.

> I didn't change too much by going abroad. I was always on time, even before going to Germany. But it helped me develop my way of working (man, 31, returned from Germany).

The returnees mentioned that for them the experience of living abroad was important for developing their skills and increasing their levels of education. It might be more difficult to reintegrate if the returnees are older, have lower levels of skills and might not have enough motivation for training upon return. However, the returnees who are skilled might still be facing difficulties when looking for a job in Armenia. Therefore, it is possible that there will be difficulties awaiting returnees across various skill levels. Some returnees mentioned that while living abroad they developed their soft skills and way of working. So if this group of returnees is able to get a job upon return, it could have some beneficial effects on their personal situation and could create a possible spill over effect.

2.3 Policy implications

This section will briefly discuss the programmes assisting the returnees in Armenia and it will outline some policy implications for the organizations as well as for the government of the Republic of Armenia and other actors. There are various organizations assisting the returnees and they differ by the audience they aim to cater for and by the type of assistance they provide. The organizations assisting returnees were briefly mentioned in Table 1. The programmes offer assistance to various groups of returnees on the scale from forced to voluntary returns, including both the participants in the AVRR programmes and the spontaneous returnees. Some programmes only offer basic assistance while others allow returnees to enhance their skills. However, returnees might struggle with finding programmes that would fit their exact needs. Many of these programmes are very similar in content, levels of assistance and the recipients targeted.

Some key informants argued that there are problems awaiting the returnees and that the physical return is often difficult. The social situation in Armenia can also appear unsatisfactory to the returnees but it can be even worse for the local residents. As one key informant warns,

> We have to be careful with the returnees because in some situations, the neighbours who never left are often worse off and they do not get any attention. This creates social tensions and increases dissatisfaction and frustration (staff member at OSCE, 26 July 2016, personal communication).

A lot of funding by EU governments is spent on the AVRR programmes in different organizations to promote returnee reintegration. There is a whole business around the AVRR programmes in Armenia. However, these organizations offer programmes that are quite similar and their work often overlaps. Moreover, cases of returnees receiving support from various organizations at the same time are not unheard of. Therefore, there should be more coordination between the programmes and more emphasis on monitoring the impacts of these programmes.

There are several organizations that work with returnees who did not avail themselves of the AVRR programmes and skilled returnees can also face many difficulties. Among these is inadequate skills recognition or problems with readjusting to a different working environment. The skilled returnees can also struggle with finding a job that correspond to their expectations. One key informant even stated that it might not be beneficial for the returnees to return at all.

> Physical return is often difficult. Maybe it is more useful for people to stay where they are at the moment. For example, if they are in Germany or France, they have a better infrastructure to carry out research at universities than in Armenia (staff member at IOM, 13 July, personal communication).

There should be policies that help skilled returnees to overcome barriers and make use of their skills. Strategies such as competitive salaries, suitable facilities for skilled workers together with the official government programme to promote skilled migration have been successfully used in different contexts. Without attracting return migration, there could still be a long way for Armenia to achieve its policy goals. However, the returnees who are interested in their return to Armenia and want to bring in new ideas or, in other words, social remittances are the key actors here so it is crucial to understand their perspectives and experiences.

Conclusion

In conclusion, it is important to note that the return experience can differ for various returnees. It depends on their age and other experience, including the experience before migrating and in the host country. On the one hand, if the returnees increased their skills during migration, they are in a better position to contribute to society in their country of origin.

On the other hand, these returnees might struggle finding a job that is commensurate with their levels of experience. There are various organizations working in the field of return migration in Armenia and they can be divided into organizations working with the AVRR programmes and those working with spontaneous returnees. Some of these organizations offer assistance to both groups.

Return migration to Armenia is important because it directly affects other states, including the EU states and their policies on return migration. While the AVRR programmes are widely hailed and seen as the stepping stone for returnee reintegration, the truth is that they fail to replace the support that returnees get from their social networks. Therefore, social capital plays an important role in returnee reintegration and it is difficult to replace it with other types of support. Human capital, or the levels of skills and education, are important for the returnees who are looking for a job in Armenia. These returnees are often welcome in public discourse and it is presumed that they will contribute to the development of Armenia. While there is no conclusive evidence for this, it is also necessary to provide support for AVRR returnees who might have lower skill levels and are in need of a long-term training or support. Finally, the return preparedness emerges as a key concept for Armenian returnees. It is crucial for them to plan for their return, have contacts in Armenia and be able to use their networks. Therefore, the programmes working with returnees should take all of these factors into account to ensure a sustainable return.

3 MOLDOVAN LABOUR MIGRANTS IN EU COUNTRIES: STATUS AND PROSPECTS (BASED ON SOCIOLOGICAL RESEARCH IN GERMANY, ITALY, PORTUGAL, UK)

Valeriu Mosneaga, Tatiana Turco and Gheorghe Mosneaga

When the Republic of Moldova became an independent democratic state, this was accompanied by its active inclusion in international migration processes. The deep economic crisis and the ineffectiveness of government-implemented reforms contributed to the spread of migration sentiments among Moldovan citizens. They began actively to migrate abroad for permanent residence, to earn money, to study, etc. Today, almost a third of the physically able population of the Republic of Moldova takes part in the process of international labour migration. The most popular destinations for labour migration, both legal and illegal, are Russia and the European Union countries.

During the course of sociological research conducted by the authors in 2016-2017, the problems of formation of Moldovan communities and diasporas in six countries (Russia, Italy, Portugal, Germany, Israel, the UK) have been surveyed. Since the goal of this article is to analyze the condition and prospects of Moldovan labour migrants in European Union countries, we have selected from the list of researched countries the ones most appropriate—Germany, Italy, Portugal, and the UK. The choice of countries was conditioned by specific factors, the study of which allowed us to obtain a more complete and versatile picture of Moldovan migration, and the formation of Moldovan communities and diasporas abroad.

In the European Union *Italy* is the main destination of Moldovan labour migrants. In large part, the affinity between the Romanian and Italian languages contributed to this and facilitated the process of Moldovan citizens' integration into Italian society. Besides, Italy as a traditional country of emigration has many years of experience of tolerant and open attitudes towards immigrants.

Portugal was one of the first countries to which Moldovan migrant workers travelled. Portugal is characterized by one of the most tolerant and well thought out policies in the field of immigrant integration in the European Union. The linguistic affinity between Portuguese and Romanian was also attractive to Moldovans.

Germany has a powerful economic potential, a huge labour market and a developed social system. Germany is only just opening up as a country of labour migration for Moldovans. This is explained by the fact that Germany only fully opened its labour market for Romanian citizens (a significant number of Moldovans use Romanian passports for entry and work in the EU countries) in 2014.

The interest in the plans and strategies of Moldovan labour migrants in *the UK* arose in the context of Brexit. The study is of interest because it reflects the psychological state, moods and plans of Moldovan citizens who are in the UK and face certain risks and fears.

Moldovan citizens are quite successful in integrating themselves into their destination countries' societies. Moldovan communities are formed in many countries as result of migration, and these gradually transform into diasporas. As the centuries-old international experience shows, diasporas can act as bridges between the country of origin and the countries of migrant destination/residence.

3.1 Reasons for the emigration of Moldovans

The Republic of Moldova actively joined the migration process in the early 1990s. In this period, political/ethno-political and ideological factors conditioned by the formation process of the independent Moldovan state and the consolidation of national state identity dominated (Mosneaga, 2000). International labour migration has become a dominant trend since the second half of the 1990s.

Starting with the traditionally familiar regions—Russia and Ukraine—Moldovan migrant workers gradually began mastering the countries of the European Union, Israel, the USA and Canada, preferring the European Mediterranean countries (Italy, Spain, Greece, Portugal, France, etc.) Since the second half of the 2000s, and especially in the 2010s, Moldovan migrants started to go beyond the "Latin world", which was attractive because of language proximity, when choosing a country of labour migration, and successfully "explored" Ireland, the United Kingdom and Germany (Cheianu-Andrei, 2013; Mosneaga, 2017, p.32).

The main reason for the migration of Moldovan citizens is the economic factor. The family's difficult financial situation, the lack of work and the need to solve various social and domestic problems remain important and are still the dominant cause of migration. People regard labour emigration as the only way out, an opportunity to change their lives for the better. But although the aspiration to solve financial problems and provide material well-being served as the basis for labour migration, the present-day economic motivation of Moldovan labour migrants has become more complicated.

At the same time, in recent years the number of migrant workers has increased: they had a job in the Republic of Moldova, normal housing and they were paid a good salary (according to Moldovan standards), which allowed their family not to be poor. The decisive reason to emigrate was the desire to get a higher salary and earn more than they could have at home for the same work in order to solve their existing financial problems or improve their current financial situation. This shows that the Moldovan labour force is becoming increasingly "capricious". It makes a choice in favour of more profitable jobs and more acceptable and human conditions of work and life.

Among the Moldovan migrants there is another, less numerous group, comprised of young people from well-endowed families. The main factor that pushes them into migration is their desire to test themselves in labour activity abroad, the intention to change their environment and to see the world while earning some money (Mosneaga, Turcan, Mosneaga, 2018, p. 88).

Moldovan politics acts as one of the "push" factors forcing Moldovan citizens to travel in search of a better life and existence abroad.

Often, this also prevents them from returning. One of the migrants in the focus group said quite frankly, "I would have returned if there was not that politics" (Mosneaga, 2017, p. 34).

A new trend in Moldovan labour migration is its reorientation to labour emigration. Earlier, this trend also occurred, but it was less noticeable and not understood by labour migrants themselves: there was no rejection of the idea of going back home, but their return was postponed to the medium term, or even became an uncertain long-term prospect. Since the late 2000s, this reorientation has become a reality. This is evidenced by the reintegration of families—the movement of family members unable to work (children and parents of migrants, pensioners) to the country of emigration.

We would also like to emphasize the factor of low societal competition in the Republic of Moldova in comparison with the countries where Moldovan labour migrants go. Moldovan migrants, having acquired legal residence and employment status in their countries of destination, have a chance to experience the attractiveness of the integration policies in the receiving countries.

Among recent trends in Moldovan migration abroad, traveling for educational purposes should be mentioned. Going abroad to study for the purpose of obtaining education at universities in the EU and other countries has become widespread since the second half of the 2000s.

Our survey showed that the main reasons for emigration by Moldovans are economic (work), educational and humanitarian (family reunification). Nevertheless, the dominant role is played by economic reasons (Table 1). For instance, if we consider the entire sample, the share of economic reasons in the overall structure of emigration reasons is about 75%. It should be noted, however, that if we speak of the reason formulated as "the family has taken this decision" (which accounts for approximately 4%), the economic aspect is also significant here. "Studies" as a reason accounts for 12.5%, while "family reunification" is a reason for 13%.

Table 1: Main reasons for the emigration of Moldovan citizens abroad

	Italy	Portugal	Germany	United Kingdom	Total
Studies	11.2%	5.4%	13.8%	19.4%	12.5%
Job was offered (found)	26.4%	45.9%	43.7%	35.5%	37.9%
Intention to find a new job	52.0%	27.0%	32.2%	19.4%	32.7%
Decision taken by the family	4.0%	8.1%	3.4%	0%	3.9%
Family reunification	6.4%	13.5%	6.9%	25.8%	13.2%

Source: Sociological research conducted by the authors in 2016-2017

Economic reasons were important to people who migrated to Italy—78%, Germany—76% and Portugal—74%. Educational reasons ("studies") are frequent among Moldovan migrants in the UK (over 19%) and Germany (14%). Humanitarian reasons ("family reunification") are most often characteristic for migrants in the UK and Portugal, accounting for 26% and 14%, respectively. In other countries, this reason is registered to a lesser extent.

Consequently, economic factors continue to influence the migration of Moldovan citizens abroad. Labour migration is the main form of Moldovan international migration. In recent years, other tendencies have also been noted: there is an increase of study migration and family reunification is also becoming a more prominent reason. In the context of the current EU visa-free regime, the significance and volume of circular labour migration (legal entry and illegal employment for up to three months) with the purpose of money-making and simultaneously substituting, and keeping the work place, for Moldovan migrants who legally reside and work in the EU countries and temporarily travel home for vacation or medical treatment, is also increasing.

3.2 Social and demografic portrait of Moldovan migrants in the countries researched

According to the Ministry of Foreign Affairs and European Integration, the number of Moldovan citizens legally residing abroad by the end of 2015, regardless of the length of stay in the country of destination, amounted to 805,509 people.

The specificity of Moldovan migration to the European Union is that, in addition to the legal form, it is supplemented, to a large extent, by illegal migration, which is mainly labour migration. Those who are in the EU countries illegally do not "fall" in the zone of visibility of the statistical structures of the receiving countries. A large number of Moldovan labour immigrants in the receiving countries have illegal status due to illegal entry, illegal residence or illegal employment (Mosneaga, 2012).

In our research we surveyed a wide spectrum of socio-demographic characteristics of Moldovan labour migrants. This chapter's length does not allow us to dwell on them in detail, so we will point out the most significant aspects.

Analysis of the distribution of migrants in the host countries shows that Italy today leads among the EU countries with the highest number of Moldovan labour migrants. According to official data from the Ministry of Labour of Italy for 2016, there were more than 150,000 Moldovan citizens with a residence permit in the country. In fact, there are significantly more Moldovans living there, as many of them are there either illegally or on the basis of Romanian or Bulgarian passports or passports of other EU countries. Since mid-2010, the process of acquiring Italian citizenship by Moldovan migrants has begun, both through naturalization and through marriage with Italian citizens. Given these factors, the number of Moldovan citizens (including those with EU passports) who are labour migrants in Italy, is according to expert estimates approaching 240,000 people (Mosneaga, 2017, p. 49-50).

The number of Moldovan citizens in Germany, according to German statistics, is small. In 2015, there were about 14,815 Moldovan citizens in Germany (Extended, 2017, p. 117). According to experts, this amounts to 25-30% of the real number of Moldovans in Germany, since many Moldovan citizens have Romanian passports and live and work in the EU as citizens of the European Union.

In Portugal, the number of Moldovan migrant workers reached a peak in 2008, when the country officially had more than 21,000 people. In 2015, 6,948 Moldovan citizens were officially registered (Extended, 2017, p. 117). This decrease in numbers is due firstly to the fact that many Moldovan citizens received Portuguese citizenship. Secondly, when the economic situation was deteriorating economic situation in 2008-2015, many Moldovan migrant workers moves to other countries as Portuguese citizens.

In the UK, the bulk of Moldovan citizens (90-95%) are living there on the basis of passports from EU countries. It is a minority of Moldovan labour migrants who possess only Moldovan citizenship and live and work in the UK on the basis of labour contracts or a British visa (somewhat more than 1,800 people). These people have legal status, a residence permit and work. According to the estimates of the Moldovan consulate and UK statistics, the number of Moldovan citizens in the United Kingdom of Great Britain and Northern Ireland is approaching 30,000 people (Mosneaga, 2017, p. 60).

The sociological survey showed that an absolute majority of respondents are of working age (Table 2). The share of persons under the age of 40 is 71.6% of the total number of respondents. However, each country has its own specifics. In Germany, the number of respondents under the age of 30 is 73%. This is the highest figure for all countries. It demonstrates the attractiveness of German universities for Moldovan citizens. The UK is the leader in the age category of 30 to 40 years. In Portugal, the number of young persons (under 30 years of age) among respondents is more than half (52.6%). Italy has the highest proportion of migrants over the age of 40—42.9%. In general, the data shows that the employable population is leaving the Republic of Moldova.

Table 2: Distribution of Moldovan migrants by age in the countries of destination

Age	Italy	Portugal	Germany	United Kingdom	Total
18-30	31.7%	52.6%	73.0%	36.4%	48.4%
31-40	25.4%	18.4%	12.4%	36.4%	23.2%
41-50	24.6%	26.4%	12.4%	21.1%	21.1%
51+	18.3%	2.6%	2.2%	6.1%	7.3%

Source: Sociological research conducted by the authors in 2016-2017

Among Moldovan migrants, men and women are almost equally represented (with a slight predominance of female migrants). A prevalence of men is seen among migrants in Germany (almost 2 times higher) and in the UK (1.5 times higher).

In Germany Moldovan citizens are mainly employed in construction and transportation. In Portugal and Italy, male Moldovan migrants mainly work in construction. In the UK, men are occupied primarily in the field of computer technology. Moldovan citizens can be found in business, in the financial sphere, in medicine, education, IT and in the hotel sphere.

The specific case of Italy is that two-thirds of all Moldovan labour migrants are women. This is explained by the demand for female labour in the field of domestic service and caring, and in the conventional social and medical services. Care for sick and elderly members of the family is the responsibility of relatives, whereas in Germany the state takes care of them. Therefore in Germany Moldovan migrant workers work in the social services, using in homes for the sick and elderly and social service centres (Davydova-Minguet, 2014).

Portugal is characterized by a more even gender balance among Moldovan migrants. Women make up more than half of all Moldovan migrants; they are occupied in the service sector (hotels, housekeeping, and caring). In Germany and Portugal, those migrants who have managed to have their medical diplomas recognised work in their profession.

An analysis of the marital status of Moldovan migrants shows that more than a half of the Moldovan migrants in the countries studied are officially married. The highest share of unmarried, single migrants is seen among Moldovan migrants in Germany (almost 60%) and Portugal (more than 40%).

An analysis of the educational status of Moldovan migrants in the countries researched shows that the level of education and qualifications is quite high (Table 3). The highest figure is in the UK, where more than 90% of migrants have university education or have completed professional training. Every second migrant has a master's degree. For other countries, this figure is somewhat different, but also quite high. In Germany, Portugal and Italy, the share of such workers is lower and equals to an average of two-thirds. Here every third migrant has a professional education. The exception is Germany, where this figure is lower (one in five migrants).

Table 3: Education of Moldovan migrants in the countries of destination

	Italy	Portugal	Germany	United Kingdom	Total
Secondary school (Lyceum)	27.0%	34.2%	36.0%	9.1%	26.6%
Vocational school	34.9%	39.5%	23.6%	21.2%	29.8%
Diploma of Licentiate	15.9%	13.2%	20.2%	15.2%	16.1%
Master's Degree	21.4%	13.2%	16.9%	54.5%	26.5%
PhD	0%	0%	3.4%	0%	0.85%

Source: Sociological research conducted by the authors in 2016-2017

According to the National Bureau of Statistics of the Republic of Moldova, about 69% of Moldovan citizens who were abroad in 2015 came from rural areas (Extended, 2017, p. 25). Our survey shows that among Moldovan migrants, natives of different types of settlements are strongly represented (rural settlements, small towns and big cities). However, the inhabitants of rural areas comprise from a third (Germany) to half (Italy) of migrants. In the UK the share of rural residents among Moldovan migrants is only 3%. In the UK there is an absolute prevalence of people from major Moldovan towns and cities.

Our survey revealed that the location of Moldovan migrants in major cities is typical for the UK (51%); every second Moldovan migrant lives in medium-sized cities in Portugal (50%) and in Germany (45%). A very small share of migrants lives in rural areas.

The survey shows that most Moldovan migrants (80.4%) have a residence permit in their country of destination (Table 4). The situation is somewhat different in the UK. The share of Moldovan citizens who have a residence permit in this country is lower, making up 63-64%. That means that almost every third Moldovan migrant (36-37%) in the UK has no residence permit.

Table 4: Availability of a residence permit in the country of destination

	Italy	Portugal	Germany	United Kingdom	Total
Available	85.6%	86.8%	85.4%	63.6%	80.4%
Not available	13.6%	13.2%	14.6%	36.4%	19.4%
No answer	0.8%	0%	0%	0%	0.2%

Source: Sociological research conducted by the authors in 2016-2017

The absolute majority (89%) of Moldovan citizens work in the countries of destination. The highest figure in this regard is among Moldovan citizens in Portugal (95%). These figures are lower in the UK (88%), Italy (87%) and Germany (78%). This is explained by the fact that these countries have a significant number of Moldovan students who are less involved in the working process.

Our survey of the Moldovan diaspora showed that 75% of migrants have a work permit. The highest percentage of persons with a work permit is concentrated in Portugal (82%) and Italy (80%). The proportion in Germany is lower. It amounts to 78%. In the UK only 60% of respondents answered that they have a work permit. Over 37% of Moldovan migrants there found it difficult to answer/gave no answer to this question. This makes one think about the reasons for the absence of an answer.

It is known that economic reasons force a migrant to emigrate in search of a higher income and means of subsistence. For this reason, the migrant is most likely to agree to take work that does not correspond to his/her level of education and qualifications. A foreign citizen who is a labour migrant is less "capricious" in this matter.

Our survey confirmed this fact. Almost every second Moldovan migrant surveyed (49.5%) has a job that does not match or is below their qualifications (Table 5). This picture is observed in all the countries studied. In Italy, the share of such workers among Moldovan migrants is 54%, in Germany 49%, in the UK 48% and in Portugal 47%. At the same time, a significant share (35.9%) of respondents indicate that the work they perform is in line with the existing qualification. Only 13% of migrants note that the work they perform is above their qualifications. The figures are above average in Portugal (22%) and in Germany (19%). The figure is below the average in Italy—12%.

Table 5: Availability of a job in the country of destination, according to the existing qualifications

	Italy	Portugal	Germany	United Kingdom	Total
Higher	11.5%	22.2%	18.6%	0%	13.1%
Lower	**54.0%**	47.2%	48.6%	48.3%	49.5%
Same	32.7%	27.8%	31.4%	**51.7%**	35.9%
No answer	1.8%	2.8%	1.4%	0%	1.5%

Source: Sociological research conducted by the authors in 2016-2017

The income in the country of destination is both an important criterion for the profitability of migration, and a condition for integration into the host society. The majority of migrants (65.4%) have incomes within the range of the average income of €500 to €1,501 per month (Table 6). 10.6% of Moldovan migrants have an income which is below €500 per month. At the same time, 24.1% of Moldovan migrants have a monthly income of more than €1,501. We note that such income is provided not only by high salaries, but also by the payment of overtime (an increase in the duration of the working day, work in two or more places, work without days off or only one day off, etc.).

Table 6: Average income of Moldovan migrants in the country of destination

	Italy	Portugal	Germany	United Kingdom	Total
Less than €500	11.4%	11.1%	13.6%	6.3%	10.6%
500-750€	13.8%	19.4%	17.0%	3.1%	13.3%
751-1000€	30.9%	22.2%	17.0%	12.5%	20.7%
1001-1500€	29.3%	22.2%	36.4%	37.5%	31.4%
1501-2000€	12.2%	22.2%	13.6%	21.9%	17.5%
More than €2000	0.8%	2.8%	2.3%	18.8%	6.2%
No answer	1.6%	0%	0%	0%	0.4%

Source: Sociological research conducted by the authors in 2016-2017

The survey outlined that 93.4% of Moldovan migrants have a valid Moldovan passport. However, many Moldovan citizens have citizenship (passports) of other countries (71.2%). Dual citizenship is allowed by Moldovan legislation. Our survey showed that the highest proportion having a second citizenship/passport is in the UK—97%. In other countries, the figure is lower. This is due to the fact that the Moldovan passport allows you to enter the countries of the European Union without a visa and stay there continuously for up to 90 days, but it does not give the right to employment in the EU. Moldovan citizens solve this issue by "restoring" Romanian or Bulgarian citizenship. Romania and Bulgaria grant their citizenship to Moldovan citizens on historical or ethnic grounds. Their citizens, as EU citizens, have the right to work in the EU.

Despite the fact that more than 70% of the respondents possess the citizenship of other countries, only a fifth of the Moldovan migrants interviewed has a passport of the host country. This is most widespread among Moldovan respondents in Portugal—37%. In the UK it is 21%; in Italy—15%; in Germany—10%.

Our survey showed that many Moldovan migrants would like to have the citizenship of the host country. Of those who do not have the citizenship of the host country/destination (in total 79% of the sample of Moldovan migrants), two-thirds (67%) would like to have it. In the various countries, context, the proportion is as follows: in Italy—63%; in Portugal—85%; in Germany—58%; in the UK—63%.

The citizenship of the host country provides for the extension of human capabilities in various spheres of life. In addition, possessing the citizenship of the host country creates more favourable conditions for the integration of migrants into the society of the countries of destination.

3.3 Moldovan business and diaspora associations in the countries of destination

The process of forming Moldovan communities, the Moldovan diaspora, abroad involves solving the problem of integration of migrants into the host society. The integration of Moldovan citizens into the host society is relatively successful. However, we must also think of the future, of the formation of a Moldovan diaspora that preserves its traditions, culture and language and cooperates with its homeland.

Business plays an important role in consolidating the diaspora. Its formation and consolidation show that among the migrants there are self-motivated and enterprising persons who, by their success in doing business, can contribute to increasing the wealth of the host country, creating new jobs in that country. Migrant businesses often not only support and employ immigrants in the host country, but also act as a sponsor for the activities of diaspora organizations.

We should note that the Republic of Moldova has no historical tradition of developing business abroad. For example, Moldovan businesses in Italy were first established only with the appearance of Moldovan labour migrants—that is, from the second half of the 1990s. Yet at the end of 2014, according to Italian statistics, there were about 4,500 "Moldovan" enterprises. The bulk of Moldovan businesses are concentrated in construction—70.2%, and in trade—8.2% (Mosneaga, 2017, p. 96-97).

Those Moldovan citizens who have opened businesses in the receiving countries point to the simple procedure for registering a company (Portugal, the UK), the provision of specific privileges during the first period of the business's existence and strict adherence to the law, to norms, and to deadlines (Germany, Italy).

The Moldovan business abroad is still at the beginning of the road. However, there are already positive examples and the main problems were identified which need to be overcome so that there will be successful and effective development and promotion of its role both in the host country and in the homeland of the Moldovan migrants.

However, Moldovan business people are afraid to invest in Moldova. The reason for this is political instability, corruption and the unfavourable investment climate. They want guarantees that they will not lose their money and business. Furthermore, there is a need for simplification of the procedure for registering a company. Therefore, the valuable experience obtained by Moldovan entrepreneurs abroad should be used to change the situation in Moldova in the field of initiating and running a business.

If business is guided by economic interests, then diaspora associations are aimed at solving the various problems faced by co-nationals. In other words, the representatives of Moldovan communities abroad, or the diaspora, are their target group.

According to statistics from the Bureau for Diaspora Relations of the Republic of Moldova, 94 associations of the Moldovan diaspora in 19 countries of the world were registered at the end of 2016 [Lista asociațiilor]. 32 associations represent Italy, and 2 associations each—Portugal, Germany and the United Kingdom. Associations of Moldovan migrants in Italy, Portugal and the UK are the most active. In Germany, the process has yet to develop widely. We should point out the specific case of Moldovan associations in the UK they have managed independently to obtain financing for their projects and are not asking for financial aid from Moldova. This is a significant indicator of a diaspora's maturity, of its role as a serious actor in social processes (Mosneaga, 2017, p. 114-5).

Ethnic/national communities of migrants are transformed into a diaspora when there is a conscious aspiration to maintain connections with their historical or real homeland. Various diaspora associations that serve as the institutionalization of the diaspora facilitate this broadly. Membership in diaspora associations shows the migrant's desire to maintain connections with the homeland not only at an individual, but also at a collective level.

Our survey showed that the absolute majority of migrants (90.3%) are not members of diaspora organizations. The proportion for all countries is above average, with the exception of the UK. The share of respondents who are not part of Moldovan associations is significantly lower there and constitutes 82%. The main reasons for the non-participation of Moldovan migrants in the activities of diaspora associations are: unfamiliarity with the Moldovan organizations in the region where they live (42.4%); lack of interest (34.5%); the opinion that "it is not important" (10%).

Although the activity and interest of Moldovan migrants (the respondents of our survey) in the activity of diaspora organizations in the countries of residence is low, people still recognize the importance of realizing diaspora goals in order to maintain and consolidate contact between Moldovan natives and their homeland.

3.4 Communication with the homeland and plans for the future

Communication with the homeland includes not only the preservation and development of relations with relatives in Moldova or abroad, with compatriots and natives of/immigrants from the Republic of Moldova in the host country, but also the maintenance of contacts and cooperation with Moldovan state structures in the host country, in particular with the embassy and consulate of the Republic of Moldova.

Our survey shows that 40% of respondents have been in contact with the Moldovan consulates abroad. Contact with the consulate by Moldovan migrants in the countries surveyed is most often related to the necessity of receiving official documents or official consultations. The absolute majority (82%) of the Moldovan respondents contacted the consulate mentioned addressing the issues related to the registration/receipt of official documents. 18% generally in the sample contacted the consulate for the purpose of consultations, more often in Portugal (26%).

Moldovan labour migrants most often stay in touch with their relatives who reside in Moldova by phone (69.8%) and Skype (86%); and they send them monetary transfers (20.5% of respondents do it often, and 48.8% do it from time to time). The majority of Moldovan migrants monitor the political, economic, and social situation in Moldova, mainly through the internet (89.5%). According to the survey, the absolute majority (86.7%) of Moldovan migrants have visited Moldova since they established themselves in the destination country. The main reason to visit Moldova for 90.5% of the respondents was to visit their relatives.

With the increase in the length of stay in the country of destination, there the perception of the goal transforms from temporary to permanent migration, and both the structure and the amount of money spent on housing, education, entertainment, etc. changes. The migrant spends more money on those spheres of life which do not have a significant meaning for them if their orientation is towards temporary migration.

Table 7: Migrants' desire to return to Moldova

	Italy	Portugal	Germany	United Kingdom	Total
Yes	62.4%	47.4%	48.9%	63.6%	55.6%
No	36.0%	50.0%	51.1%	36.4%	43.4%
No answer	1.6%	2.6%	0%	0%	1.1%

Source: Sociological research conducted by the authors in 2016-2017

Based on this, an important topic in our research was the analysis of the Moldovan migrants' plans for their future, and the place the Republic of Moldova holds in that future. When asked if they were going to return home after spending some time in another country, three-fifths of the Moldovan migrants polled answered that they do plan to return home (Table 7). By country, the situation is as follows: in the UK—64%, in Italy—62%, in Germany—49% and in Portugal—47%. The higher proportion of those who desire to return home in the UK is linked to Brexit.

Our research has revealed three main groups when estimating the migrants' future and return to Moldova. In *the first group*, the Moldovan migrants are convinced defectors. A significant number of migrants (young people primarily) clearly do not want and do not plan to return to their homeland. They have a job and property in the host country, their children were born (or were brought up) and are being educated there. They seek to integrate into the new environment and to become law-abiding citizens and workers in their host countries. But these people are not always inclined against Moldova; they can be and are activists of the associations of the Moldovan diaspora.

The second group of migrants is comparable in number with the first and close to it in what they say. These people are still at a crossroads. In fact, they have not definitely decided on the future yet. Therefore they postpone their return to the more distant future. Their return is conditional on both their own successes in gaining material prosperity in the host country and on positive changes in their country.

The third group of migrants, which intend unequivocally to return home, is considerably smaller in number than the previous ones. There are primarily older people who could not adapt to the way of life in the host country among those who declare they will definitely return.

The Moldovan labour migrants' return or non-return home strongly depends on the Moldovan authorities' policies to change the situation in Moldova. At the same time, the Moldovan state must strive to build relationships with those citizens who have clearly decided not to return home. The diaspora is becoming an independent actor in migration politics. With this in mind, new approaches are necessary, approaches that are conditioned by the changing migration situation in Moldova itself, and in the countries that accept Moldovan migrants.

Conclusion

The results of the study of Moldovan labour migrants in the countries of the European Union make it possible to draw the following conclusions.

Firstly, economic factors continue to cause the migration of Moldovan citizens abroad. Labour migration is the basic form of Moldovan international migration.

Secondly, the absolute majority of migrants are persons of working age. Moldovan migrants are educated people. However, migrants are often engaged in unskilled labour or work which requires lower qualifications and education than those they received.

Thirdly, Moldovan communities abroad differ in the number of their members. The absolute majority of Moldovan migrants successfully integrate into their countries of destination.

Fourthly, Moldovan business abroad is developing and gaining experience, best practices and success stories. Nevertheless, migrants are rather reserved in terms of investing in business in Moldova.

Diaspora associations strengthen and institutionalize the diaspora, serving as an instrument for transforming the communities into a diaspora. The associations of the Moldovan diaspora are characterized by the tendency to preserve and promote national cultural values, to consolidate the diaspora and to work on a voluntary basis.

Fifthly, contacts with the native land, relatives and friends remain an important aspect of the life and behaviour of a migrant. People are quite actively interested in the events and the life in their homeland. Most migrants are eager to visit the Republic of Moldova during their vacation. A large portion of migrants transfers money home to their relatives.

Sixthly, there are three main concepts regarding the future prospects among Moldovan communities abroad. A significant number of migrants definitely do not intend to return to their homeland. The second group has not actually taken any final decision about their future. The third group of migrants unequivocally intends to return home.

The Republic of Moldova has to continue cooperating with, and expanding the forms and methods of working with, Moldovan migrants and diasporas abroad, and in involving them in investing funds, technologies and skills for the sustainable development of the Republic of Moldova, and encouraging them to return to their homeland.

PART III:
MIGRATION: CZECHIA AND SLOVAKIA

1 THE THEORY AND PRACTICE OF MIGRATION WITH A FOCUS ON CZECHOSLOVAKIA IN THE 20TH CENTURY

Ľudmila Maliková and Josette Baer Hill

What did migration in practise and theory look like in the politically contested Central European space? With a focus on Communist Czechoslovakia (1948–1989), we present facts and figures of immigration and emigration, respectively. Our paper investigates also what political thinkers and philosophers had to say about a regime that citizens wanted to leave. Before that regime collapsed in November 1939, waves of emigration had occurred; those who left Czechoslovakia did not only commit a criminal offence; they put their relatives and families who stayed in the country under political pressure. The totalitarian system was, first and foremost and since Lenin, the principal result of the totalitarian mind-set, a particular way of thinking we explore at the end of our paper.

1.1 The case of Czechoslovakia in the 20th century

1.1.1 The immigrants' story: the Wheeler family in communist Czechoslovakia[13]

If we look at it in the context of what would become the Cold War, the story of the Wheeler family is a telling example for Soviet propaganda in the grand theatre of the ideological war of the 20th century. The Cold War

---

[18] Note that minor parts of this subchapter appear in Baer (2018).

was in formation from 1945 on; it became visible for the first time in 1948, when the Central European states were not allowed to participate in the Marshall Plan for the reconstruction of post-war Europe. One could therefore say that participation in the Marshall Plan was the litmus test for a country's independence—and non-participation a demonstration of Soviet hegemonial power.

Immediately after the end of WWII, the former Allies GB, USA and USSR drifted apart because of their different ideological orientation. While the Western states advocated market economy and democratisation, hence a system that protected the individual in a rule-of-law state, the Soviet Union under Stalin followed quite a different agenda: only planned economy, Marxism-Leninism as state theory and the rule of the Communist Party would make the world a safer place, forfeiting Fascism and National Socialism forever. In Marxist-Leninist theory, wars were power games of the ruling bourgeoisie that had always been eager to enslave and exploit the working class by bourgeois political currents such as Liberalism, Nationalism, and Fascism. In 1945, Germany was defeated, under immense sacrifices of the Soviet people; millions of Soviet citizens did not die to have the West German zone, the legacy of Hitlerism, prosper again under Allied command—or so Stalin must have thought. The East German zone was firmly under Soviet command. Not yet, or so it seemed to the Western view, were the Central European states Poland, Czechoslovakia and Hungary.

Czechoslovakia's fate was particularly painful for democratically minded citizens: unbeknownst to Western politicians, the first step on the path that would lead to Communist rule, had been the Soviet-Czechoslovak Treaty of Cooperation President Edvard Beneš and Stalin had signed on 12 December 1943 in Moscow. The three years of limited democracy ruled by the Czechoslovak National Front (NF) did not bode well for liberty and market economy: the Czechoslovak Communist Party led by Klement Gottwald used intrigues and demagoguery to convince the citizens of a Czechoslovak own way toward Socialism, with no intervention from Moscow. Post-war Czechoslovakia from 1945 to 1948 was neither a Republic nor a parliamentary democracy, but it was no totalitarian state either—not yet. In constitutional terms, the political system was a hybrid, a democracy limited by the stipulations of the Košice Agreement that had, under the psychological and political authority of Beneš and Stalin, secured the NF's dominant position:

> "This fact was of key significance, and worked to the disadvantage of the non-Communist parties. These parties jointly shared in building up the new system, and they accepted the political conception of a regulated democracy. Beneš was the prominent advocate of the latter as a defensive measure taken to prevent a repetition of Munich. A regulated democracy was a limited democracy and was conditional on the fact that if one or more government parties were to try to take full power, it would limit the forces of democracy to acting in its own self-defence. A regulated democracy can be justified only when there is cooperation between democratic parties with equal representation in the coalition." *(Kaplan, 1987, p. 189)*

Limited democracy is legitimate in terms of political morality, if all involved parties agree on fair play and keep to the rules of democratic procedure—which the KSČ (Komunistická Strana Československa, Czechoslovak Communist Party) blatantly did not. The post-war atmosphere was not conducive to democratic procedure or fair play; the people were exhausted after five years of Nazi occupation in the Czech lands and clerical-fascist propaganda and rule in Slovakia:

> "The war had radicalized the population, and a large part considered fundamental political and social reforms a solution for the difficult situation. That was why a critical part of the population supported the nationalization of the key industries, banks and insurances, pushed forward by the Communists, the Social Democrats and the trade unions. The presidential decrees of October 1945 realized the nationalizations. The Communists also pushed forward a radical land reform, which the poor farmers and the agricultural workers welcomed. In general, radical and apparently simple measures seemed attractive to improve the difficult post-war situation." (Kováč, 2007, p. 246)

The KSČ had the full support of Stalin and was ready to assume power. The government crisis the KSČ had artificially created in February 1948 seemed to be solved with the support of President Beneš—which suggested that the NF was working and Czechoslovakia was still a democracy. Yet, as soon as the KSČ was in control of the country, it embarked on a brutal course of Sovietization:

> "The terror that was unleashed hit everybody. Even in the tiniest village citizens suspected of political opposition were found. The purges were carried out ruthlessly in all social strata. Privacy, a private life was completely eliminated, which hit the farmers and tradesmen particularly hard. Those who stood up against the terror had to expect that their families' fates were at stake." *(Kalous, 2012, p. 89)*

In the purges from 1948 to 1954, between 250,000 and 280,000 citizens were imprisoned, and 23,000 sent to labour camps (Kalous, 2012, p. 91). The rationale of the persecution and oppression unfolded in three phases: first, mass purges to terrorize the population; second, elimination of politicians of the oppositional parties, and third, a thorough purge of the Party's top ranks, demonstrating that not even high-ranking Communists could be trusted. The third phase would become known as the 1952 show trial of the Titoist conspiracy of Slánský and co-accused. Now, how did the Wheeler family fit into this historical context?

In 1947, the American economist John Shaw Wheeler, his wife Eleanor and their four children moved to Czechoslovakia; under suspicion of being a Communist or at least not reliable in political terms, Wheeler had lost his job in the US administration in the West German zone (Geaney, 2015, p. 25). The couple was particularly critical of US foreign policy and believed that the East European states under Stalin's grip embodied the camp of Peace and Socialism. They believed that the US government was mounting a new war against the Soviet Union and her Socialist allies and hence frequently held lectures in Czechoslovakia about the politics of the West. Were the Wheelers naïve or true believers—or both?

The fact that the Wheelers could meet up with US journalists, diplomats and foreign correspondents in Prague *kavárny* (coffee houses), while normal Czechoslovak citizens, safe of course for StB agents, could not, did not cause them suspicion; they did not seem to notice that they were a particularly valuable asset for the Interior Ministry's propaganda policy. Why did the Wheelers ask for political asylum in Czechoslovakia in 1950? After all, the demand for political asylum is the demand for protection from physical and psychological torture, abrogation of one's civil rights and the fear that the regime would take one's children away.

On 24 March 1950—former Foreign Minister Vladimír Clementis was already imprisoned in Prague-Ruzyně and being 'prepared' for the show trial planned for November 1952, while unsuspecting Rudolf Slánský was enjoying his last three months in freedom and power in the Castle—three Czechoslovak pilots fled to the West with three Dakota planes, landing at the US air force base in Erding in Bavaria (Michálek, 2013). It was a fantastic operation, because the three pilots had coordinated their flights. The passengers of the routine ČSA flights to Brno and Bratislava, who had no clue what happened, had the choice to stay in Germany or return to Czechoslovakia. Most of them returned. The Communist regime reacted with a wave of arrests, while the West, from its point of view, applauded the courageous men, all former air force pilots during WWII. The Erding action (Michálek, 2013, pp. 149-216) and the histrionic propaganda of the regime prompted the Wheelers to ask for political asylum in Prague. Let us have a look now at how John Wheeler reacted:

> "The immediate impulse for my statement is the brutal and unlawful steps taken by the American occupation offices in West Germany against 58 Czechoslovak citizens who became victims of a carefully prepared and typically gangsterish dragging across the borders of their country. […] I personally had the occasion to experience how this constantly stressed 'real' American democracy looks like in reality. When the word democracy is used by warmongers and aspirants to world rule, it means an impudent profanation of the term. […] I felt so ashamed in front of my host nation when the spy jiggery-pokery of the American embassy was uncovered, be it the spy trials with Rajk, Kostov or the American diplomats in Prague. […] I confront the America of Wall Street, Trumans, Achesons, warmongers and atomic gangsters with the honest efforts of Czechoslovakia to strengthen the peace front." *(Geaney, 2015, p. 30)*

The StB must have had a field day—most probably, they did not even have to give Wheeler a script, so precisely did he present the Stalinist worldview. The Wheelers were naïve and true believers, hence particularly prone to the psychologically refined manipulation by the regime, unaware that Czechoslovak 'friends' who shared their beliefs and encouraged them to hold speeches about the US warmongers of the Capitalist West were StB agents set on to them (Geaney, 2015, p. 31). Let us now have a look at emigration.

1.1.2 Czechoslovak emigration with a focus on the end of the 1960s

In our recent history, waves of emigration were connected mainly with events in Czechoslovakia, the common state of Czechs and Slovaks. They manifested themselves always after significant political or economic changes. We can say that the Czechoslovak emigration was divided into three waves: The first wave was in the inter-war period linked to the economic crisis (1921-1923 and 1929-1934): as incentive factors for the exit from the Republic were the poverty, high unemployment and the social emigration of the Slovaks. "Target states" were Germany, France, Belgium, Austria, and overseas Canada, Australia and partly Argentina. The second one was after the Communist assumption of power on 25 February 1948; and here internal political changes and their impact on the character of the state were the main motivating factor (push factor). Mostly it was a political emigration that headed to Germany, Austria, Switzerland, Sweden, France, but also to the US, Canada, Australia and partly to South Africa.

The third wave occurred after the invasion and occupation of Czechoslovakia by Warsaw Pact troops on 21 August 1968. It had its specific features and connections that we will continue to talk about.

What did the emigration at the end of the 1960s look like and why is it important to talk about it today?

In the second half of the 1960s, the political atmosphere gradually changed in Czechoslovakia, and a new Communist elite headed by Alexander Dubček came to power, which began a process of revival of society based on the reconstruction of the institutions and the mechanisms of management. The "Prague Spring" 1968 brought the liberalization of totalitarian practices and allowed the inhabitants to participate in discussions on the democratization of society. However, this "revival process" did not last long and was stopped by military intervention from the outside. This interference was not expected by most citizens, and society became chaotic with the uncertainties about the future of life in the country.

From the perspective of the timing of the emigration we have to bear in mind a specific process which had started before the invasion of Warsaw Pact troops on the night of 21 August 1968: in this time many young people used the opportunity to travel abroad. The occupation took place while they were out of the country. Considering the situation back home, many citizens, particularly students, decided not to return to the Republic. They became involuntary emigrants, that is, refugees. In this case, the reasons for the exodus originated not in Czechoslovak domestic affairs but were the consequences of interference in Czechoslovakia

From 1968 to 1971, approximately 74,000 refugees left Czechoslovakia; some sources (Navara, Albrecht, 2010) put the figure at more than 80,000 for the period from 1968 to 1969; one estimate counts even more than that (Dennik N, 2015). The daily newspaper SME estimated 140,000 to 150,000 (from 1969 to 1989) persons left Czechoslovakia, 24% of them children and 41% young people between the ages of 16 and 30. The office of the UN High Commissioner for Refugees UNHCR estimated up to 250,000 people (UNHCR, 2018). In view of this high figure, this third and last wave was a phenomenon in itself, which should be analysed also in academic studies.

That part of the emigrants who left after the invasion of the Warsaw Pact troops, mainly in the years of the normalization, left involuntarily with the intention of returning home; they were the category of citizens who felt themselves to be in exile, that is, forced to live abroad. In connection with the post-August emigration, the StB called some citizens *uloženka*: they were persons the StB thought might come back. Presumably they did not engage in any conspicuous anti-communist activity. Some of them were people who didn't so much emigrate as go on holiday in August 1968 and then stay abroad to see what happened after the invasion. They posed as regular emigrants and did not draw attention to themselves abroad. Their goal was to settle in the country of 'choice' as quickly as possible, achieve new citizenship and professional status and prepare for long-term support of Czechoslovakia in the future.

What was the regime's position on emigration in the years of normalization?

The process of normalization had begun with political purges; the regime considered emigration a criminal offence. The law against leaving the republic was added to Socialist legislation; it was a crime to leave the country. The state confiscated the property emigrants left behind, and their relatives were punished with a note in their official files, while persons who were in contact with emigrants were legally persecuted and condemned to prison.

In 1977, the regime introduced a *smernica* (regulation), which made it possible for emigrants to normalize their relationship with Czechoslovakia; this meant the legalization of the emigrants' relations with the state, a change in their legal status. Emigrants could return to the country, remain Czechoslovak citizens abroad, or, after five years, legally end their Czechoslovak citizenship; then the Czechoslovak state considered them foreigners, treating them as such in the administration. This option was open to persons who had not engaged in politics or acted against the Communist regime, or who had sufficiently repented, and, in both cases, promised not to engage in future subversive activities.

Who were the post-August emigrants?

After August 1968, many specialists, scientists and artists emigrated. According to the historian Adam Hudek, *"among the Czechoslovak refugees, highly qualified specialists, scientists, artists and young, university-educated persons were over-represented"* (Po udalostiach v auguste 1968 odišlo z Československa množstvo odborníkov, vedcov a umelcov, 2017). We can single out the writers Ladislav Mňačko and

Milan Kundera, the singer Karel Kryl and the film director Miloš Forman among the best-known emigrants. "It is, however, not well-known that from 1968 to 1970, approximately 10% of the country's scientists left; logically, these were the top ones who had good contacts abroad," stresses Hudek, explaining that these emigrants had no problem to find well-paid positions abroad. The regime was aware of this fact; thus the condition for regaining Czechoslovak citizenship, which the refugees automatically lost by leaving the country, was to make them pay back the cost of education and training they had accomplished in Czechoslovakia (Po udalostiach v auguste 1968 odišlo z Československa množstvo odborníkov, vedcov a umelcov, 2017).

In the period after November 1989 many emigrants, refugees and exiles returned and their memories of the period outside Czechoslovakia that have survived appeared in the public media. Looking back at their life stories, it is possible to interpret the period of third wave emigration as specific in terms of the push and pull factors of migration. Regarding the motivation of these immigrants, refugees and exiles we can say that it was predominantly fear of returning to their occupied homeland, of the loss of freedom, and unwillingness to subject themselves to the rule of "shut up, keep up" (Kryl). Push factors did not result from internal changes in society, but from the armed intervention from outside in the domestic affairs of the country. In terms of pull factors, it can be said that most refugees from Czechoslovakia did not pick their goal destinations entirely voluntarily, but for many of them it was staying in refugee camps and waiting for a residence permit in some western country. Only part of emigrants was lucky enough to be able to rely upon the help of relatives or friends who lived abroad. Perhaps the only common positive factor for the emigration wave at the end of the 1960s was that they were welcome as foreigners who refused to live in a totalitarian society. They obtained great support from the beneficiary western states as well as various non-governmental and charitable associations.

A specific feature of this wave of emigration should be seen in the social and political context of the period of the Cold War. It was connected with an atmosphere of mutual hostility, mistrust of different ideologies, communist (totalitarian) and capitalism (plural, liberal) society. Czechoslovakia was seen in the West as one of the totalitarian regimes, where the results of the Helsinki Convention (Helsinki Final Act, 1975) did not reach and where there are violations of human rights and freedom of speech. Not until November 1989 and the collapse of the Soviet bloc did Czechoslovak society return to the ideas of Dubček's reforms and the liberalization of society.

1.2 Thoughts on totalitarianism from political philosophers

1.2.1 Hannah Arendt on totalitarianism

From what exactly did Czechoslovak citizens flee, some voluntarily, others not so voluntarily? There are three principal pillars in Arendt's (1906–1975) theory of totalitarianism (Arendt, 1973). They explain, first, how the two totalitarian ideologies of the 20th century, Stalinism and Nazism, came to power; second, how they stayed in power; and third, what happened to the believers in higher positions of the Party when the totalitarian regime collapsed. Let me quote from Arendt with added key words:

Assuming power:

> "*The important factor for the movements is that, even before they seize power, they give the impression that all elements of society are embodied in their ranks.*" (Arendt, 1973, p. 371)

Key words: children and youth organizations; women's associations; sport clubs; cultural associations; newspapers; journals; professional associations—the entire society is about to become 'integrated' into the movement. Everybody not yet a member of the Party or the movement is viewed with suspicion, and feels threatened, excluded. I rush to join the movement, because I don't want to be the only one left out.

In power:

> "The claim inherent in totalitarian organizations is that everything outside the movement is 'dying', a claim which is drastically realized under the murderous conditions of totalitarian rule." (Arendt, 1973, p. 381).

Key words: terror; observation; spying; *Blockwart* (block monitor) mentality; general mistrust among citizens; fear. Leaving the movement or Party is impossible now; they are in total command. Although I don't want to obey, I obey because of fear, not only for myself, but also for my children, parents, friends—if they are my friends? Whom can I really trust?

Loss of power:

> "It is in the moment of defeat that the inherent weakness of totalitarian propaganda becomes visible. Without the force of the movement, its members cease at once to believe in the dogma for which yesterday they still were ready to sacrifice their lives. [...] they will quietly give up the movement as a bad bet and look around for another promising fiction or wait until the former fiction regains enough strength to establish another mass movement." (Arendt, 1973, p. 363)

Key words: turncoat; adaptation; search for a new truth or political goal to believe in; lack of regret; eagerness to embark on a new career; personal moral failure. Yes, I did quite well under the old regime—I am not guilty, I just followed orders. But that new Party around the block looks attractive ... they have a good take on national identity, I think I could join them ...

Why did totalitarian and post-totalitarian regimes,[19] like the Normalization regime under Gustáv Husák,[20] dislike migration? The

---

[19] Juan J. Linz was the first to coin the concept 'post-totalitarianism', adding a new category to the types of authoritarian, democratic and totalitarian government. A post-totalitarian regime distinguishes itself from a totalitarian one in the characteristic tolerance of a limited social pluralism, which manifests itself in the so-called parallel society or parallel structures founded by dissident artists and intellectuals; Linz (1975). Václav Havel (1936-2011) mentioned the concept 'post-totalitarian' in his famous

answer is really and truly banal: the state cannot exercise total control of citizens' minds and bodies if they can move freely, even emigrate. It seems a psychological[21] banality, but we can say that most ideological leaders, save perhaps for Stalin, are not cynics—they are idealists who believe in their creed so strongly that they are willing to kill, torture and persecute everybody who expresses the slightest criticism. In Stalin's understanding of Marxism-Leninism and its principal element of Materialism, the human soul did not exist; man is machine, determined by the laws of biology, physiology and chemistry. He is flesh, matter and dies, but while he is alive, his thinking, class-consciousness and behaviour can be improved by sheer political and psychological mechanics: writers were the 'engineers of human souls', who took care of man machine steering it to the proper class consciousness (Baer, 2015, p. 133).

1.2.2 The totalitarian mindset

What is the totalitarian mindset? The Russian-born British political philosopher Sir Isaiah Berlin (1909–1997) described the totalitarian mindset with his unrivalled insight:

> *"If I know that I am right, if I know that what I seek is the true good, then people who oppose me must be in error about what it is that they themselves seek. No doubt they too think that they are seeking the good, they assert their own liberty to secure it, but they are seeking it in the wrong place. Therefore I have a right to prevent them. In virtue of what have I this right to prevent them? ... It is because if they knew what they truly wanted, they would seek what I seek. The fact that they do not seek this means that they do not really know."* (Berlin, 2003, p. 45-6)

The British historian of ideas Tony Judt (1948–2010):

> *"It is one thing to say that I am willing to suffer now for an unknowable but possibly better future. It is quite another to authorize the suffering of others in the name of*

---

essay "Moc bezmocných" ("The Power of the Powerless") from 1977, published in 1990 in O lidskou identitu. Praha: Rozmluvy, 55-133.

[20] The best biography of Gustáv Husák known to us is S. Michálek, M. Londák et al (2013). See also a psychological interpretation: Baer (2015).

[21] Recommended is J. Kabát (2011).

that same unverifiable hypothesis. This, in my view, is the intellectual sin of the century: passing judgement on the fate of others in the name of their future as you see it." (Judt, 2012, p. 91)

At the end of 1951, some French Marxists committed an intellectual sin that is truly shocking in its blatant ignorance of the suffering of others. Claude Roy (1915–1957) on New Year's Eve in Paris at his friends' house, and how French Marxists dealt with the news from the show trials in the Eastern bloc:

"Everyone was very happy. In fact, everyone was quite drunk. 'You're the one we were waiting for,' said all my friends. They explained the game to me. Jean Duvignaud [an art historian and sociologist] said that every epoch invents its own literary genre or form: the Greeks had had tragedy, the Renaissance the sonnet, the classical age the five-act play in verse with the three unities, etc. The socialist age had invented its own form: the Moscow show-trial. These partygoers, who were all slightly the worse for drink, had decided to play at being on trial." (Roy, 1980, pp. 389-390).

Confronted with the crimes under Stalin, the Soviet invasions of Hungary in 1956 and Czechoslovakia in 1968 and finally, the publication of Solzhenitsyn's *The Gulag Archipelago* in 1974, some French comrades began to distance themselves from Soviet Communism. As if they had learnt nothing at all, they started to praise Mao Tse-tung's peasant Marxism[22] in China (Kołakowski, 2008, pp. 1183-1205). Jean-Paul Sartre (1905–1980) was one of them:

"*Various leftist sects and individuals seem to have seriously believed that it [Chinese Communism, add. JB] was the perfect cure for the ills of industrial society, and that the United States and Western Europe could and should be revolutionized on Maoist principles. At a time when the ideological prestige of Soviet Russia had collapsed, utopian longings fixed themselves on the exotic East, the more easily because of the general ignorance of Chinese affairs.*" (Kołakowski, 2008, p. 1203)

Before he found his intellectual refuge in Maoism, Sartre had visited Prague in 1963 with his partner Simone de Beauvoir:

---

[22] The best biography of Mao Tse-tung known to us is J, Halliday, J. Chang (2007).

> "And the great writer justified his big illusion in front of a public that was surviving that 'experience' first-hand and regarded contemporary socialism as a pointless error of history: "Socialism, whether it has a future or not, is moulding the mind of our entire epoch, it might be hell, but hell too can be a subject for literature— disappointed hopes, the deaths of comrades—is this not the most modern perfection of tragedy?" By no means might few of the shocked listeners have thought exactly the same as the writer Ivan Klíma: "Hell is a great subject, as long as one doesn't have to live in it." (Jaksicsová, 2017, pp. 448-9)

Sartre was a French leftist intellectual, author and poet, but analytical skills in terms of the brutal realities of Cold War politics were not his forte—his totalitarian mindset forbade him to look at the naked reality. In 1974, Sartre visited German RAF (Rote Armee Fraktion) top terrorist Andreas Baader in Stuttgart Stammheim prison (Bohr, Wiegrefe, 2013). Apparently, they immediately disliked each other; Baader did not feel respected by Sartre in terms of political theory, while Sartre disliked Baader's arrogance. Allegedly, Sartre told reporters after the meeting that Baader was an arsehole. Sartre's essay about Baader, Meinhof and Ennslin's conditions of imprisonment was published in *Libération* on 7 December 1974 (The Slow Death of Andreas Baader, 2004). In his last sentence, Sartre demanded that political prisoners and common criminals be treated the same way. This is a practice perfected in Stalin and Hitler's prisons and camps. The failure to distinguish between politically active intellectuals that are critical of the regime and common criminals, that is, murderers, bank robbers and rapists, is a practice of totalitarianism, of a state where the rule of law has ceased to exist. Lawlessness is a core element of a totalitarian regime, a historical fact Sartre did not consider important enough to even think about.

Conclusion

Finally, we can say that any political theorist worthy of the name would agree on two things: first, mobility is a human right. If I don't like it here for whatever reasons, I should be allowed to move somewhere else. Any political system that criminalizes emigration thus violates the human right to mobility. Second, political philosophers would also agree that, in dealing with the current refugee crisis, one has to apply a sober and unimpassioned mind, analysing details and contexts of the crisis and search for solutions. What one should not do is be nice, that is, apply political correctness. Hermann Lübbe, a neo-Kantian, had already addressed political correctness very early in the late 1980s, revealing its totalitarian character when it first appeared on US campuses, then swiftly swapping over to Europe; to him, the euphemistic concept 'political correctness' was political moralism—which was the "triumph of attitude over reason." (Lübbe, 1987)

2 THE CZECH EXTREME RIGHT OF THE 21st CENTURY AT THE TIME OF THE MIGRATION CRISIS

Jan Rataj and Jaroslav Mihálik

In this chapter, we focus on the growing mobilization of far-right movements and political parties in the recent electoral cycle in the Czech Republic. We argue that the current wave of far-right populism is largely driven by the migration crisis and the inability of collective action in decision-making at the European level. The populists have significantly changed the political map of the European countries, including Czechia. Similarly, a large part of far-right parties' political manifestos and public meetings are aimed at open criticism of European political mechanisms, the dictatorship of the European political leadership and intervention in domestic policy-making. These problems are inevitably linked to the changing nature and moods and political processes as well as social and economic deprivation in different regions. Another tipping point is also the strained international relationship, escalated through the current refugee crisis and tidal migration into Europe. The spread of fear, paranoia and national securitization campaigns as well as negative campaigns mobilize voters to focus on the position of the nation state in Europe and to support, sometimes in the wake of an undemocratic political agenda, more authoritarian and populist views and an antagonistic approach to democratic values. EU countries have seen a specific scenario linked to economic and social deprivation, but the human dimension is also very important. The recent influx of refugees, coupled with the rise in terrorist attacks, is only the peak of a crisis spreading throughout the continent.

2.1 Migration and the rise of far-right populism in Europe

Many authors argue that the peak in refugee arrivals in Europe since 2015 has significantly influenced the position of radical right political parties and movements and has shifted the role of traditional parties (Schain, 2018; Steinmayr, 2018; Davis-Deole, 2018). Across Europe, far-right parties have gained significant electoral successes and attracted substantial popular support. This is the story of many European countries including Sweden, Italy, France, Germany and Austria, where all of them have rich experience with the previous immigration waves from the 20th century. Apparently, such trends of anti-immigrant policy making from "big" countries have impacted the Visegrad group countries: Czechia, Hungary, Poland and Slovakia. The new fertile ground of anti-immigration discourse is also present in those countries that do not yet have strong experience with a foreign population and integrating third-country nationals but are strong in their nationalism and securitisation strategies. Stirring fears about immigrants is a very popular tactic in the rhetoric of all the leaders in Central Europe, which was confirmed by the joint resolution of the V4 prime ministers against the quota system for reallocating refugees in EU Member States. As Davis and Deole state *"not only does the rise of far-right parties challenge the center-left consensus on which European institutions have come to rely, brought to the fore by Britain's decision to exit the EU; it also raises fundamental questions related to the role of ethnic identity in European societies and the potential for ethnic conflict in Europe"* (Davis-Deole, 2018, p. 10). The authors studied a large amount of academic research trying to investigate the impact of the migration crisis on the success of the current far-right platforms in the wider Europe. Their analysis has shown that increases in immigration play an important role in the success of contemporary far-right parties in a number of European countries (Davis-Deole, 2018, p. 10). This is an important finding since the rise of new political platforms is being significantly driven by the crisis scenarios and finding new enemies. The series of terrorist attacks have only strengthened the far-right positions and given them strong levers in their hands. Recently, the far-right leaders in Europe have used populist topics that may vary from country to country but in general have several common features:

- A sense of exclusive nationalism;
- Belief that national identity is threatened by foreign (non-European) cultures;
- Desire to sharply cut immigration rates;
- Distrust of elites (Schain, 2018).

Similarly, the relative ease of carrying out a negative campaign, gaining from national populism, and spreading fears and paranoia among citizens has also impacted on the situation and the role of established political parties that have also found themselves in strong opposition towards European policy making, blurring the centre-left political orientation and stepping on the train of thought typical for radical-right parties. They have responded in particular to the growing economic and social inequalities, the imbalance between rich and poor, problems of labour immigration to the domestic market, ethnic grievances and ethnic diversity, security and crisis management. However, the plethora of topics used by the far-right is not restricted nor limited to the above-mentioned challenges. The general consensus revolves around open criticism of the governance status quo, the limits of liberal democracy and opposition towards Western democratic values, globalization and the world economy. From the analytical point of view, and specific for anti-immigration policies in the Czech Republic, but also in Slovakia and Hungary, the migration crisis did not strike these societies directly with huge numbers of migrants seeking asylum and political protection. On the contrary, the immigration discourse was largely abused by political leaders, public debates and news media. Furthermore, this topic has become widespread during the 2017 parliamentary elections, similar to other elections in Central Europe and Slovenia, for example. The discourse was primarily aimed at securitization and designed to openly ignore and oppose the EU and German-led proposals for solving the problem. Such negativism was countrywide and reached its peak with the re-election of President Miloš Zeman, who is famous for his critical and radical positions towards immigrants in the Czech Republic. As Věra Stojarová notes, the migration crisis brought a new topic for the parties and their attitudes towards immigrants. She explains that political leaders only present refugees and immigrants in a negative manner, as a threat creating a *"breeding ground for spreading terrorism in Europe and the world."* Such narratives started the new wave of open criticism towards the EU for accepting refugees, followed by the rejection of the EU's solidarity principles (Stojarová, 2018, p. 36).

2.2 The position of the Czech far-right in the 21st century

The anti-systemic far-right in the Czech Republic is fragmented, inconsistent in its ideas, and without a charismatic leader. Just as before 1945, it consists of radically conservative, fascist and Nazi platforms. But it is not just a revitalized footprint from the past. It talks of its historical roots but responds promptly to changes in 21st century Czech society of the and to contemporary globalization and integration movements. The main core of its ideas is copied from the more successful extreme right in Western and Southern Europe. One fundamental change is the shift away from its own national emphasis and uniqueness and a shift towards ultra-right transnational Europeanism under the motto *"the White Fortress Europe"*, which is nothing more than a substitute term for Aryan Europe without Jews (Vejvodová, 2015). These ideas are well presented in the relevant Czech literature (Mareš, 2003; Bastl et al., 2011; Háka, 2016; Dlouhý, 2018).

Radical conservatives and traditional Czech fascists are brought together in the political party National Democracy, which proclaims itself to be the successor of Kramář's Czechoslovak National Democracy in the interwar First Republic. However, they are aware of the substantial differences between Masaryk and Kramář's understanding of democratic governance (Rataj, 2009). It shares authoritarian traditionalism, the rejection of Masaryk's democratic modernization and Masaryk's concept of human democracy and open society, and scepticism about the political system of representative democracy. The real national state is a fascist professional state. National Democracy remained anti-German, anti-Nazi and anti-Communist. It popularizes the former Czech fascist leaders Radul Gajda and Jan Rys-Rozsévač. It stands against the anti-Western Slavic orientation using the radical and illiberal sense. In Putin´s Russian Federation it finds the coveted example of a sovereign, powerful, illiberal state with a leading authority and the predominance of traditional values.

The conflict of the West and the Russian Federation is perceived by Adam Bartoš, chair of National Democracy, as a *"dispute between Jews and Slavs"* (Bartoš, 2014, p. 69). It is also strongly influenced by clerical Slavicity with a focus on the present extreme right in Poland (especially the Falanga organization) and Slovakia. The chair of National Democracy told the leader of the Slovak far-right Marian Kotleba that he was convinced that his party could change Slovak policy, the life of Slovak citizens and the international status of the country, which suffers from the Brussels dictatorship and neo-Marxist indoctrination: *"Thanks to the inability of the European Union elites to deal with the invasion of migrants ... the Slovak nation faces a threat ... The Slovak political elites are similarly corrupt and have sold out to alien interests like the Czechs ... At the same time ... we realize ... the international dimension of our efforts: the resurrection of Europe of Free Nations is unthinkable without cooperation. Two nations that are so close should cooperate"* (Bartoš, 2016). National Democracy has joined the World National Conservative Movement.

A new feature that has nothing in common with the non-denominational pre-war National Democracy is the influence of clerical fascism and ultra-conservative Catholic circles in the party (lefebvrists), who reject the reforms of the Catholic Church after the Second Vatican Council. Today's crisis of democracy, consumerism, relativism and moral values, hedonism, the deterioration of family life, a new round of emancipation and the growth of Muslim stances in Europe links the lefebvrists with the political far-right. National Democracy interprets modern history from the Great French Revolution through the optics of the Jewish-Masonic conspiracy. The Liberal Democratic regimes of the First Republic and the present Czech Republic are referred to as part of the Jewish plan for world domination and the destruction of nations. Under the pretext of initiating a discussion about the Jewish questions, National Democracy launched anti-Semitic activities, e.g. trying to re-politicize the taboo affair of Leopold Hilsner, who in 1899 was accused of carrying out a Jewish ritual murder. Public networks and demonstrations brought the political culture of lists of political and racial enemies of which they will be free after their victory, symbolic gallows and the burning of German "multicultural" chancellor Angela Merkel as Moran. The propaganda of such purges and violence corresponds to the concept of the Czech militia forces. The party has begun building paramilitary units of the National militia, which include shooting training.

The Red-White Organization already refers in its name to the first Czech fascist formation founded in 1922. The youth organization Generation of Identity belongs to the distinctive transnational of European fascist group and was formed on the basis of foreign fascist models from France and Italy. It corresponds to the horizon of the youngest nationalized generation of Czech youth, who rejects modern democratic Czechoslovak and Czech traditions and symbols, including the flag of the *"blue Masonic wedge"* and the national colours, and prefers a unifying European fascist identity with ancient and medieval roots, value traditionalism and anti-European Union positions.

The neo-Nazi political orientation in the Czech Republic is mainly represented by the Workers Party of Social Justice and the militant association National Revival. The patron of the Workers Party of Social Justice has since 2007 been the National Democratic Party of Germany, from which the Czech Radical Conservative leadership of the Workers Party, headed by Tomáš Vandas, took on a national socialist plan, tactics and strategy, including a pact with activist neo-Nazis.

At present, dogmatic pan-German Nazism, based on the adoration of Hitler's Third Reich including the division of European nations into Aryan Nordic and racially inferior, is still in the background. Czech followers experienced a sense of shame for their *"spoiled Czech blood and tongue"* and tried to become Germans. Contemporary globalized neo-Nazism already recognizes the Aryan status of all native European nations. It strives for the global unification of the white race. It represents the national socialist international White Aryan movement against the global US-Israeli *"Jewish Occupation Government"* and alien coloured races to build a White Fortress Europe. The change facilitated the breakthrough of Nazism among Czech youth under the motto *"Nothing but a Nation!"* Within the framework of White Europeanism, Czech regional autonomy is preserved, but Czech nationalism with the slogan *Nothing but a nation* is condemned as a chauvinist provincialism that shatters the struggle for European white racial unity. Earlier conflicts among white European nations should be forgotten under the slogan *"No more fratricidal war."* As some authors put it, World War II was allegedly misinterpreted between the white race. It was not ended by the victory of the Allies but by the Jews (Piskač, 2016).

The far-right movement is characterized by the youngest membership base in the current political spectrum. The current young Czech generation lost its immunity against the recruiting slogans of the Nazi ultra-right, which, in previous generations, has been clashed by personal experience or an awareness of the threat of Pan-German or Nazi expansion. The defensive position of being anti-German, which was as an essential component of Czech emancipation nationalism of the 19th and 20th centuries, has disappeared. Some young Czechs, unlike in the past, are no longer inhibited about becoming members of the neo-Nazi organizations that are now numerous in the Czech Republic.

The Workers' Party of Social Justice develops German historical revisionism among its members. In the years of the economic crisis (2008-2014), the party interconnected the antisystem critique of the regime of representative democracy with the revolt against global capitalism in the interests of the national socialist welfare state. At the same time, the party acted as a representative of the majority society in the regions where the Roma were socially excluded, complaining about criminal activity and the non-adaptability of a significant part of the Roma ethnic group to the generally applicable socio-cultural patterns and norms. The party exploited the failure to provide political and social solutions for Roma issues in the Czech Republic, as well as the inaction of politicians and of the local public administration together with politically radicalized part of the citizens (Rataj, 2003, pp. 75-6).

National Democracy and the Workers' Party of Social Justice often expressed their solidarity and admiration for the Slovak People's Party Our Slovakia of Marian Kotleba. On the other hand, it is to be noted that the electoral gains and political achievements of the Czech far-right parties (parliamentary elections in 2017—ND—0.72%, DSSS—0.20%) were considerably less than those of the Slovak People's Party (parliamentary elections in 2016—8.04%). The legacy of the World War II Slovak Republic led by Jozef Tiso, whose historical link Kotleba is trying to re-establish, is considered to be the only sovereign and independent statehood in the modern history of Czechs and Slovaks (excluding the episode of the post-Munich authoritarian and anti-Semitic Czechoslovakia). The adoration of the war period and the existence of the Slovak Republic in 1939—1945 is witnessed in the speech of former DSSS party member, Ladislav Malý:

> The historical memory of the Slovak nation is a living memory of the first free, independent state under the leadership of the modern Slovak martyr Mons. Jozef Tiso. Honour his memory! People's Party Our Slovakia headed by Kotleba is quite logically and continuously connected to the spiritual tradition of the Slovak nation ... Unfortunately, in modern history, Czechs have no historical memory of their own sovereignty and emancipation, they have nothing to follow; the so-called First Republic was a Jewish construction, and so it fell. The period of the Second Republic, when there was hope for a more just social and national order, was soon undermined by the occupation of Nazi Germany ... Moreover, from the 19th century in Bohemia, a systematic and purposeful campaign for the Christianization of Bohemia was carried out by Masons and a part of the Jewish intelligence ... The authentic Czech right, which undoubtedly belongs to the Workers' Party, must thus build its structure and programme from scratch—unlike the Slovak brothers, our situation is much more difficult (Malý, 2017).

There are good contacts between the Czech and Slovak far-right. For example, Workers' youth from the DSSS organized voluntary work together with Slovak ĽSNS representatives in April 2017 to clean up the forest, which transformed into political training on how migrants in Europe are harming nature and not respecting environmental standards.

The situation in interwar Czechoslovakia is being repeated, when the weaker Czech far-right sought reinforcement and participated in Hlinka's People's Party protests against Czechoslovak liberal and secularized democracy. Nowadays, both Kotleba and Vandas are united by membership in the far-right European Alliance for Peace and Freedom.

The Czech far-right has not yet been successful in the eyes of Czech voters, unlike in some European Union states where the parties of the far-right have received so much popular support that they have become part of the governmental coalitions (Mudde, 2011; Tejchman, 2017). During the migration crisis, however, it demonstrated its activist ability to communicate directly with citizens, then to infiltrate and control legal demonstrations by ordinary citizens and to identify the anti-immigrant movement with an anti-systemic message, often with a neo-Nazi discourse.

2.3 Czech far-right and anti-immigration discourse

Since 2015, migration has brought into Europe an uncontrollable massive influx of immigrants. According to Czech far-right these come predominantly from Arab and African regions with rooted standards of Islamic fundamentalism, and a lifestyle diametrically opposite from the free-minded secularized values of the Western European modernity of the enlightenment type and the democratic concept of rule of law.

These claims are associated with the arguments that previous experience with immigrant minorities from the Islamic world has shown that even future generations have been unable to integrate into the values of Western democracy. They have kept and secured their cultural, often linguistic exclusivity, fundamental intolerant theocratic codes, they have not successfully integrated into the labour market, and some have found their life mission in Islamic terrorism and in the support of the Islamic State. In the words of the appreciated but controversial French writer

Richard Millet: *"multiculturalism ... creates a mosaic of ghettoes in which the host nation no longer exists"* (Millet, 2012).

Immigration from the Muslim world has begun to jeopardize the internal security of some European countries not only by the demonstrably increased crime rate towards the domestic population but also by the actions of Islamic religious terrorism as interpreted by Petr Robejšek: *"an unknown but significant proportion of migrants, I would say at least a quarter, represent a different intensity risk. From the 'sleepers' sent by terrorist organizations to those who fail to escape in Europe and are slipping to religious radicalization or 'only' to criminality"* (Robejšek, 2015).

The situation is all the more complicated because most immigrants from Islamist countries do not come to the territory of the European Union from the desire for democracy and human rights or pluralism but with the vision of the Western social system and the illusions of easy personal prosperity. "Faithless" and "decadent" Western society is more a target of their contempt than admiration since they are forced to continue to reach a better life, preferably in a European country that is rich and wealthy. What is worse, some radical wings of Islam in the captivity of the Jihad are not abandoned with the idea of Islamization of European territories. Humanitarian visions can be easily overwhelmed by the inability to rationally interfere into the roots of the problems. The fear and paranoia of migrants and refugees is mostly spread through the national media and political leaders. Although support for migrants is widely rejected in society at large, political parties and their elites in practice identify themselves with such measures (Vejvodová-Smolík 2013).

An incomprehensible fact that helped extreme right-wing conspiracy theories about the background of migration was the finding that the European Union had lost the will and ability to protect the external Schengen border and to prevent people smuggling. Germany's free immigration policy without clear rules caused confusion or corruption in asylum policy and the compliance of the Sharia law in violation of German law and human rights.

The largest number of foreigners (5%) among all post-communist countries lives and works in the Czech Republic. The Czech Republic, with a minimum rate of unemployment (around 3% in 2018), good GDP growth (4.5%) and a labour shortage on the one hand and low wages and profits abroad on the other hand, does not close the door for immigrants who have shown good will and value preconditions for integration (e.g. Vietnamese, Ukrainians).

Basically, there is no conflict with the large Asian minority of Vietnamese, who have achieved such a degree of integration into Czech society that they have acquired the status of a national minority. The results of the Czech Centre for public opinion research showed that Czech sympathy for the Vietnamese is growing The Vietnamese ranked fifth in the most likeable nations after Slovaks, Poles, Greeks and Jews. For the least likeable peoples, the Czechs mentioned Arabs and the Roma (CVVM, 2018).

Czech society is open to foreigners and its attitudes are not primarily determined by racial prejudice. About 51% of Czechs believe that the number of foreigners does not need to be increased. There is disagreement with economic immigration, unless justified by the need to maintain ethnic identity, but, for example, fears of rising unemployment, lowering the standard of living and the wages of the domestic population are considered legitimate and within the framework of democratic national interests.

External pressure on the admission and settlement of immigrants from Islamic countries has radically influenced the Czech public as well as the policies of traditional and populist parties (Action of Unsatisfied Citizens—ANO, and Freedom and Direct Democracy—SPD of national populist Tomio Okamura). New movements have arisen, such as "We don't want Islam in the Czech Republic", "For Our Culture and Safe Country", "Block against Islam" and others; the theme overwhelmed the Internet and was prominent in street demonstrations.

Czech far-right uses arguments against the forced and uncontrolled influx of immigrants and has pointed to the fact that, according to the experience of Western democracies, immigrants are largely unemployable and will become the permanent social burden of a new homeland at the expense of the living standards of the domestic population. It pointed to genuine security and health risks as well as to the incompatibility of the Christian foundations of Europe and Islamic fundamentalism. There was also a serious objection that the concerned cohabitation of a community with a democratic political culture and community with an undemocratic political culture and the absence of tolerance is difficult, if not impossible (Loewenstein, 1995).

Resistance to immigration is one of the long-term activating issues of the Czech far-right. From the legitimate substantive justification of disagreement with the influx of immigrants to Europe, the far-right is distinguished by racist and anti-democratic forces. The subject of Islamic dangers as interpreted by party leaders such as Okamura from SPD party that dragged citizens into the streets was used by extremists to attempt to influence the public by their doctrine. For this reason, populist movements have refused to hold joint demonstrations with National Democracy and the DSSS, for which it earned the immediate accusation of collaborating with Jews. There have been rallies in which some extremists warn the public against other extremists in order to gain imaginary points against liberal democracy.

In public speeches, debates with citizens and hateful posters, Nazi and fascist activists persuaded citizens about their conspiratorial explanations of the causes of the migration crisis that finds the culprit in the alleged global Jewish domination: *"We must not only stand against Islam. The immigrant wave of intruders is a tool of Jews destroying white Europe and white races. If we want to survive and if we want our culture, the nation and the whole of Europe to survive, we must rise up against the international practices of Jewry, who organize and stealthily manage everything"* (Piskač, 2016). The American Zionists are said to be behind the backdrop of contemporary neo-Marxism, which is *"a Masonic ideology of human rights"* aimed at *"changing the composition of the European population, a systematic attack on the white race and its destruction; our will has been paralyzed in advance by political correctness, consumerism, gender ideology, constant emphasis on tolerance and their perverse love, and all of this deprived most of our nation of internal defence mechanisms; it is literally and virtually an attack on the existence of our nation, in fact, it is all about life"* (Malý, 2017).

The alarming rhetoric of anti-Jewish hatred helped the far-right to continue threatening or hideous illustrations on posters. On the other hand, political posters of populists against Islamist migration have used puns, humour and jokes in anti-immigrant propaganda.

Alternative für Deutschland used a banner poster titled *"Islam, it does not belong to our kitchen."* Another poster with a smiling pregnant woman stated: *"The new Germans? We will do ourselves. Children! Do! Entertainment!"* (Novotný, Šárovec, 2018, pp. 108-9).

At the demonstrations against the crimes of Islam, which were taken over by the neo-Nazis from the National Revival in 2016, Jews were pillaged as guilty of today's war conflicts, architects of liberalism, the Islamic state and the European Union, who want to crush the Czech nation and the white race through migration: *"We are not governed by the Presidents, nor the Governments, but the US Jewish Corporations ... And that's why we will stand together and deny this Zionist disease!"* (Piskač, 2015).

At the National Democracy demonstration in 2015 it was said: *"We must crush the steel fist of the left-wing, false humanists, intellectuals and all who stand in the way of the Czech nation. Traitors will hang!"* (Matějný, 2015). Speakers tribunals on anti-immigration protests have been used by contemporary fascists and Nazis to promote anti-democratic systems such as the Italian fascist corporativist state (Malý, 2017).

From the electoral point of view, the Czech far-right did not receive the same support and increase in sympathizers as the similar part of the political spectrum in some West European countries. The Czech Republic has not yet been hit by an influx of Arab and African Islamic migrants, and the government as well as the president are implementing a strict policy so that it does not happen in the future. The Czech

Republic has a policy of preventing Muslim immigration and prefers assistance to the regions from which migration originates, i.e. before the borders of the European Union. The second cause of the current marginalization of the Czech extreme right lies in the fact that some of the new extremist parties of radicalized voters who have lost confidence in the Czech democratic party and the policy of established –traditional political parties (the Czech People's Party, the Czech Social Democratic Party, the Civic Democratic Party, TOP 09) give great support to anti-government populist parties and movements that are anti-corruption and protesting, openly critical but not anti-democratic, anti-pluralistic or racist. An example of such can be seen below:

> We have not talked about race in my life, I am personally a mix of two races ... I told Mr. Bartoš the simple thing: I refuse to be on a demonstration where flags are burned, where someone has a noose or someone announces that he will make lists of enemies ... We will not take part in events and cooperate with subjects that suggest undemocratic processes. We are a parliamentary party and we would like to be successful in the framework of the Constitution. I cannot imagine another way (Okamura, 2015).

Conclusion

The principle of representative democracy reflects the relationship between political parties and their leaders who need their supporters, in this sense their voters. However, if political actors fail to deliver the political will of civil society, we can argue with a reduced interest in public affairs as a voting deficit. This creates a new space for alternative parties that do not always bring comprehensive and strategic concepts of society management, nor do they address long-term societal and economic problems, such as unemployment. We can also see that traditional, conventional political parties do not fulfil their commitments and promises to the citizen, at least in terms of ideology and, ultimately, pragmatically because they are unable to cope with sudden and unforeseen circumstances that they cannot directly influence. Among the main domains of the success of the new political parties in the parliamentary elections in wider Europe including the Czech Republic, we can see the growth of populism, radicalism and extremism, which is both a combination of failure and a negative interest in the political process. It may seem that traditional parties have created some vacuum and possible entry into politics for new political platforms, visions as well as instruments for gaining political power and support. These trends include the growth of popular and radical rhetoric directly supported by the deteriorating economic and social situation of citizens, rising euro-scepticism and the general decline of voter confidence over conventional politics and political elites.

The Czech public holds a reserved and reluctant attitude to a far-right ideology with a vision of violent anti-systemic revolt. Nevertheless, a pointer to the possible future crisis is the fact that a large number of people took part in the protest demonstrations of the far-right in Prague and Brno in 2015 and 2017. In a generally open media and political atmosphere, people no longer mind expressing dissatisfaction alongside ultra-conservative authoritarians, fascists or Nazis. The recent migration crisis and the inability of European political representatives to bring acceptable solutions only supports the antitheses to democratic standards and proposed European values. As the results of the elections in the Czech Republic and many other countries together with the research implications show, the pattern of continuous support for radical and extreme variations in policy-making is visible and observable. There are many ongoing academic and public debates on how to cope and combat the rise of political extremism, although the success of the political parties representing the far-right or populist measures are not the immediate sources of such society moods but, more specifically the outcome of the problem.

3 MIGRATION AS AN ISSUE IN THE 2017 GENERAL ELECTIONS IN THE CZECH REPUBLIC

Ondřej Filipec

The 2017 general election to the Czech Chamber of Deputies resulted in a political earthquake. It was a demonstration of protest voting leading to the victory of populism and anti-establishment parties. The populist Alliance of the New Citizen (ANO), the movement of "Czech Berlusconi" Andrej Babiš, became the dominant party by securing almost 30% of the popular vote, leaving the centre-right Civic Democratic Party (ODS) second with just slightly over 11%. The anti-establishment Pirates (Piráti) came third with 10.79% and the nationalist, populist and anti-immigration Freedom and Direct Democracy (SPD) gained fourth place with 10.64%. The Czech Social Democratic Party (ČSSD), who had come first in the previous elections, was unable to survive being in government with the more assertive ANO movement and lost 35 of its 50 seats, the party's worst result in modern history, and gained just over 7% of the popular vote (Czech Statistical Office, 2017). The elections were a great defeat for liberal democracy.

The elections were strongly affected by both internal problems and external issues, among which migration played the most important role in at least in two respects. First, the 2015 migration crisis was associated with the weak response of the EU, where "hostile Brussels" pushed for a relocation mechanism for asylum-seekers, which was met by a negative response from Czech citizens. Secondly, the flow of migrants itself was portrayed as a danger for a homogenous country with limited experience of foreign migration. This perception intensified further after the terrorist attacks in Paris and Brussels. Fighting migration became an important topic, with parties seeing the promise of political capital being transformed into electoral support.

The main aim of this chapter is to assess the communication of political parties about migration with a special focus on party leaders and party programmes. The programmes are assessed from both a qualitative and quantitative perspective in order to reveal how much space was given by political parties to migration within their programmes. The attitude of leaders and visual materials (such as billboards) are presented to provide a more detailed picture. Unfortunately, this contribution cannot also deal with communication on social media as it has limited space and such communication requires more extensive assessment.

Instead, the assessment focuses on a higher number of actors. It assesses not only the parties that entered parliament—ANO, ODS, the Pirates, SPD, the Communist Party of Bohemia and Moravia (KSČM), ČSSD, Christian Democratic Union–Czech Peoples Party (KDU-ČSL), TOP 09 and Mayors and Independents (STAN)—but also parties with a high profile in using migration to communicate with their voters. These include the Party of Free Citizens (Svobodní), the Greens (Zelení), Reasonable People (Rozumní lidé), the Realists (Realisté), the Workers Party of Social Justice (DSSS) and the Coalition for the Republic-Republican Party of Czechoslovakia (Republikáni). The involvement of non-parliamentary parties will add better contrast to the content and methods of communication of the issue.

The main claim verified in this chapter is that radical and populist parties dedicated more space to the issue of migration within their programmes and used more radical vocabulary than traditional parties. While the first part of the claim can be verified by quantitative assessment of the programme, the second part requires content analysis and a qualitative approach. The method of coding or data analysis within the quantitative approach is described more closely in the second part of the chapter.

This chapter may be considered as an exploratory case study using mixed methods of analysis in order primarily to reveal how much space has been given to migration within the political programmes of Czech political parties for the 2017 elections, and how this issue was communicated. The visual presentation of the issue is secondary to the aims of the chapter but is important for providing context. Because it does not focus on social media communication and references to migration in the printed media and on TV, the scope of this contribution is limited and produce complex and comprehensive conclusions about migration and party communication. Instead, it represents one piece of a complex puzzle.

3.1 Party programmes: Qualitative assessment

Political parties had already started to develop an anti-immigration profile at the beginning of 2015. On 25 September 2015 the Czech Republic was outvoted in the Council of the European Union on the issue of redistribution quotas for refugees. The Czech Republic was against, together with Slovakia, Romania and Hungary, and was legally bound to accept 1591 refuges (Česká televize, 2015). From then onwards, refugee quotas became the most controversial issue connected to migration and fuelled negative attitude towards the EU. The issue of migration and quotas filled considerable space in party political programmes. The parts of the text that follow describe and analyse further how the issue of migration was communicated by individual political parties.

ANO movement

The ANO programme for the 2014 elections to the European Parliament already contained a reference to immigration policy, indicating that immigration policy had quite a high importance for ANO even before the 2015 migration crisis. The party dedicated 389 of the 5,353 words in their election programme (7.3%) to migration (ANO, 2014). It considered EU immigration policy as a policy which "has a good concept". ANO understood immigration policy as an opportunity to overcome negative demographic trends if the negative effects of migration, including the integration of migrants, would be managed. ANO supported the fight against illegal migration and securing external borders. Special focus was put on cooperation with countries of origin or transit countries with the aim of reducing or eliminating illegal forms of migration. ANO is in favour of common asylum standards within EU member states (ANO, 2017). However, there is a considerable shift in the election programme for the Chamber of Deputies and a departure from the positive tone of 2014.

The importance of migration is visible right from the first topic deal with, security: *"In the light of the migration crisis and terrorist attacks in Europe the security of citizens is the most important issue"* (ANO, 2017). Throughout the whole programme migration is mentioned mainly in terms of security and it is also raised in Chapter 5: Clear and active foreign policy. According to ANO, decisions about refugees should be the competence of member states and the party promises that it will do everything possible to stop illegal migration at the EU level to "stop migration to Europe". ANO stresses that Czech and European policy should focus on a solution for the migration crisis through reduction of migration flows from the countries of origin. They call for international operations (EU, NATO) in conflict areas in order to prevent migration waves. Moreover, ANO wants change in development programmes which should be aimed at war-torn countries (Libya, Syria, Iraq, Afghanistan) or countries with low living standards (Eritrea, Sub-Saharan Africa). Border protection is key for ANO and it will push NATO to actively protect borders (ANO, 2017).

ANO already communicated security as an issue in 2016, in the run-up to the regional elections, with their billboard (see Picture 1). ANO also used other billboards with the slogan "Strengthen security and not just blab".

Picture 1: ANO Billboard

Source: ANO, 2016.
Note: ANO leader Andrej Babiš claims "We want a better Czechia" and Bohumil Šimek: "A more secure one".

Civic Democratic Party (ODS)

The issue of migration is also present within the ODS programme. The party twice stressed that it refuses compulsory relocation quotas. It promises to establish a responsible and strong immigration policy which makes access to the Czech Republic easier for migrants who are of benefit for the country and makes things harder for immigrants who do not respect Czech laws, values and habits or are misusing the Czech social system. The party also promised to gain opt-outs from the common asylum and migration policy at the EU level (ODS, 2017, p. 11).

As for their visual campaign, ODS put the emphasis on emotions: "So we don't have to be afraid" is the message on billboard with party leader Petr Fiala (see Picture 2).

Picture 2: ODS Billboard

Source: ODS 2017.
Note: "So we don't have to be afraid", with the picture of Petr Fiala, the chair of ODS.

ODS further communicated the issue on its websites and developed its programme. The party stated that integration has failed in Muslim communities and that EU quotas are "a monstrous idea". The party also criticised Turkey and states that are unable to secure the Schengen border. As Petr Fiala pointed out, it is at place to expel those states from Schengen (ODS, 2016). The party is in favour of creating hot spots in Africa and outside Europe and increasing penalties for human trafficking (ODS, 2016).

Pirates

The Pirates referred to migration in their programme restrictively in one sentence: "We have a rational attitude towards immigration crises: we are against extreme requirements (see statement on migration). We support help closest to areas of conflict and humanitarian crises" (Piráti, 2017, p. 14). For this reason, the Pirates did not develop the issue of migration in their programme.

The main stances of the party are summed up in their statement from 22 October 2015. The Pirates call for a rational attitude towards migration and stress that the Dublin system does not work. They did not consider quotas as a solution but call for solidarity with overburdened states. The Pirates refuse radicals steps such as sinking ships with illegal refugees or automatic acceptance of refugees: they are in favour of a common asylum procedure based on country preference. The Pirates provide a detailed overview of facts and figures and later lay down several principles for EU policy and state attitude towards immigration. State policy should focus on nine issues: (1) the Czech Republic should voluntarily accept a reasonable number of refugees; (2) the Czech Republic should discuss and cooperate with other countries about finding a common solution; (3) the Czech Republic should establish the preferred characteristics of immigrants and later accept them; (4) keeping the Schengen system working; (5) supporting better treatment in refugee camps; (6) the involvement of local authorities; (7) allowing asylum-seekers to work during their asylum application in the Czech Republic; (8) a better focus on refugees' integration into society and (9) transparent dealing with public funds (Piráti, 2015). Thanks to the almost 2000 words long statement regarding refugees and its set of principles for both the national and European level, the programme of the Pirates is one of the most complex, rational and constructive despite being missing as a main issue for 2017 elections.

SPD

The programme of the SPD has the most sharply defined attitude towards migration, which is stated with reference to the EU: "*The current project of European integration directly threatens freedom and democracy in Europe. Part of this process is the managed Islamization of Europe. The ongoing illegal migration is the first phase of a conflict which will in the end threaten freedom, democracy and the existence of Czech Republic and our nation*" (SPD, 2017). The party stated that it wants a strict immigration policy: they do not want "*maladjusted migrants or the arrival of Islamic religious fanatics*" (SPD, 2017). The motto is "*No to Islam, no to terrorism*". The party refuses the forced acceptance of illegal immigrants and refuses "*the Islamization of our country under the pretext of multiculturalism*" (SPD, 2017). The programme also promises to prevent the creation of a fifth column of radical Muslims and to outlaw Sharia and the Islamic Jihad. In relation to law, the party *"says that it is unacceptable to let migrants stand above the law as is observed in other countries"* (SPD, 2017). Migrants are referred to in the programme on a number of occasions. For example, under the topic *"Money for working families and the retired, not for immigrants, not for parasites"* (SPD, 2017). The motto *"no to Islam, no to terrorism"* was also put on billboards with party leader Tomio Okamura (picture 3).

Picture 3: SPD Billboard

Source: SPD, 2017.
Note: *"No to Islam, no to terrorism" with the picture of Tomio Okamura.*

It is important to note that SPD leaders lied about migration. For example, Jana Lévová, head of party in the Plzeň region, created and spread a fake massage about 30 refugees who ran from the bus into the forest in Southern Bohemia. Police later denied this event (Kochová, 2016). In this sense the party programme and the information spread may be considered incorrect and manipulative. This conclusion is also supported by the Czech intelligence services.

In its yearly overview the Security Information Service (BIS)—the Intelligence Service of the Czech Republic—stresses that the BIS observed Okamura and his party and noted that: *"activities of the anti-immigration movement contributed to the polarization of Czech society and the increased radicalization of opinions within society (not only among the anti-immigration public but also among the pro-immigration public) and its distrust in democratic values. Some citizens with anti-immigration stances gradually became aggressive without any significant difference to right-wing extremists*" (BIS, 2017). This trend was mostly visible on the internet and social networks, which contributed to the spread of much fake news regarding migration and contributed to polarization.

Social networks were one of the domains of SPD. Tomio Okamura has more than 270,000 followers and he (or his team) deletes unpopular statements or alternative opinions and purposefully restricts the plurality of opinion. Followers of Okamura or members of SPD groups on Facebook preserve a homogeneity of opinion and members of the community assure each other that their opinion is correct. If someone penetrates the group and posts real facts on the wall, they are immediately banned. For this reason, approximately 20,000 people created their own group entitled "Tomio Okamura mi dal ban" (Tomio Okamura banned me).

Communist Party (KSČM)

For the Communist Party (KSČM) migration was a very important issue as it was mentioned in first topic (out of 5) called "Life without fear", where migration is addressed in the first point "*Let's solve the causes of migration crises, we are against forced quotas on refugee relocation*" (KSČM, 2017, p. 7). The party in its simple manifesto stresses that emphasis should be put on crisis solution, the stabilization of the environment in the place of origin and greater responsibility by the state which participated in or caused destabilization of that regime. From the EU, KSČM requires regulation of migration on its territory with respect to the sovereignty of member states and humanitarian aid for the needy. It refuses to accept refugees relocated under the quota mechanism (KSČM, 2017, p. 21).

At its 17th meeting, the General Committee of KSČM adopted (12 December 2015) a document entitled "Attitudes of KSČM towards migration and its causes", which was updated later in 2017. In the original document KSČM strongly criticizes the government, which did not succeed in avoiding quotas, and urges the government to be more active at the level of international institutions including the UN, OSCE and NATO in solving the causes of the immigration crisis. It also stresses that the government is not fulfilling its obligation to provide 0.33% of GDP for development aid (KSČM, 2015). The demands of KSČM are, however, very general. For example, the party calls for "Resolving the status of people who have no country to return to" or "to discuss alternative humane attitudes to migration policy with other left parties in Europe, to coordinate views and build a European asylum policy from the bottom up with respect for the needs of socially weak EU citizens" (KSČM, 2015). In the updated version KSČM strongly refuses quotas and calls for resolving the causes of migration in the countries of origin. Even here, there is a reference to the poor: KSČM calls for "measures which are effective and targeted and at the same time do not worsen the living standards and problems of our citizens" (KSČM, 2017).

Media associated with the party have also consistently presented hard-line attitudes to migration and refused quotas. For example *Haló noviny* in one of its June 2016 issues presented criticism by the KSČM shadow minister of interior Zdeněk Maršíček, who claimed that "accepting any immigrant is a security threat. As we can see in France or Germany, they are attacking individuals who are very quickly radicalized" (Haló noviny, 2016).

Social Democrats (ČSSD)

Contrary to ANO, the Social Democrats (ČSSD) communicated the topic of migration for the first time on page 9 of their programme in relation to wages: We will not allow a decrease in the cost of labour in the Czech Republic through unregulated economic migration (ČSSD, 2017). Security issues related to migration are dealt with later, on page 28: *"We will support the creation of preventative measures to stop illegal migration, mostly targeted and conditional humanitarian and development aid for African and Asian countries from where people come. We refused and are refusing models based on compulsory relocation quotas"* (ČSSD, 2017, p. 29). Compared to ANO and other parties the issue of migration is rather lost in the programme.

It is important to note that ČSSD was criticized for the way it communicated the migration issue, although the minister of interior Milan Chovanec tried to act very decisively and refused EU quotas. Chovanec claimed that his hard-line and uncompromising approach to refugees resulted in situation when refugees tried to avoid the Czech Republic. This is true: refugees were placed in detention facilities where men were separated from women and children. Moreover, they had to pay for their detention and sometimes their valuables were used for covering the debt, as reported in the documentary movie Czech Allah by Zuzana Piussi (2016). For these and similar reasons the Czech Republic was criticised for violating human rights.

Picture 4: ČSSD billboard.

Source: ČSSD, 2017.
Note: Minister of the Interior Miroslav Chovanec claims that *"Refugees are not flooding towards us or through our country. This success did not come by itself. It took a lot of work, nerves and dedication".*

The party also used other billboards aimed at security with the slogans "Vote for a safe country" or with the face of the Minister of the Interior and the slogan "We are and will be safe country".

Christian Democrats (KDU-ČSL)

KDU-ČSL made reference to migration in the middle of its programme under the specific topic "Solution of the migration wave", where they stress that one of the priorities of Czech foreign policy should be the regulation of migration flows and the elimination of illegal migration together with an increase in financial contributions to development aid programmes. KDU-ČSL also expressed support for securing the EU external borders and internal security assurance in cooperation with other member states. They support asylum policy reform with the aim of stabilizing countries in the European neighbourhood and having an effective return policy (KDU-ČSL, 2017, p. 11).

TOP 09

Migration was a very important topic for TOP 09, which dedicated several paragraphs to the issue under the title "controlled migration". TOP 09 sees the EU as a platform for an effective solution of the immigration issue. The party calls for the preservation of the Schengen area, which is crucial for the Czech Republic. The party highlights that securing borders requires the help of the common border and coast guard and the development of the Schengen Information System in order to prevent illegal migration. TOP 09 also stresses that the Czech Republic shall contribute to sustainable conditions in the countries around Europe, especially through conditional development aid, investments and projects which will help to decrease the impact of climate change (TOP 09, 2017, p. 17).

However, the party also highlights the moral dimension of aid: the Czech Republic shall provide international protection to people from the most persecuted and vulnerable groups on an individual basis and fulfil its humanitarian obligations. In the following six points the party develops a vision for immigration policy: (1) the creation of safe areas where refugees will be not in danger; (2) support of a return policy for those who fail to gain protection; (3) a flexible and justified immigration policy meeting the needs of the Czech economy; (4) the independence of the Czech Republic in decisions about the number, origin and qualifications of immigrants; (5) not compromising the values of developed European society and (6) supporting EU countries facing immigration waves (TOP 09, 2017, p. 18).

Other parties

Migration was also an issue for other parties who did not pass the 5% threshold for gaining seats in parliament (see Table 2). For example, the eurosceptic Svobodní (Free) put a point in their programme labelled "We refuse the redistribution of people", claiming that the Czech Republic has one of the best asylum policies in Europe and it would be a mistake to adopt a common EU policy which would undermine the possibility for prompt responses to world changes. Moreover, as the programme states, the EU has demonstrated in recent years that it is not able to solve crises effectively. Svobodní believe that every person has the right to fight for a better place to live, but *"We have the duty to protect our security and public finances"* (Svobodní, 2017).

Table 2: 2017 Elections to Chamber of Deputies in the Czech Republic (Results II)

Party	% of votes
Party of Free Citizens	1.56
Greens	1.46
Reasonable People	0.72
Realists	0.71
Workers Party of Social Justice	0.20
Coalition for Republic—Republican Party of Czechoslovakia	0.19

Source: Czech Statistical Office, 2017.

Piture 5: Svobodní billboard.

Source: Svobodní, 2017.
Note: Party leader Petr Mach claims on the billboard that "We can remain a safe country without quotas".

The Czech Green Party also dedicated considerable space to migration. In their programme the Greens want to create a specialized ministry for human rights, equal opportunities and migration, as human rights protection are one of the key areas for the party (Zelení, 2017, p. 36). The Greens also call for making development aid stronger and more effective in order to prevent forced migration. According to party reservations to the Lisbon Treaty, coalitions with other non-liberal

Visegrad countries and the blind refusal of redistribution quotas is a waste of political capital which might have been invested in real priorities. As mentioned later, the real challenge is Brexit, the integration of refugees, Eurozone stability, internal reform, an ambitious climate policy, working opportunities for young people and the harmonization of social systems (Zelení, 2017, p. 41). Greens are in favour of a real common asylum policy based on solidarity to help the needy but at the same time to minimalize the security risk of uncontrolled migration. The party is positive about the Czech experience and optimistic about its capacities: with the cooperation of public institutions and NGOs we can without difficulties take care of several thousand refugees (Zelení, 2017, p. 44).

Other parties remain marginal. However, in some cases migration played important role: for example, the party Reasonable People: Stop Migration and the EU Dictate and Block against Islamization—Defence of the Homeland also expressed their attitude towards migration in the name of their party and used visual campaign. Block against Islam posted a picture where the party claims that they can "stop them" (picture 7).

Picture 7: Block against Islamization material.

Source: Block against Islam, 2017.
Note: "Block against Islamization—Home Defence. We can stop them! Vote no. 13".

Other far-right parties such as the Coalition for the Republic—Republican Party of Czechoslovakia call for strict anti-immigration laws and protection of the borders. In the party programme they call for ensuring the security of state borders and refuse any acceptance of "dagos" without exception. The party also calls for rethinking EU membership if acceptance of "economic dagos" and criminal elements continues (SPR-RSC, 2017). The party refuses EU quotas as an attempt to destroy nation states. Moreover, it is against the family reunification of refuges which should be allowed only in their native lands. The party also addresses the issue of migrant smuggling with prison and fines several times higher than the payments from dagos (SPR-RSC, 2017).

Also a new project "Realists", led by political scientist and the face of Institute 2080 Robejšek, used the migration issue in order to attract voters. In their programme they call for zero tolerance of illegal immigration. They are in favour of setting strict selection and integration criteria which will prevent the entry of unwanted migrants. The protection of borders and the assimilation of immigrants are key tools for changing the situation (Realisté, 2017).

Picture 8: Realisté billboard

Source: Realisté, 2017.
Note: "Do you think there is a difference? Realists thinks there is!"

The Workers Party of Social Justice (DSSS) adopted the main slogan "DSSS Against Migration!" As noted by party member Lukáš Brandtner: "Part of the DSSS programme is a clear and radical solution: labour camps for immigrants, where they pay their costs for staying in Europe before forced deportation to their native countries when the situation has cooled down and where they cannot get in touch with regular inhabitants, who will be not put under the risk of becoming the next victim of immigrant animals" (Brandtner, 2017) On a party webpage, there are several articles strongly attacking immigrants, calling for their deportation and punishment for "traitors". Moreover, the party supported many anti-immigration protests, including those in Germany organized by ThüGIDA and the NPD in Greiz (DSSS, 2017). As President of the party Tomáš Vandas said already in 2015: "The only solution how to save Europe is to deport all immigrants. We shall start with those who came last year!" (DSSS, 2015). However, the party has not changed its programme since 2015 and thus migration is not reflected in the official party programme.

The billboards and analysis of communication presented show that the two most successful parties during the 2017 general election addressed the issue of migration visually within a more general message about security. Small non-parliamentary parties, on the other hand, were more open to using pictures with greater impact, which is mainly visible on the billboards of the Realists or the Block against Islam. These parties were also more prone to use dramatic, expressive and non-standard labelling of refugees within their communications.

3.2 Quantitative assessment

The main aim of the quantitative assessment is to measure the length dedicated to the issue of migration within party programmes. In relation to this issue it is important to stress several methodological aspects. Coding the passages related to migration may be subjective as the border lines between migration and other issues are sometimes not very clear. Does the migration issue also cover security issues? What about NATO involvement? Or the issue of protecting identity? In order to avoid double standard within the analysis it is important to formulate coding rules. For this purpose the author used programmes available on party web sites without discrimination relating to their form. Some programmes were directly on the web page, some in a pdf document. The total length of the programme was calculated by transferring the text from the website to the MS word editor and using the word count function. For pdf documents the Monterey Language Services online application was used, which provides information about the word count of pdf documents.

Coding followed in two steps. In the first step sentences containing words such as "migration", "migrant", "refugee", "quotas", "Schengen" or "asylum" were counted as relevant. In the second step all other sentences with reference to migration were considered as relevant even if they did not contain the key words, but only if they referred to migration from outside the EU. References to terrorism or security were considered relevant only in relation to migration.

The length of the party programmes varied as some parties put emphasis on clarity and short message while other focused on more developed principles and positions. Among the parties which succeeded in the elections to the Chamber of Deputies, the longest programme was that of ANO (15,645 words) and the shortest that of KDU-ČSL (2,043 words). The TOP 09 party dedicated the most words to migration (437). This was due to the party's attempt to explain its stances, and sentences sometimes had an instructive character. However, in relative numbers the populist SPD dedicated the highest proportion of its programme to migration (4.59%) and often referred to migration and terrorism (in relation to migration). Unsurprisingly, the least space was dedicated to immigration by STAN, which is a party that previously operated mainly at local level. Table 3 summarizes quantitative assessment.

Table 3: Immigration as % of main party programme documents

Party	Incumbent	Programme length (words)	Words dedicated to migration	As % of programme
ANO	Yes	15,645	398	2.54
ODS	Yes	4,725	105	2.22
Piráti	Yes	4,416	53	1.2
SPD	Yes	3,576	164	4.59
KSČM	Yes	4,278	94	2.2
ČSSD	Yes	8,734	129	1.48
KDU-ČSL	Yes	2,043	69	3.38
TOP 09	Yes	14,178	437	3.08
STAN	Yes	14,827	153	1.03
Party of Free Citizens	No	4,484	116	2.59
Greens	No	29,494	312	1.06
Reasonable People	No	641	46	7.18
Realists	No	7,676	271	3.53
Workers' Party of Social Justice	No	-	-	-
Coalition for the Republic—Republican Party of Czechoslovakia	No	1,259	146	11.6

Source: Author, based on party programmes.

At first sight there is no correlation between the success of political parties and the space dedicated to migration within the party manifestos or party rhetoric. There are several explanations for this. Most significantly, parties are using other communication channels apart from political programmes, and voter support is constructed on a multidimensional basis.

On the other hand, we can note that there has been a significant increase in the number of words dedicated to migration within political programmes. For example, the ANO movement in the shortened version of its 2013 election programme did not mention migration at all. The longer version, "Resort Programme", is 7,205 words long, but just half a sentence (6 words) is dedicated to migration (ANO, 2013). The full programme of the Pirates for 2013 was 9,011 words long and the issue of migration was avoided completely, which was also the case with KSČM, whose programme "With the People for the People" consists of 3,730 words, but the issue of migration is missing (Piráti, 2013; KSČM, 2013). Likewise, in the almost 9,000 words long programme of TOP 09 the issue of migration is missing (TOP 09, 2013), and the same applies for ČSSD (whose programme was 8,133 words) as well as for STAN, which at the beginning of its existence did not refer to the migration issue.

However, there were parties which already mentioned migration in their programmes for the 2013 general elections. For example, in a 2,640 word programme, ODS dedicated one small paragraph, consisting of 47 words, to migration, which is approximately 1.8% of the programme (ODS, 2013). Similarly the populist SPD (at that time registered as the Movement for Direct Democracy of Tomio Okamura) dedicated two sentences amounting to 15 words to migration in a 728 word long programme 728 words, which is approximately 2.1% (UPDTO, 2013). Likewise, KDU-ČSL dedicated one paragraph (55 words) of a 5,399 word long programme to migration, which is approximately 1% (KDU-ČSL, 2013). The changes are summarized in the Table 4.

Table 4: Changes in migration coverage between 2013 and 2017

Party	Words dedicated to migration in 2013	Words dedicated to migration in 2017	Change in words between 2013 and 2017	As percentage of programme in 2013	As percentage of programme in 2017	Change in percentage between 2013 and 2017
ANO	6	398	+392	0.01	2.54	+2.53
ODS	47	105	+58	1.8	2.22	+ 0.42
Pirates	0	53	+53	0	1.2	+1.2
SPD	15	164	+139	2.1	4.59	+2.49
KSČM	0	94	+94	0	2.2	+2.2
ČSSD	0	129	+129	0	1.48	+1.48
KDU-ČSL	55	69	+14	1	3.38	+2.38
TOP 09	0	437	+437	0	3.08	+3.08
STAN	0	153	+153	0	1.03	+1.03
Average	*14*	*178*	*+163*	*0.44*	*2.41*	*+1.97*

Source: Author, based on political programmes.

To sum up, among incumbent parties only ODS, SPD and KDU-ČSL made substantial reference to migration in 2013, so the 2017 election brought an important politicization of the issue, or the "migrationization" of party political programmes, as all incumbent parties without exception increased the length of references to migration. Next to the populist SPD and ANO movement, migration also became very important for TOP 09 and remained a topic for ODS and KDU-ČSL. Other parties adjusted their programmes similarly.

Conclusion

Elections to the Chamber of Deputies in the Czech Republic in 2017 had a significant impact as they resulted in losses for traditional parties and the strengthening of populism. This was partially caused by the issue of migration, which became one of the most important topics raised during pre-election campaigns. This is to an extent a paradox as the country is not in the path of the main migration flows and does not accept a high number of refugees.

Despite this paradox, parties soon realized that the issue of migration presents political capital and used this topic extensively in communicating with voters. As above analysis shows, all parties created a stance towards migration and developed their political programmes and communication on this issue. For some parties (SPD, ODS and KDU-ČSL) this topic was not new as it was already communicated in the run-up to the 2013 elections. However, the elections of 2017 led to important changes as the space within political programmes dedicated to migration is on average more than 10 times higher than during the 2013 elections and parties on average dedicated 2.4% of their total length to the issue, with greater space allocated by populist parties, although traditional parties (KDU-ČSL and TOP 09) also publicised the issue, but on a more pro-European basis.

Despite the considerable importance of the issue, some more radical subjects did not succeed in the elections and even their sharp vocabulary and emotional visualisation did not prove helpful. As the latest results of the Eurobarometer survey shows (2018), migration is still seen as a very important issue and continues to have mobilization potential. However, it is not the only topic on which competition is based and it may be expected that it will lose significance as the public discourse changes in favour of different topics which have more real basis in the everyday life of the Czech Republic than the virtual threat of migration.

4 IMPACTS OF MIGRATION ON PUBLIC ADMINISTRATION

Ondrej Mitaľ

The reality of the 21st century should be characterized by intensive global interdependence, deterritorialization of social life and by the porosity of state borders. States and public administration are fundamental and irreplaceable parts of contemporary democratic societies. Yet public administration faces many challenges. Transformations of public administration are determined by factors from outside the sovereign state. The cross-border movement of people is one of the crucial factors and its potential to influence the conduct of public administration is not insignificant. Migration, one of the most examined global phenomena, is mostly discussed as an important factor of social development. Therefore European states should consider the impacts of migration on the sphere of public affairs and public administration.

However, the relationship between these two dynamically progressing phenomena—public administration and migration—is a relatively unexplored field of interest. Yet these issues should be perceived as a very important and attractive field of research. Given the complexity of public administration, the aim of this text is to focus attention on the limits and perspectives linked to the challenges of public administration which should be identified in the context of international migration. The hypothesis is that migration affects the conduct of public administration. This contribution examines, with the help of analysis and synthesis methods, the impacts of international migration on the conduct of public administration in the Slovak Republic.

The contribution tries to reflect the current state of the contemporary globalized world. The introductory part deals with the importance of migration. Attention is paid to issues related to democratic states and the social reality of the 21st century. The following part deals with the conceptual and strategic framework formulated at global,

European and national level. The core part of the chapter is devoted to current perspectives and challenges for public administration linked to the impacts of migration. It is important to note that the text concentrates on regular international migration. The issues of irregular migration and refugees are not a major part of this analysis. However, given the importance of these issues it is clearly impossible to overlook these contemporary global problems and they will be mentioned where of importance.

4.1 Migration and contemporary democratic states

The traditional concept of public administration was born without any need to consider issues from outside the territory of the state. However, contemporary states should implement policies in accordance with perspectives and challenges which have international and global proportions, and at the same time some activities of public administration need to consider cross-border cooperation (Raadschelders, Vigoda-Gadot, 2015). International flows should be perceived as an important factor in the decision-making process. States try to manage the movement of goods, services, financial capital and people. Yet some processes should not be dealt with by sovereign states. Globalization limits state sovereignty and leads to a loss of exclusivity when regulating international movement. States should try to mitigate the negative aspects of these movements. On the other hand, states need to take advantage of the opportunities offered. Migration should be perceived as an important process in contemporary society which has the potential to change our world significantly.

4.1.1 Social reality of the 21st century and the determinants of migration

The multidimensional character of globalization and integration processes is changing the world and social reality as intensively as any other process in our history. Isolation caused by natural and environmental characteristics has been eliminated in the last century and people of different cultures, religion and ethnicity live together (Singer, 2016). Contemporary states regarding the level of global interdependence could not expect that movement of people would not be significant factor of decision-making processes in the future. In this sense international migration grew enormously in consequence of extensive social and political changes in the world and was directed towards European countries (Priecel, Belo-Caban, 2016). The modern world is getting smaller and people and their cultures, values, traditions and ideas are getting closer.

The primary motivation to cross-border movement of individuals is the vision of a better life. This motivation has been important in the ancient times and in the Migration Period as well. Moreover, the prosperity, welfare and quality of life have been significant factors of resettlement both in the times of Industrial Revolution and in the 20th century. Migration is not a new phenomenon, it is a stable part of our history. But, current impacts of migration are qualitatively and quantitatively different. Anyway, there is one key perspective of contemporary migration flows. Different levels of states' welfare are one of the main reasons of regular and irregular migration. What's more, welfare disproportions are getting more intensive between the states. The result of this tendency is the fact, that some parts of the world are getting richer and some parts of world are getting poorer.

We might argue that the international position of the Slovak Republic has changed over the past decades. Slovakia became one of many destinations for international migrants. Since the accession to the European Union, the tensions remain between the attempt to close oneself off to new immigrants and realization that one has become an immigration country that must make a greater effort to integrate the immigrants (Zeitlhofer, 2011). However, Slovak Republic needs to respect international commitments and human rights.

Regarding the growing population of migrants, we could identify some contradictions linked to this international flow, such as hostile attitude of majority, employment issues, social issues related to discrimination and standards of living or ethnic tensions. Obviously, these issues are typical for high-income democracies. Mentioned issues linked to the migration are mostly caused by lack of interest from legitimate authorities. The migration policy should be adjusted in accordance to contemporary migration trends to gain positive effects both for immigrants and Slovak Republic (Bolečeková, 2010). On the other hand, it is quite illusory to expect, that Slovak Republic could be competitive without migrants in modern globalized world. Moreover, using the words of F. Briška (2008) we may argue, that global system does not recognise the oasis of untouchability and in spite of that possible future problems will have impact on whole world and especially on relatively open and dependent Slovak Republic. The importance of contemporary tendencies reflection is confirmed by the issues of demographic features, foreign direct investments, openness of economy and relatively exhausted labour market.

States should accept their international responsibility and implement adequate migration policies in accordance with the wider interests of global society. Powerful liberal states should set the trend on how to manage migration for the rest of the world, but construction of a truly international regime can only become reality when the asymmetry of interests between the developed and developing worlds are eliminated (Hollifield, 2012). Besides that, an important part of migration strategies is the integration of migrants. European states should choose the direction of their integration strategy because contemporary problems linked to migration could become more and more complicated without a well-prepared strategy (Halász, 2012). This trend should be reflected by various types of public policies carried out by public administrations.

4.1.2 Migration and public administration

Migration is an important process in the contemporary globalized world. The international movement of people influences the formulation and implementation of public policies. According to the text of the "Migration Policy of the Slovak Republic: Future prospects until 2020" (2011), migration should be perceived as a historical phenomenon which determines politics, economy and society, as well as the security situation. Moreover, the movement of people could be the source of conflicts which could influence the future of states and whole world. This document was adopted by the Government of the Slovak Republic and selected statements indicate respect for the potential and current impacts of migration.

We might conclude that there is general agreement about the relationship between public administration and the state. Public administration carries out fundamental roles and functions of states, such as safety, security, the regulation of economic activities, public health, public education and public culture. These roles and functions have a permanent social importance. Consequently public administration functions are mainly social functions, which reflect public expectations, public needs and the interests of various entities (Erneker, Pána, 2017). Therefore migration transforms these important aspects of public administration, especially public needs and the structure of the population. Particularly, programming function, regulation function, informational function or social-political function should be perceived in the context of new limits and perspectives.

Moreover, movement of people influences another important feature of the public sphere and public administration. Migration is an important factor which in the context of globalization, transnationalism and global economy influences public interest (Hanyane, 2015). In this sense, the attributes of public interest are changing because of migration. Another question regarding the relationship between public administration and public interest should be represented by public opinion. It is necessary to pay attention to issue of public opinion on migrants to avoid ethnic tensions, and at the same time enthusiasms linked to integration of migrants in to our society demonstrates our maturity (Žaková, Berová, 2014). According to the words of J. Liďák (2016) there is an important question on how to solve issues related to meeting on ethnic base, rejections of migrants by the majority, removal of dogmatic positions and other issues, which need to be solved by public authorities. Moreover, any distinction between political declarations and real actions is unacceptable.

However, we might identify various approaches on how to manage impacts of migration. According to Z. Števulová (2017) public goals should be achieved by building trust of migrants in the system through the programs such as resettlement, visa schemes, scholarships and measures, which could help motivate refugees to settle in countries with confidence in a hope for the future. Mentioned public policy tools should be perceived as generally widespread. But, are these general activities everything what are we responsible to do? On the other hand, integrated approaches to migration consist of activities such as intervening, networks, intermediaries and any types of connections (O´Reilly, 2012). Anyway, the most important are real practical activities, which need to be realized on each level of public administration.

Generally, we might agree with the words of P. Scholten (2018), that migration influences all policies and institutions in the cities. Local self-government units should actively cultivate conditions, through which migrants should be integrated in social life on local level, and in this context, migrants, as a part of local community help to cultivate quality of life in the local community (Integration Policy of Slovak Republic, 2014). We might say that this relationship should be mutually advantageous both for migrants and local community. Local entities are important actors when it comes to managing the impacts of migration. In this sense, we should highlight positive example from the Western Europe. British local government capacity moderated the negative impact on performance of migration from Eastern Europe after 2004 (Andrews, Boyne, O'Tolle, Meier, Walker, 2013). But, there must be stressed one important paradox. According to the newest World Migration Report (2017) cities are not part of national migration policy development, even though they are increasingly among the principal determinants of migration.

We might sum it up, that migration is changing both organizational and functional aspect of public administration. Practical activities of public administration are very important. On the other hand, conceptual and strategic documents represent outcomes of specialized and complex evaluation of contemporary conditions. These documents should be perceived as important and general guidelines on how to manage impacts of migration.

4.2 Managing of migration—conceptual framework

Migration is a global phenomenon, which is not discussed only by the theoreticians and academics. International movement of people is also the centre of attention at platforms established by governments, non-governmental organizations and international organizations. The results of these debates are mostly presented by various types of conceptual documents. The ambition of this part of text is to point out parts of selected documents, which concentrate their attention on examined impacts of migration on public administration. But, the attention will not be put on documents, which are relatively older and do not reflect contemporary reality linked to migration.

4.2.1 Managing of migration at global and European level

Firstly, migration is a phenomenon, which could be quantified. According to the newest report processed by International Organization for Migration, international migrant population globally has increased in size but, remain relatively stable as a proportion of the world's population in last two decades (World Migration Report, 2017). United Nations Department of Economic and Social Affairs provides accurate statistics about international migration. Overall, the estimated number of migrants was 152 million in 1990 (2.9% of world's population), 172 million in 2000 (2.8% of world's population), 220 million in 2010 (3.2% of world's population), and 257 million migrants in 2017 (3.4% of world's population), what was the highest overall number since the beginning of measurements (International Migrant Stock: The 2017 Revision, 2017). Globally, nearly 57% of international migrants lived in developed regions "North", while only 43% of international migrants were hosted by developing regions "South" (International Migration Report, 2017). This antagonistic distinction of the world is relatively clearly defined in the theory. Using the words of A. Heywood (2011) globalization channels benefits to the rich North at the expense of the poorer South, helping to maintain, if not increase, between-country inequality. Anyway, prosperity and welfare is one of the strongest sources of migration in the world. Moreover, governments could not expect that presented trends would not continue in next years and decades.

As it was mentioned indirectly before, the question is not if impacts of migration should be managed by governments and public administration. The question is how we should maximize positive aspects and minimize negative aspects of migration. The delivery of services to migrants happens for a large part at the local level and in this sense, cooperation across sectors of national economy and across levels of governments is more than required (World Public Sector Report, 2018). Moreover, managing of migration is implausible without public administration and the reason is simple. Administrative tools are based on a wide array of recording systems, usually operating as part of the management or control of international migration, such as record visa issuance, work permits, residence permits, border control statistics and regularization drives (Toolkit on International Migration, 2012).

The European Union is challenged by the migration significantly for a very pragmatic reason in last decade. It consists of highly developed states, especially Western Europe. In this sense, the European Union represents territory, where many migrants want to spend the rest of their lives. Almost one third of the world's international migrants (75 million) lived in Europe in 2015 (World Migration Report, 2017). The migration priorities of the European Union were set by the document called European Agenda on Migration. According to this document fundamental aims of European Union and member states are restoring confidence of ability to bring together European and national efforts, meeting international and ethical obligations, working together in an effective way and working in accordance to principles of solidarity and shared responsibility (European Agenda on Migration, 2015). Besides that, migration is a topic, which is also discussed by the public.

According to the special Eurobarometer survey published by European Commission, Europeans tend to agree on the main factors that may facilitate integration of immigrants, such as offering language courses upon arrival (88%), improving integration programmes (85%) or supporting job finding (83%). (Integration of immigrants in the European Union, 2018).

We might sum it up, that European Union and member states should formulate and implement policies related to migration very carefully. Rational solutions and compromise should be found between taking international responsibility and abusing of social systems. Moreover, responsibility of European Union and member states should be defined fairly and clearly.

4.2.2 Managing of migration in the conditions of Slovak Republic

Based on database of the Ministry of Interior of the Slovak Republic, there were almost 105 thousand migrants hosted by the Slovak Republic in 2017 (Statistical Overview of Legal and Illegal Migration in the Slovak Republic, 2017). This population of migrants represents 1.92% of total population. The total migrant population has increased in size, but remain relatively stable in comparison to total population in last decades.

Slovak documents related to migration are formulated very pragmatically. If society will ignore impacts of migration, growing population of migrants can cause problems in the political, economic and social life (Migration Policy of the Slovak Republic Perspective until 2020, 2011). Besides that, we should mention principles of migration policy, which are principle of sovereignty, legality, regulation of legal migration, cooperation with the European Union, non-discrimination and flexibility (Conception of migration policy of Slovak Republic, 2008). On the other hand, Slovakia and few other member states of European Union hold negative stance towards quotas and redistribution scheme of asylum seekers and migrants. But, one important attribute of contemporary globalized world should be mentioned once again. Migrants take advantages of existing social and economic divergences and they are heading to states, where social benefits reach wages in poorer states, but the same states are thanks to their unwillingness to accept migrants blamed of lack of solidarity and punished by quotas (Keller, 2017). Anyway, goals declared by documents correspond with actions identified on European and global level.

Based on integration policy, public administration provides some basic public goods and services related to housing, cultural and social integration, health care, education, employment or social protection. This document formulates some additional activities of public administration, such as social, legal and psychological advice. Besides that, this document tries to emphasize importance of integration through the helping services, such as finding accommodation, job search assistance, organization of courses or assistance to disadvantages groups (Integration policy of Slovak Republic, 2014).

Moreover, local self-government units should perform some activities too. This part of public administration is the closest one both to citizens and migrants. Local self-government regions should provide counselling activities, guarantee the quality of social, healthcare and educational services, support participation of migrants on various regional events and promote self-presentation of migrants (Integration policy of Slovak Republic, 2014). Local authorities should be very effective in managing impacts of migration and some solutions should be implemented very quickly. These entities should promote creating an ambassador position, support language training and the remission of taxes or local fees in the context of tenant living (Possibilities of Cooperation of Migration Office of Ministry of Interior of the Slovak Republic and ZMOS on Integration of Persons under International Protection, 2016).

Finally, we might conclude that there is an evident effort to maximize positive impacts of migration and minimize negative and contradictory impacts of migration. This tendency should be clearly recognized at global, European and national level. Nevertheless, we must say that public administration could not influence migration flows significantly. But, according to mentioned documents, public administration organizations play important role in migration and integration policy.

4.3 Challenges of public administration

Talking about impacts of migration in Germany, Great Britain, France or Belgium is not that same, as talking about migration in Central European countries. The problems such as radicalization, integration difficulties and ethnic tensions, security issues, organised crime, people trafficking or terrorist attacks are not so intensive and frequent in the Slovak Republic. Current situation is not ideal, but intensity of these problems is not so serious. But, impacts of migration is something what should be discussed and managed by democratic states. In this sense, there are various spheres of public life, which are continuously transformed by international movement of people. Regarding the complexity of public administration, various types of contradictions are linked to the migration in the conditions of Slovak Republic. But, this part of the text will be focused on those, which should be perceived as the most urgent.

Regarding the openness of Slovak Republic, the perspective of labour market and employment issues is one of the key sphere of social life, which needs to be managed by public administration. Labour market is relatively exhausted in the Slovak Republic. In this context, we are not able to fulfil market needs by our citizens. Nevertheless, there are various explanations of this situation, such as irrational policies or non-perspective decisions of government. But, regardless the reason, the lack of qualified labour force needs to be solved. Especially big transnational corporations must solve this problem. In the context of examined issue, bringing people from other countries is the easiest solution for big corporations, such as automotive, logistics or financial companies. In this sense, migration should be perceived as an important part of our economy. Moreover, this interpretation of international migration is typical for high developed countries around the world.

Moreover, there is another crucial problem linked to mentioned issue, which is mostly called as social dumping. In this sense, the key role of public administration is to secure equal working and salary conditions. If state and public administration organizations could not handle this challenge, then integration of migrants could be more difficult. States could not overlook problems linked to these contradictions. Tensions in the factories and in the local communities should be identified especially in western Slovakia, where big companies compensate insufficient labour force through the potential of migration. Regarding the future direct foreign investments, the delaying of solutions could be very contra productive. Besides that, there was mutual problem linked to migration in western countries of Europe approximately 15 years ago. Anyway, it is not an absolute parallel, but some common attributes are more than evident. Anyway, generally we might argue that equal working conditions should be perceived as a characteristic sign of developed democratic state. Using the words of V. Žofčinová (2015) antidiscrimination policy in labour law legislation is not as effective as it should be and the importance of equal wage for the same work, non-discrimination and equal treatment should not be even more decreased by ambiguous interpretations.

Migrants are coming to Europe, they are coming to the Slovak Republic as well. But, they are coming to cities and local self-government regions. What´s more, many important competencies were decentralized on local self-government units. In this sense, these entities can create and realize some activities related to healthcare, education, culture or issues associated to social aspects of everyday life. On the other hand, active participation of other local entities is more than necessary. More often the local governments must move toward the common decisions and widen their cooperation with other subjects to fulfil their goals (Adamcová, Ondrová, 2017). Besides that, achieving goals of public policies is more challenging without this cooperation. Significant part of public goods and public services is not provided by public administration anymore. According to the European Agenda on Migration (2015) wider cooperation of relevant entities, such as states, European Union institutions, international organizations, civil society and local authorities is more than necessary. In this sense, public administration should cooperate with all entities involved in the processes related to providing of public goods and services.

As it was mentioned in the first part of the text, the isolation of cultures disappeared thanks to globalization. But, this process is accompanied by some negative aspects. Fears of cultural heterogeneity linked to global migration flows are particularly salient in Western European democracies and have given rise to defensive forms of mobilization by the indigenous populations (Kreisi, 2015). But, these tendencies should be perceived in wider social circumstances. As it is expressed by J. Mihalik (2017), if there is a relationship between the migration crisis and the rise of alternative political leaders and parties in the Slovak Republic, we may concur that it has been continuously supplemented by the previously unresolved social and economic inequalities. In this sense, the minimization of negative atmosphere is another important role of public administration. Otherwise, the respect for cultural, religion and social diversity should be irreplaceable quality of contemporary society (Innocenti, 2015). We may sum it up, that governments should find some compromise between promoting rights of migrant and maintaining of national identity.

Otherwise, migration is complex phenomenon, which transforms many spheres of public administration, such as healthcare, education, participation or employment issues. Activities of local entities should reflect specific conditions in concrete territory. But, financial, personal and professional capacity is often limited in the conditions of many local self-government units.

Based on abovementioned, there should be used those information tools, which could help to enrich awareness about migration. Such public policy tools should reflect golden middle way between centralization and decentralization. Governments should create conditions, where migrants and refugees would not be trapped in protracted displacement, their household will not be integrated into local labour market and migrants and refugees would not sink to poverty or dependence on public sources (Newland, 2017). According to this interpretation, centralization should be very beneficial. On the other hand, international organizations could formulate more complex recommendations and guidelines. These types of entities have quality personal substrate, which is supported by relatively high financial resources. Moreover, using the knowledge of international organizations should be very perspective, especially using proved information campaigns, workshops, brochures and many other informational tools. International organizations process various types of statistical reports, guides or documents, which could be very inspirational for state, public administration and local self-government units.

Mentioned issues should be perceived in the context of problems of public administration in the Slovak Republic. The changes after 1989 have raised issues, which have not been solved satisfactory so far. As it is presented by V. Džatková (2016) it is necessary to give attention to common historical background, consisting of centralized power and non-existence of dialogue between state and citizens. Reforms, transformations and modernizations of public administration are discussed by both academics and public (Župová, 2017). Contemporary public administration should manage the impacts of migration in a generally beneficial way. On the other hand, public administration is often restricted by legal, organizational, personal and financial limits and perspectives. What's more, some imperfections should be identified especially in the conditions of local self-government.

Fragmentation of local self-government is one of the major problems of public administration in Slovakia. If we consider almost 3000 local self-government units, more than 1150 of them have less than 500 residents (Palúš, 2017). Based on this fact, financial and personal potential to handle impacts of migration by these local self-government units is quite limited. On the other hand, there needs to be mentioned, that most of migrants are concentrated in economic attractive regions with big cities. Anyway, migration is another important issue of contemporary society, which could not be effectively solved by local self-government units because of their fragmentation.

As it was mentioned before, some key competencies were decentralized on local self-government units. But, financial resources of these entities are often very limited. Local self-government units, especially those with less than five thousand residents, have some serious problems with their functioning. Local self-government units associate together and main benefits of this cooperation are cost savings and solving problem of personal capacity. In this sense, some local self-government units have problems with providing some basic public goods and services. Using the words of V. Bobáková (2017) in order to ensure the further economic and social development of Slovakia a higher attention should be paid to an optimization of the process of decentralization of public funds. In this sense, better personal and financial capacity of local self-government units should result in better quality of public goods and public services both for migrants and citizens.

Finally, we might argue that the Slovak Republic should solve specific and relatively different challenges than other member states of European Union. But, the efforts of the Slovak Republic need to be perceived in the wider context of managing impacts of migration in the Europe.

Conclusion

International migration is global phenomenon, which could influence almost every sphere of social life. Governments could not expect, that international movement of people would not be significant factor of decision-making processes in the future. Contradictions negative and positive factors of globalization and integration processes, which determine international migration would not disappear in a short time. In this sense, states should manage positive and negative impacts of migration.

We might sum it up, that the question is not if impacts of migration should be managed by the governments and public administration. The main question is how we should maximize positive aspects and minimize negative aspects of contemporary migration. International migration is phenomenon, which could not be managed absolutely. But, the priorities on how to manage the migration are mentioned in various types of documents processed on national, European and global level. Such documents represent outcomes of some unavoidable centralization linked to managing of migration and its impacts.

We might sum it up, that migration is changing both organizational and functional dimension of public administration. The hypothesis has thusly been proved. The ambition of this text was to examine the impacts of migration on public administration. The attention was put on contradictions linked to employment issues, working conditions and social dumping. Besides that, the adequate part of text concerns issues related to minimization of negative atmosphere and building up awareness to cultural and religious diversity. At the same time, the attention was put on importance of cooperation across the entities of national economy and across all levels of public administration. Moreover, mentioned contradictions were discussed in the context of specific problems of public administration in the Slovak Republic, such as fragmentation of local self-government and decentralization of public funds.

Finally, we might sum it up, that migration will be a centre of attention in the next years and decades. The political, natural, social and economic inequalities, which determine movement of people will probably be more intensive. Moreover, traditional barriers, especially political, cultural, natural barriers and natural resources, should be the crucial factor of possible future massive migration. In this sense, governments and public administration organizations should be prepared for such big tests, which might be more challenging than contemporary impacts of migration. Anyway, contemporary and possible future intensive migration should be successfully managed by systematic effort of state and public administration.

PART IV:
MIGRATION: BEYOND EUROPE

1 IMMIGRATION POLICY IN AUSTRALIA, CANADA, NEW ZEALAND AND THE UNITED STATES

Sven Krüger

In many Western countries immigration policy has changed significantly due to domestic economic challenges caused by an aging population, decline in fertility and internal population migration to more prosperous from less prosperous regions. The economic criteria presiding over social factors in many countries is that family class immigration is now dominated by economic class immigration.

This has put pressure on citizenship and settlement policies as a result of changes in the source country composition of immigrants. Partnership with settlement agencies by Governments in most countries facilitates economic and social integration and immigrants' settlement. More focus is given to attracting international students, as they generate a potential pool of skilled immigrants without educational recognition barriers. Often immigration policies incite intense debate and controversy as the migration occurs from non-western countries and is sometimes unpopular amongst western citizens.

In 2009 the United Nations projected an increase of 10 per cent since 2005 of the total number of international migrants around the world; the total number being about 214 million in 2010. The largest increase in the migrant stock was projected to impact the more developed regions. These regions were expected to gain an additional 45 million international migrants representing an increase of 55 per cent. In 2010 in the more developed regions international migrants would make up 10 per cent of the overall population, an increase from 7.2 per cent in 1990. The growth in the migrant stock between 2000 and 2010 was anticipated to be highest in Northern America, at 24 per cent, followed by Europe (21 per cent) and Oceania (20 per cent).

In 2010, in the US immigrants made up 13.2 per cent of the population, a massive increase from 9.1 per cent in 1990. Whilst in each of the other three countries immigrants account for less than five per cent of world migrants, they represent more than twenty per cent of the country's population. These percentages represent gains of 5 to 6 per cent since 1990 for Canada and New Zealand, while in Australia there has been no increase in the proportion of immigrants in the population since 1990. The mass movement of immigrants to these countries and the greater proportion of the total population they now represent has created a wide-reaching public debate concerning the economic and social integration of immigrants.

Australia, Canada and New Zealand are international co-operating competitors when it comes to skilled migration. Over the last ten years they have developed large permanent migration programs, agreeing on two common priority goals: nation-building and economic growth. From a policy perspective, their primary focus is on skills, covering for two-thirds of permanent intakes. Over the last twenty years each country has grown quotas, diversified source countries and fields, and grown considerably temporary labour flows (motivated by state and employer sponsorship). They have generated 'two-step migration', enabling category-switching by non-permanent employed workers, and retaining former international students. They have cultivated substantial migration databases, including longitudinal surveys to ensure frequent monitoring and development of policy strategies. By 2014 Australian, Canadian and New Zealand strategies had merged to a considerable degree, founded on the national and international research evidence. Each country seeking to attract 'the best and brightest' in an growing competitive international environment, where skilled migrants are demonstrably capable of procuring fiscal benefits for each nation.

1.1 Population growth

Population growth has two elements; firstly, the natural growth rate, evaluated as the difference between birth and death rates, and secondly; net international migration, evaluated as 4 Per cent the difference between emigration and immigration. Consistent data for Australia, Canada and the United States shows that for the period 1972 to 2008, population growth rates have been low and almost intransigent. There is long term declining population trend for New Zealand caused by emigration (Bedford Spoonley, 2013), and greater growth rate fluctuations than the other countries. The downward declines (which tend to come at the end of decades) reflect the rises in emigration.

Each country's population growth is shown in their falling or low natural growth rates and is an indicator of the growing importance of immigration. Between 1972 and 2012 in the United States the natural growth rate has been slow, there was, until early 1980s, however, a steep decline in Australia and New Zealand, following which their rates stabilized. The steepest decline since the late eighties was experienced by Canada and in 2010 it also saw the lowest natural growth of the population (on a per capita basis) among the four nations. In New Zealand, natural growth has stayed high due to the number of births per fertile woman has remained high in comparison to other countries, with a major part of that provided by Maori and Pasifika women, whose average birth rates (numbers per women) are still relatively high, albeit declining.

Declining natural growth rates of population in each country has seen a response through immigration policy. This is shown in immigration arrival rates per thousand population. Unlike the other three countries, in the United States policy concerning legal immigration has stayed less sensitive to natural decline in population growth. However, this solid population growth rate in the US could be a factor of its growing population of illegal immigrants.

Immigration policy in Canada adjusted sufficiently to enable immigrant arrival rates to grow enough to sustain low population growth despite Canada having experienced the steepest decline in its natural growth rate. Australia and New Zealand were also able to sustain greater population growth rates throughout the period due to immigration. Concerning New Zealand, fluctuations in arrival rates seem to follow more closely the variations in natural growth rates.

Since 2000, overall, NZ has seen of the highest rates of immigration in the OECD (third in 2012 but on occasion greater than that). In terms of rate per population New Zealand's immigration is higher than Australia and Canada and it has a very flexible immigration system which accepts (perhaps not on purpose) the reality that circular migration is a fact of life. New Zealand has the third highest diaspora in the OECD. It has a very large diasporic population of around 800,000 (in addition to a New Zealand-based population of 4.5 million).

1.2 Immigration policy developments in the post-World War II period

Before World War II, all four countries facilitated immigration for nation building. Examples include; to promote societal culture, the priority being the population's cultural homogeneity. (Kymlicka, 2007). Canada, in 1910 introduced an Immigration Act which contained a "preferred country" clause and prioritized the admittance of Western Europe immigrants, as these immigrants had a greater chance of cultural integration into Canadian society. Due to colonial ties, the majority of immigration came from Britain, and other western European countries. However, some immigrants from Asia, mostly from China, were also accepted as cheap labour to work in mining, agriculture and in railway industries. Following the completion of the railway a head tax (1885) was introduced to discourage Chinese immigration and this was followed by the Chinese Immigration Act of 1923, in policy shift towards the promotion of cultural homogeneity (Kymlicka, 2007).

Economic conditions in Europe which had been adversely affected by the War had begun to improve in the period following the end of World War II. There was a growth in prosperity. Incomes were rising and more labour was in demand. In the late1950s, as a result, emigration from Europe to other developed regions of the west began to reduce pace. In all countries the economic prosperity that followed the War caused in increased demand for skilled labour. The unification of Europe, through the forming of the European Union enabled greater mobility of workers within Europe, which put the brakes on European emigration. The reunification of Germany in the 1990s and the EU's expansion created wider mobility within the continent of European workers, and expanded economic opportunities. The outcome was a shortage of skilled labour within developed economies outside of Europe which for many years had benefitted from European workers. This shortage was exacerbated by the baby boom period at the end of the World War II.

The West's future economic activity was threatened by these emerging Labour shortages. European countries and the aforementioned host countries felt this pressure. Immigration was thought to be a key tool to reverse the demographic trends impacting economic activities. However, if nations were reliant on immigration to turn around some of their demographic decline, it became obvious that they were required to widen their admissions criteria by expanding immigration from other parts of the globe.

As early as 1953, Canada adopted this approach when admission became essentially free for the prospective immigrants originating from the "most-preferred" countries. However, for Asian immigrants restrictions were still the tightest. The 1962 Immigration Act was introduced and Canada sought to get rid of racial discrimination and the criterion of country preference. In 1967, a "Points System" was formalized, evaluating each applicant on the basis of his / her human capital content. This covered skills, education and intended occupation. Immigration policy now became universal and immigrants were to be selected in accordance with their potential contribution to the economy, decided by their human capital content and not on the foundation of their country of origin.

The aspects of immigration of a more humanitarian nature were strengthened. Those in the country of origin which were based on family reunification and political persecution. As a result, Australia, New Zealand and the United States also developed the human capital model of immigration. Stalls in some countries development towards changing demographics may be attributed to differences in localized public opinion on immigration. However, these policy changes are reflected in the changing composition of annual immigration flows by local areas.

Public opinion regarding immigration altered along with economic conditions. Eventually, by the late 1980s, the importance of immigration to economic growth and job creation through augmentation of human and physical capital was begun to be explicitly recognized by governments. There was an increase in professional, or technical fields, of the proportions of immigrant occupation.

1.3 Australia, Canada, New Zealand and the United States recent trends in immigration policy

In each host country, over the past fifteen years immigration policy has become more sensitive to economic outcomes given the significance policymakers assign to the role of immigration in economic development. However, several economists and other social scientists in each country have conducted evidence-based research have demonstrated that the economic performance of post-World War II immigrants has become progressively worse.

A rise in unemployment, declining earnings, and mismatching of human capital and occupations in which immigrants work serves to evidence the deterioration. These worsening economic outcomes are put down to the immigrants weak language skills which makes them less suitable in terms of human capital acquired in their native countries coupled with labour market discrimination. Studies have concluded that host nations, and indeed the immigrants themselves are not reaping the rewards or experiencing the full economic benefit of immigration. For this reason, in all countries, policy makers have been amending the immigration policy to improve economic outcomes of immigration.

These adaptations are formed in the following ways:

- focus towards labour market demand for specific skills and a shift away from human capital
- increasing focus on temporary foreign workers program to support immediate labour market requirements
- attraction of international students with the potential to create a possible pool of skilled immigrants
- regionalization of immigration and a review of refugee system

Aside from these changes, the legalization of illegals in the United States continues to be a key policy debate. In more recent times with arguments emphasizing the economic benefits of immigration to the country of legalization.

1.4 Less focus on the human capital model of immigration

The nations Australia, Canada and New Zealand are now centering their efforts on the and human capital model of immigration towards meeting specific labour market needs moving away from family class-based and human capital model of immigration. To illustrate further, Australia, and New Zealand have adopted an "Expression of Interest" (EOI) model to identify skilled immigrants. Canada in March of 2014 adopted this model, under which potential migrants in each country submit their details into a database online.

The United States policy focus concerning legal immigration remains on the family class and human capital model of immigration. However, some economists, such as Duleep, (Duleep, 2013) have suggested that for immigrants coming into the United States without immediately transferable skills, there is a higher inclination to invest in new human capital and that this propensity is more significant among those who enter with higher education. In the United States policy regarding legal immigrants Duleep recommends instead combining the family class and human capital approaches. Chiswick (Chiswick, 2012) On the other hand, is in favor of choosing skilled immigrants on the basis of specific labour market needs and argues in support of this approach.

1.5 Temporary foreign worker programs

Temporary foreign worker (TFW) programs are established to fulfill short-term needs of employers. They allow employers to hire foreign workers on a temporary basis, when local citizens and permanent residents are unavailable to do the jobs and therefore underpin immediate skills and labour shortages. Over the past decade in the West increased reliance on TFWs to meet labour market needs has grown.

The number of TFWs rose, in all countries, the maximum increase in Australia (85 per cent) and with the minimum increase being in the United States (29 per cent). Additionally, increases were seen in immigrants who are granted permanent residence status. The number of TFWs each year, in the United States, was greater than the number permitted permanent residency. The second highest recipient of temporary foreign workers per permanent resident was Canada. Overall, in each of the countries the relative significance of TFWs grew over the period, the most dramatic increase being in Canada. In sum, reliance, by all countries, on temporary foreign workers to meet their labour market needs grew.

1.6 Attracting International students

Regardless of western countries seeking skilled immigrants to fulfill their labour market requirements, lack of recognition of the educational credentials and labour market experience acquired in their countries of origin by immigrants has led to under usage of their human capital in host countries. This lack of recognition of their human capital has also created a major obstacle to their economic integration. As previously stated, since the 1970s, research on economic performance of immigrants in their host countries has shown increasingly reduced economic performance. Increasingly, a number of these immigrants are from developing countries of Asia, Africa and the Middle East. Credentials obtained in these developing countries are often discounted and not valued by employers in the west.

In order to help new arrivals update their skills to meet the local requirements host governments have introduced various programs and are introducing towards proper assessments of foreign credentials attempts to motivate employers to not rely on prejudiced and preconceived value judgments. Concurrently, all countries are recognizing the important role and contribution international students can make in meeting the demand for skilled labour.

As stated by Hawthorne (Hawthorne, 2005), "International graduates are "young, with advanced English language skills, with fully recognized qualifications, locally relevant professional training and a high degree of acculturation." By regarding International students as potential new immigrants, these elements are believed to better support integration into both the labour market and the social sphere. Martha Justus of Citizenship and Immigration Canada in the October 2006 International Metropolis Conference held in Lisbon, presented Canadian estimates, which indicated that it is expected that between 15 and 20 per cent of international students would eventually settle and work in Canada.

In all four countries, governments have undertaken measures to attract international students and sought to keep them after they complete their education. Measures such as allowing international students to work part-time on campus at the same time as pursuing their education. However, work permits are needed for off-campus jobs; but also some dependent family members can be eligible to apply for work permits.

1.7 Revising refugee systems

The studied nations are all key destinations of refugees who are forced out of their countries of origin due to political, religious or racial conflicts. Immigration policy focused towards humanitarian, or refugee migrants, is a key element of each country's overall immigration policy. Refugees can be individuals recognized as refugees on the basis of the

1951 Geneva Convention, sponsored by the government or by private groups, or individuals being re-settled for humanitarian reasons.

The population of refugees and asylum seekers dropped in all four countries over the five-year period ending in 2011. Australia, Canada and New Zealand accept applications for the resettlement of refugees, i.e., from those who are settled outside of their native country and cannot return for fear of persecution. The United States, however, does not accept resettlement applications. Applicants must be either in already in the United States or their country of origin.

Following tragic events of September 2001, for security reasons and also out of concerns of misuse of the system, there has been a tightening of rules for each country for refugee admission. There is co-operation amongst the Countries in processing of applications. In December 2001, in accordance with the Smart Border Declaration, signed by both Canada and the United States, Canada and the U.S. now cooperate on the processing of applications for asylum. In 2004 the Safe Third Country agreement came into force and some asylum seekers in Canada and the U.S. now must make their claims in the country in which they were previously present.

To summarize, in each country changes to refugee immigration system seem to be more motivated by security concerns and the impact on public treasury instead of concern for refugee protection and was the original intention of each country's refugee admissions policy.

1.8 Immigration regionalization

Several economic challenges in all advanced countries have occurred as a result of population aging due to slowing down of population growth. In each country, the smaller and less prosperous regions, including rural areas, are impacted more due to the added phenomenon of outmigration of youth seeking better economic opportunities into the larger and more prosperous regions. The outcome of this is an increasing regional imbalance of population, which in turn is creating regional imbalances of growth and economic development.

The media are reporting more and more the effects of population changes and as a result have captured the attention of regional policy makers and community organizations. New initiatives are being developed to reverse the regional population declines and to grow the regional labour force. Better incentives for business investments are offered to create more job opportunities for youth and to also encourage their return or discourage their departure. To retain university graduates monetary incentives are also available. Labour training programs are being invested in by Governments. Smaller regions are also playing a more significant role in their national immigration programs.

Settlement by immigrants tends to be in larger regions and urban centers of their host nations. The reasons for this are as follows:

- generally there are greater economic opportunities
- there is already a presence of large immigrant population to provide a network to support the easier settlement of new arrivals
- there is a presence of ethnic goods.

Special programs have been created in immigrant receiving countries, through federal-regional collaborations, to attract immigrants to smaller areas and retain them. With the main focus attraction and retention of regional/provincial and state policies in western countries being the skilled immigrant. Australia, in 1995, introduced the State Specific and Regional Migration (SSRM) visa schemes; these schemes developed the role of state and regional authorities in Australia's immigration program.

Along the same lines as Australia's SSRM visa schemes is Canada's Provincial Nominee Program (PNP). Under this scheme, an individual for immigration to Canada, is nominated by a province or a territory nominates and they will reside in that same province or territory. This relevant individual immigrant has the skills, education and work experience required in order to contribute and make an instant economic contribution to the nominating province or territory.

Greater geographic distribution of immigrants can either result in the improved, or adverse economic performance of immigrants, according Akbari (Akbari, 2011). These economic performance improvements do not occur if the initial distribution was not optimal. This means if the immigrants could not select their location in a manner that maximized their marginal product in the host nation. This could be due to a lack of information about the host country's regional labour markets because of the limitations of social networks and/or government programs.

1.9 Illegal immigration

More people and more people want to move to the developed world, especially as political and /or economic situations in the sending countries of the developing world continue to worsen. But as the host nations of the developed world are more selective regarding immigrants, greater numbers of people wishing to leave their country of origin are more likely to try and enter the countries in illegal ways. 11 million immigrants reside illegally in the United States and illegal immigration is the highest in the United States, most of whom arrived from Mexico. In the United States, immigration policy mainly focuses on legalization of illegals. Generally, illegal immigrants are poorly educated, work in low-paid jobs and without the rights and privileges of legal citizens.

Whilst the exposure to illegal immigration has been less for Australia, Canada, and the New Zealand, they may see further increases as a result of worsening conditions elsewhere in the world, especially in Asia, Africa and the Middle East.

1.10 Policy refinement—key developments to 2014

Australian, Canadian and New Zealand employers showed a strong preference for skilled migrants especially those with advanced English ability and training in OECD countries (including onshore). With regards to the skilled migration policy in recent years the three nations have co-operated, using shared research evidence, and implementing the most effective selection strategies.

From 2006 to 2014 these are as follows:

Skilled migration pathways:

Each nation now offers three skilled migration pathways, enabling the entry of:

- Permanent skilled migrants better monitored for human capital attributes
- Temporary sponsored workers chosen by employers or states to work in allocated positions for up to 4 years
- International students with a capacity to 'category-switch' by the study-migration pathway

60-68% of permanent migration intakes are skilled, with targets established following national (and in the case of Canada and Australia) state or provincial discussions.

1.11 Ability to integrate

A New Zealand study recently discovered that English language skill was central to the successful employment of migrants in the age group 24-54. It discovered that immigrants of Eastern European origin with conversational English had an employment rate of 62.4%, yet those less fluent and could not converse was 26.6%. Similar studies in the US, Canada, and Australia have found evidence to support this.

Critical influencers in the settlement country to successful settlement and language skills were demographic and geographic factors. In destination countries with more heterogeneous, multicultural populations, cannot speak the dominant language is not as much of a barrier to integration than in smaller, more monolingual countries such as New Zealand where the immigrant communities are smaller.

With regards to education and skills, the research discovered that a male immigrant of non-English speaking background with a university degree needed 16 years in the country until he reached the earning level of a New Zealand born male with matched qualifications. Whereas a male immigrant with a school leaving certificate but non-English speaking required 25 years to catch up to his New Zealand born equivalent. Further, at the initial stage of immigration, skilled immigrants incur greater wage differentials versus New Zealand-born workers with the same qualification than less skilled immigrants do in comparison to their counterparts.

Conclusion

Over the last century, in each of the four countries under consideration immigration policy has followed a common course in response to widely similar obstacles. Immigration policy favored western European source countries, by responding first to the requirements for settlement and nation building. After World War II, countries moved to a more universal immigration policy, in the face of new labour shortage challenges. Canada pioneered forward by adopting a system in immigrant selection, which emphasized potential economic contribution, or human capital. This was followed suit by other countries. However, the increased flows of immigrants from developing countries resulted in worsening situations for immigrants, albeit because of language issues, skills and education recognition, or discrimination. In response to the challenges of population aging and declining birth rates, and in light of this, in recent years immigration policy has shifted.

Noted are several common policy responses. Firstly, there has been a decreased emphasis on family class immigration and humanitarian concerns and economic considerations have become dominant. Additionally, there has been a shift in the economic criteria from wide human capital measures to more targeted selection founded on specific labour market requirements. This has included temporary foreign worker programs targeted at filling both high skilled and low skilled labour shortages, regionalization of policy to fulfill local labour market needs outside of the main urban areas that traditionally draw immigrant populations. Efforts have been made to recruit and retain international students, as they have less adjustment challenges than other immigrants. There are of course differences, within these wide trends, which are dependent on both national economic conditions and policy levers—such as, Australia and Canada have stripped down some authority to their states and provinces, respectively and policy stays more centralized in New Zealand and in the United States.

Australia has increased the use of temporary foreign workers the most, whilst in the United States the rise of their numbers has been relatively slowly. This is possibly because of the predominance of illegal immigrants, populating the low skill labour shortages whilst other countries use temporary foreign workers. A common policy trend amongst the four countries, motivated by security concerns post 9/11, is that have tightened their refugee admission systems.

These recent policy trends, in each country, have created debate about rights and citizenship. In the United States this can be seen in the ongoing political debate concerning legalizing illegal immigrants. In Canada, the exploitation of temporary foreign workers is of concern. Consequently, the changing racial and ethnic composition of immigrants, and the documented decline in economic outcomes all serve to flag concerns about discrimination in the labour market.

For Australia, Canada and New Zealand the development of skilled migration policy is still challenging, especially where global migration is an early 21st century shaping phenomenon. The rise of short-term people movement, and the openness of one immigrant-receiving country can affect the level of demand in another immigrant-receiving country. In this trend dynamic environment, governments with pro-active immigration programs need to amend their entry policies, whilst facing 'difficulties in harnessing their immigration programs to achieve diverse and often incompatible policy goals—(in) economic development, human resource development, population and foreign affairs' (Stahl, 1992). In the battle for skills, to some extent Australia, Canada and New Zealand have developed shared skilled strategies and data Meanwhile, they are in competition with each other and other OECD countries, to draw and keep the 'best' global workers.

REFERENCES

ADAMCOVÁ, M., ONDROVÁ, D. (2017). Centralization, Decentralization, Local Administration and Ethical Impacts: Negative Aspects Evident in the Contemporary Public Administration. In: *European Journal of Transformation Studies.* Vol. 5, No. 2, 2017, pp 18-34.

AGGESTAM, L. (1999) *Role Conceptions and the Politics of Identity in Foreign Policy.* ARENA working papers, 99/08. Oslo: Centre for European Studies University of Oslo.

AGGESTAM, L. (2006). Role theory and European foreign policy: a Framework of analysis. In: *The European Union's Roles in International Politics. Concepts and Analysis.* London: Routledge, 2006, pp. 11–29.

AKBARI, A. (2011). Labour Market Performance of Immigrants in Smaller Regions of Western Countries: Some Evidence from Atlantic Canada. In: *Journal of International Migration and Integration / Revue de l'integration et de la migration internationale.* Vol. 12, No. 2, 2011, pp. 133-154.

AL JAZEERA. (2017). *Syrian Refugees Improve Armenia's Social Fabric.* [online]. Available at: https://www.aljazeera.com/indepth/features/2017/12/refugees-improve-armenia-social-fabric-171214061224398.html. [Accessed 23/8/2018].

ALJAZEERA. (2015). *Refugees rush into Croatia as borders open.* [online]. 20.10.2015. Available at: http://www.aljazeera.com/news/2015/10/refugees-rush-croatia-border-opens-151019191242689.html. [Accessed 2/11/2015].

ANDERSON, B. (1983). *Imagined communities. Reflections on the Origin and Spread of Nationalism.* London: Verso, 1983.

ANDREWS, R., BOYNE, G., O'TOLLE, L., MEIER, K. WALKER, R. (2013). Managing Migration? EU Enlargement, Local Government Capacity and Performance in England. In: *Public Administration.* Vol. 91, No. 1, 2013. pp. 174-194.

ANDRIJASEVIC, R., WALTERS, W. (2010). The International Organization for Migration and the International Government of Borders. In: *Environment and Planning D: Society and Space.* Vol. 28, No. 6, 2010, pp. 977-99.

ANDROVIČOVÁ, J. (2015). Sekuritizácia migrantov na Slovensku—analýza diskurzu. In: *Sociológia*, Vol. 47, No. 4, 2015, pp. 319-339.

ANDROVIČOVÁ, J. (2016). The Migration and Refugee Crisis in Political Discourse in Slovakia: Institutionalized Securitization and Moral Panic. In: *Studia Territoralia*. Vol. 16, No. 2, 2016, pp. 9-64.

ANO. (2013). *Resortní program*. [online]. Available at: goo.gl/d5JZ1V. [Accessed 11/5/2018].

ANO. (2014). *Náš program pro volby do Evropského parlamentu*. [online]. Available at: goo.gl/PFTibk. [Accessed 11/5/2018].

ANO. (2017). *Teď nebo nikdy. Ten jediný program, který potřebujete. Program hnutí ANO pro volby do Poslanecké sněmovny 2017*. [online]. Available at: goo.gl/SdGD54. [Accessed 11/5/2018].

ARENDT, H. (1973). *The Origins of Totalitarianism*. Orlando, FL: Harcourt Brace, 1973, 527 p.

BADE, K. J. (2005). *Evropa v pohybu. Evropské migrace dvou staletí*. Praha: Nakladatelství lidové noviny, 2005, p. 497.

BAER, J. (2015). *Seven Czech Women. Portraits of Courage, Humanism and Enlightenment*. Stuttgart, New York: ibidem, Columbia University Press, 2015.

BAER, J. (2015). Trusting Nothing except Power, Gustáv Husák (1913-1991): An Attempt at a Political Psychological Profile. In: *COMENIUS II*. No. 1, 2015, pp. 43-52.

BAER, J. (2018). *Alexander Dubček Unknown (1921-1992). The Life of a Political Icon*. Stuttgart, New York: ibidem, Columbia University Press, 2018.

BAHNA, M. (2011). *Migrácia zo Slovenska po vstupe do Európskej únie*. Bratislava: VEDA, 2011.

BAKALIAN, A. (1993). *Armenian Americans: From Being to Feeling Armenian*. New Brunswick: Transaction Publishers, 1993.

BARŠOVÁ, A., BARŠA, P. (2005). *Přistěhovalectví a liberální stát*. Brno: Masarykova univerzita—Brno, 2005.

BARTOŠ, A. B. (2014). *Zpověď. Jsem antisemita?* Praha: ABB, 2014.

BASTL, M., MAREŠ, M., SMOLÍK, J., VEJVODOVÁ, P. (2011) *Krajní pravice a krajní levice v ČR.* Praha: Grada Publishing, 2011.

BAUEROVÁ, H., HLAVÁČKOVÁ, H., CABADA, L. (2014). *Politika rozšiřování a země Západního Balkánu.* Praha: MUPPress, 2014.

BAUMAN, Z. (2017). *Cizinci před branami.* Olomouc: Broken Books, 2018, 94 p.

BBC. (2015). *Migrants crisis: Slovakia 'will only accept Christians'.* [online]. 2015. Available at: www.bbc.com/news/world-europe-33986738. [Accessed 23/9/2015].

BENEŠ, V., HARNISCH, S. (2014). Role Theory in Symbolic Interactionism: Czech Republic, Germany and the EU. In: *Cooperation and Conflict.* Vol. 50, No. 1, pp. 146–165.

BEN-SIRA, Z. (1997). *Immigration, Stress, and Readjustment.* Greenwood Publishing Group, 1997, pp. 7–10.

BERLIN, I. (2003). *Freedom and its Betrayal. Six Enemies of Human Liberty.* London: Pimlico, 2003, p.182.

BERNARD, A. (2008). Immigrants in the Hinterlands. In: *Perspectives on Labour and Income.* Vol. 9, No. 1, 2008. (Statistics Canada Catalogue number 75-001-XWE).

BIGO, D. (2002). Security and Immigration: Toward a Critique of the Governmentality of Unease. In: *Alternatives: Global, Local, Political.* Vol. 27, No. 1 (Special Issue), 2002, pp. 63-92.

BIS. (2017). *Výroční zpráva Bezpečnostní informační služby za rok 2016. Bezpečnostní informační služba.* [online]. Available at: goo.gl/AelsYh. [Accessed 11/5/2018].

BLACK, R., GENT, S. (2006). Sustainable Return in Post-conflict Context. In: *International Migration.* Vol. 44, No. 3, 2006, pp. 15-38.

BLACK, R., KOSER, K., MUNK, K., ATFIELD, G., D'ONOFRIO, L., TIEMOKO, R. (2004). *Understanding voluntary return. Technical Report.* London: Home Office, 2004.

BOBÁKOVÁ, V. (2017). The Formation of Regional Self-government in the Slovak Republic and its Sources of Funding. In: *ADMINISTRAȚIE ȘI MANAGEMENT PUBLIC.* Vol. 16, No. 28, 2017, pp. 97-115.

BOHR, F., WIEGREFE, K. (2013) *The Philosopher and the Terrorist. When Sartre Met RAF Leader Andreas Baader.* [online]. 6.2.2013. Available at: http://www.spiegel.de/international/germany/transcript-released-of-sartre-visit-to-raf-leader-andreas-baader-a-881395.html. [Accessed 8/4/2017].

BOLEČEKOVÁ, M. (2010). *Migračná politika.* Banská Bystrica: Univerzita mateja Bela v Banskej Bystrici, Fakulta politických vied a medzinárodných vzťahov, 2010, p. 127.

BRANDTNER, L. (2017). Jedině DSS zatočí s imigranty a ochrání naše obyvatelstvo. In: *DSSS.* 28.8.2017. [online]. Available at: goo.gl/hG9Meo. [Accessed 11/5/2018].

BREUNING, M. (2007). *Foreign Policy Analysis: A Comparative Introduction.* Palgrave Macmillan, 2007.

BREUNING, M. (2011). Role research: genesis and Blind spots. In: *Role Theory in International Relations. Approaches and analyses.* New York: Routledge, 2011, pp. 16–35.

BRIŠKA, F. (2008). Perspektívy Slovenska v procese globalizácie. In *Formovanie nového strategického postavenia SR.* Banská Bystrica: Univerzita Mateja Bela v Banskej Bystrici, 2008, pp. 69-73.

BRUBAKER, R. (2005). The 'diaspora' diaspora. In: *Ethnic and Racial Studies.* Vol. 28, No. 1, 2005, pp. 1–19.

BUNCE, V. (1995). Should Transitologists Be Grounded? In: *Slavic Review.* Vol. 54, No. 1, 1995, pp. 111-127.

BUZAN, B., WÆVER, O., DE WILDE, J. (1998). *Security: A New Framework for Analysis.* Boulder and London: Lynne Riener, 1998.

CANADIAN BROADCASTING CORPORATION. (2013). *Temporary Foreign Workers at Risk of Abuse, Advocates Say.* [online]. 1.5.2013. Available at: http://www.cbc.ca/news/canada/montreal/temporary-foreign-workers-at-risk-of-abuse-advocates-say-1.1305145.

CASSARINO, J. P. (2004). Theorising Return Migration: The Conceptual Approach to Return Migrants Revisited. In: *International Journal on Multicultural Societies.* Vol. 6, No. 2, 2004, pp. 253-279.

CASTLES, S. (2000). *Ethnicity and Globalization.* London: SAGE publications Ltd., 2000, p. 228.

CASTLES, S. (2010). Understanding global migration: A social transformation perspective. In: *Journal of ethnic and migration studies*. Vol. 36, No. 10, 2010, pp. 1565-1586.

CAUCASUS RESEARCH RESOURCE CENTERS. (2013). *Migration and skills in Armenia: results of the 2011/12 migration survey on the relationship between skills, migration and development*. [online]. Available at: http://www.crrc.am/research-and-surveys/completed-projects/58-migration-and-skills?lang=en. [Accessed 30/5/2018].

ČESKÁ TELEVIZE. (2015). Ministři vnitra přijali uprchlícké kvóty, Slovensko je odmítá respektovat. In: *Česká televize*. 23.9.2015. [online]. Available at: goo.gl/2YtJyN. [Accessed 11/5/2018].

ČESKÉ NOVINY. (2017). Naši klekli na FAU, říká Babiš na nahrávce o firmě v konkurzu. In: *České noviny*. 27.8.2017. [online]. Available at: goo.gl/ydECDq. [Accessed 11/5/2018].

ČESKÝ ROZHLAS. (2015). "Mám střet zájmů, ale já ho nezneužívám". Anketu o výrok roku ovládl Andrej Babiš. In: *Český rozhlas*. 31.12.2016. [online]. Available at: goo.gl/eYn4Ex. [Accessed 11/5/2018].

ČESKÝ ROZHLAS. (2016). Migranty nepřijímat. Vytvořilo by to podhoubí pro barbarské útoky, vzkázal Hrad. In: *Český rozhlas*. 2.8.2016. [online]. Available at: goo.gl/TkYnw4. [Accessed 11/5/2018].

ČESKÝ ROZHLAS. (2017b). Vedou proti mě kampaň, pracují na ní desítky lidí, tvrdí Andrej Babiš. In: *Český rozhlas*. 24.5.2017. [online]. Available at: goo.gl/tCW2Zr. [Accessed 11/5/2018].

CHEIANU-ANDREI, D. (2013). *Cartografierea diasporei moldovenești în Italia, Portugalia, Franța și Regatul Unit al Marii Britanii*. Chișinău: OIM, 2013, p. 142.

CHISWICK, B. R. (2011). *Immigration: High Skilled vs. Low Skilled Labour?* IZA Policy Papers 28. Institute for the Study of Labour (IZA).

CICI, D. (2011). *Regional Cooperation and European Integration in the Western Balkans. The Effectiveness of Regional Cooperation Policies on Albania Achievements and Shortcoming*. Berlin: Lambert Academic Publishing, 2011.

CLANCY, R. (2013). *Decline in International Students Studying in Australia*. Australian Council for Education and Research. 1/2013.

COAKLEY, L. (2011). *Where do I go from here? The leading factors in voluntary return or remaining in Ireland.* Dublin: IOM, 2011, 96 p.

COLLIER, P. (2013). *Exodus: How migration is changing our world.* Oxford: Oxford University Press, 2013.

COLLYER, M., CHERTI, M., LACROIX, T., VAN HEELSUM, A. (2009). Migration and development: the Euro–Moroccan experience. In: *Journal of Ethnic and Migration Studies.* Vol. 35, No. 10, 2009, pp. 1555-1570.

Competing for Skills: Migration policies and trends in New Zealand and Australia. (2011). Government of Australia, Department of Labour, 2011.

Conception of Migration policy of the Slovak Republic. (2008). [online] Bratislava: Government of the Slovak Republic, 2008, 16 p. Available at: https://www.minv.sk/?zamer-migracnej-politiky-slovenskej-republiky&subor=10500. [Accessed 20/4/2018].

CONVENTION de Genève du 28 juillet 1951, relative au statut des réfugiés entrée en vigueur le 22 avril 1954.

Council of Ministers of Education Canada. [online]. Available at: www.education au-incanada.ca.

COURT OF JUSTICE OF THE EUROPEAN UNION. (2017). *Press Release No 91/17: The Court dismisses the actions brought by Slovakia and Hungary against the provisional mechanism for the mandatory relocation of asylum seekers.* [online]. 2017. Available at: https://curia.europa.eu/jcms/upload/docs/application/pdf/2017-09/cp170091en.pdf. [Accessed 26/5/2018].

CRINES, A., HEPPELL, T. HILL, M. (2016). Enoch Powell's 'rivers of blood' speech: A rhetorical political analysis. In: *British Politics.* Vol. 11, No. 1, 2016, pp. 72-94.

ČSSD. (2013). *Prosadíme dobře fungující stát.* [online]. Available at: goo.gl/AH8Ebx. [Accessed 11/5/2018].

ČSSD. (2017). *Dobrá země pro život. Volební program ČSSD pro volby 2017.* [online]. Available at: goo.gl/EQuBfJ. [Accessed 11/5/2018].

ČSU. (2017). *Míra zaměstnanosti, nezaměstnanosti a ekonomické activity—září 2017. Český statistický úřad.* [online]. Available at: goo.gl/Rj6PXY. [Accessed 11/5/2018].

ČTK. (2018). *Únia rokuje s východoeurópskymi štátmi povýšenecky, myslí si Seehofer.* [online]. 18.3.2018. Available at: https://spravy.pravda.sk/svet/clanok/462687-unia-rokuje-s-vychodoeuropskymi-statmi-povysene-mysli-si-seehofer/.

CVVM. (2018). *Vztah k národnostním menšinám žijícím v ČR 3.-15. 4. 2018.* [online]. Available at: https://cvvm.soc.cas.cz/media/com_form2content/documents/c2/a4584/f9/ov180409.pdf.

DAILY TELEGRAPH. (2007). *Enoch Powell's 'Rivers of Blood' speech. 6 Nov. 2007.* [online]. 2007. Available at: https://www.telegraph.co.uk/comment/3643823/Enoch-Powells-Rivers-of-Blood-speech.html. [Accessed 25/4/2018.]

DAVIS, L., DEOLE, S. S. (2018). Immigration and the Rise of Far-Right Parties in Europe. In: *ifo DICE Report*, Vol. 15, No. 4, pp. 10-15.

DAVYDOVA-MINGUET, O., MOSNEAGA, V., POZNIAK. O. (2014). Gendered Migration from Moldova and Ukraine to the EU: Who Cares? In: *Borders, Migration and Regional Stability in the EU's Eastern Neighbourhood.* Joensuu: Karelian Institute of the University of Eastern Finland, 2014, pp. 225-240.

DÉCLARATION universelle des droits d' homme. (1948).

DENNIKN. (2016). *Premiér Fico je opäť svetový, prerazil s výrokmi o moslimoch, ktorých k nám nepustí.* [online]. 8.1.2016. Available at: https://dennikn.sk/338314/premier-fico-opat-svetovy-prerazil-vyrokmi-moslimoch-ktorych-nam-nepusti/. [Accessed 8/10/2018].

DESOUZA, R. (2013). *Finding more humane solutions: New Zealand's refugee deal with Australia.* [online]. 16.2.2013. Available at: http://www.ruthdesouza.com/2013/02/16/finding-more-humane-solutions-new-zealands-deal-with-australia/. [Accessed 24/11/2013].

DIVINSKÝ, B. (2016). Nelegálna migrácia—jej podstata, základné črty, význam a trendy v slovenskom kontexte. In: *Nelegálna migrácia na slovensko-ukrajinskej schengenskej hranici.* Prešov: Výskumné centrum Slovenskej spoločnosti pre zahraničnú politiku, 2016, pp. 6-13.

DLOUHÝ, M. (2018). *Neonacismus a neofašismus v České republice na počátku 21. století (2010-2017).* Disertační práce. Praha: Fakulta mezinárodních vztahů, Vysoká škola ekonomická, 2018.

DOMONKOS, T., PÁLENÍK, M., RADVANSKÝ, M. (2010). *Saturovanie dopytu po pracovnej sile prostredníctvom migrácie v SR. Národná štúdia pre Euópsku migračnú siet*. Bratislava: European Migration Network, International Organization for Migration, 2010.

DSSS. (2015). *Vandas v ČT: Deportujme imigranty z Evropy. Tiskové centrum DSSS*. 14.12.2015. [online]. Available at: goo.gl/cCib2b. [Accessed 11/5/2018].

DSSS. (2017). *DSSS podpořila protimigrační protest německých nacionalistů. Tiskové centrum DSSS*. 23. 5. 2017. [online]. Available at: goo.gl/zU8fVU. [Accessed 11/5/2018].

DULEEP, H. (2013). *US Immigration Policy at a Crossroads*. Discussion Paper Number 7136.IZA Discussion Paper Series. Bonn, Germany, 1/2013.

DULEEP, H. O., REGETS, M. C. (2013). *The Elusive Concept of Immigrant Quality: Evidence from 1970-1990*. Working Papers 138, Department of Economics, College of William and Mary, 2013.

DŽATKOVÁ, V. (2016). The Role of Civil Society in Public Governance. In: *Rocznik Administracji Publicznej*. Vol. 2, No. 2, 2016, pp. 373-383.

EC. (2011). The Global Approach to Migration and Mobility. [online]. Brussel: European Comission. Available at: http://eur-lex.europa.eu/LexUriServ/LexUriServ.do?uri=COM:2011:0743:FIN:EN:PDF. [Accessed 1/6/2018].

ELGSTRÖM, O., SMITH, M. (2006). Introduction. In: *The European Union´s Roles in International Politics. Concepts and analysis*. Abingdon: Routledge, 2006, pp. 1-10.

ERNEKER, J., PÁNA, L. (2017). *Systémové aspekty veřejné správy*. České Budejovice: Vysoká škola evropských a regionálních studií, 2017, p. 117.

EUROBAROMETER. (2015). *Standard Eurobarometer No. 83. European Commission*. [online]. Brussels, 2016. Available at: goo.gl/AkC6gC. [Accessed 11/5/2018].

European Agenda on Migration. (2015). [online]. Brussels: European Commission, 2015, p. 22. Available at: https://ec.europa.eu/anti-trafficking/sites/antitrafficking/files/communication_on_the_european_agenda_on_migration_en.pdf. [Accessed 20/4/2018].

EUROPEAN COMMISSION. (2015). *Communication from the Commission to the European Parliament, the Council, the European Economic and Social Committee and the Committee of the Regions EU Action Plan Against Migrant Smuggling (2015—2020).* [online]. 2015. Available at: https://ec.europa.eu/anti-trafficking/sites/antitrafficking/files/eu_action_plan_against_migrant_smuggling_en.pdf.

EUROPEAN COMMISSION. (2018a). *Special Eurobarometer 469. Integration of immigrants in the European Union: Report.* [online]. 2018. Available at: http://ec.europa.eu/commfrontoffice/publicopinion/index.cfm/survey/getsurveydetail/instruments/special/surveyky/2169. [Accessed 24/4/2018].

EUROPEAN COMMISSION. (2018b). *Standard Eurobarometer 89. Public opinion in the European Union: Annex.* [online]. 2018. Available at: http://ec.europa.eu/commfrontoffice/publicopinion/index.cfm/Survey/getSurveyDetail/instruments/STANDARD/surveyKy/2180. [Accessed 2/6/2018].

EUROPEAN PARLIAMENT AND COUNCIL OF THE EUROPEAN UNION. (2008). *Directive of 16 December 2008 on common standards and procedures in Member States for returning illegally staying third-country nationals, 2008/115/EC.* [online]. Available at: https://eur-lex.europa.eu/legal-content/EN/ALL/?uri=celex%3A32008L0115. [Accessed 30/5/2018].

EUROSTAT. (2018a). *EU citizens living in another Member State—statistical overview.* [online]. 2018. Available at: http://ec.europa.eu/eurostat/statistics-explained/index.php?title=EU_citizens_living_in_another_Member_State_-_statistical_overview. [Accessed 2/7/2018].

EUROSTAT. (2018b). *Migration and migrant population statistics.* [online]. 2018. Available at: http://ec.europa.eu/eurostat/statistics-explained/index.php/Migration_and_migrant_population_statistics. [Accessed 23/5/2018].

EUROSTAT. (2018c). *Asylum statistics.* [online]. 2018. Available at: http://ec.europa.eu/eurostat/statistics-explained/index.php/Asylum_statistics. [Accessed 22/7/2018].

Extended Migration Profile of the Republic of Moldova 2010–2015. (2017). [online]. Available at: https://publications.iom.int/books/extended-migration-profile-republic-moldova-2010-2015. [Accessed 30/4/2018].

FAIRCLOUGH, N. (1992). *Language and power.* New York: Longman, 1992.

FAIRCLOUGH, N. (1995). *Critical Discourse Analysis. The Critical Study of Language*. London: Longman, 1995.

FOSTER, J. (2012). Making Temporary Permanent: The Silent Transformation of the Temporary Foreign Worker Program. In: *Just Labour: A Canadian Journal of Work and Society*. Vol. 19, 2012, pp. 22-46.

GAZDÍK, P. (2015). Interview ČT24. In: *Česká televize*. 26. 9. 2015. [online]. Available at: goo.gl/84XYLs. [Accessed 11/5/2018].

GCIM. (2005). *Migration in an Interconnected World—New Directions for Action: Report of the Global Commission on International Migration*. [online]. Geneva: Global Commission on International Migration, Available at: https://www.unitar.org/ny/sites/unitar.org.ny/files/GCIM%20Report%20%20PDF%20of%20complete%20report.pdf. [Accessed 1/6/2018].

GEIGER, M., PÉCOUD, A. (2010). The Politics of International Migration Management. In: *The Politics of International Migration Management*. Hampshire: Pallgrave. Macmillan, 2010, pp. 1-21.

GEORGI, F. (2010). For the Benefit of Some: The International Organization for Migration and its Global Migration Management. In: *The Politics of International Migration Management*. Hampshire: Pallgrave. Macmillan, 2010. pp. 45-73.

GFMD. (2007). Report of the First Meeting of the Global Forum on Migration and Development. [online]. Belgium 9–11 July 2007, Available at: https://gfmd.org/files/documents/gfmd_brussels07_final_report_en.pdf. [Accessed 1/6/2018].

GHOSH, B. (2000). *Return Migration: Journey of Hope or Despair?* Geneva: IOM, 2000.

GREEN, A. (1976). *Immigration and the Postwar Canadian Economy*. Toronto: Macmillan of Canada/Maclean-Hunter, 1976.

HÁKA, A. (2016). *Dělnická strana sociální spravedlnosti*. Disertační práce. Praha: Fakulta mezinárodních vztahů, Vysoká škola ekonomická, 2016.

HALÁSZ, I. (2012). *Medzinárodná migrácia, krajania a volebné právo: Podoba a volebné hranice moderného politického spoločenstva v štátoch strednej Európy*. Praha: Ústav štátu a práva Akademie věd České republiky, 2012, p. 330.

HALLIDAY, J., CHANG, J. (2007). *Mao. The Unknown Story*. New York: Vintage, 2007, p. 1200.

HALÓ NOVINY. (2016). KSČM: Nechceme žádné migranty! In: *Haló noviny*. 28. 7. 2016. [online]. Available at: goo.gl/7Wew6n. [Accessed 11/5/2018].

HANYANE, R. B. (2015). Exploration of transnationalism as a concept and phenomenon in Public Administration. In: *The Journal for Transdisciplinary Research in Southern Africa*. Vol. 11, No. 4, 2015, pp. 47-59.

HARNISCH, S. (2011). Role theory: Operationalization of key concepts. In: *Role Theory in International Relations. Approaches and analyses*. New York: Routledge, 2011, pp. 7–15.

HAWTHORNE, L. (2005). Picking Winners: The Recent Transformation of Australia's Skill Migration Policy. In: *International Migration Review*. Vol. 39, No. 3, 2005.

HEATH, A., RICHARDS, L. (2016). *Attitudes towards Immigration and their Antecedents Topline Results from Round 7 of the European Social Survey*. [online]. 2016. Available at: https://www.europeansocialsurvey.org/docs/findings/ESS7_toplines_issue_7_immigration.pdf. [Accessed 6/10/2018.].

HENDERSON, K. (2017). Euroscepticism and the "missing left": The Slovak case study. In: *Czech Journal of Political Science*. No 3, 2017, pp. 229-48.

HEYWOOD, A. (2011). *Global Politics*. London: Palgrave Macmillan, 2011, p. 585:

HLAVÁČKOVÁ, H. (2017). *Role Slovinska v integraci zemí západního Balkánu do EU: analýza diskurzu slovinských zahraničně-politických aktérů. 1. vyd.* Praha: Metropolitan University Prague Press, 2017.

HOFREITER, L. (2004). *Bezpečnosť, bezpečnostné riziká a ohrozenia*. Žilina: Žilinská univerzita v Žiline, 2004, p. 146:

HOLLIFIELD, F. J. (2012). Governing Migration. In: *Global Migration: Challenges in the Twenty-first Century*. New York: Palgrave Macmillan, Pages, 2012, pp. 183-209.

HOLLIFIELD, J. C. (2004). The Emerging Migration State. In: *International Migration Review*. Vol. 38, No. 3, 2004, pp. 885-912.

HOLSTI, K. (1970). National Role Conceptions in the Study of Foreign Policy. In: *International Studies Quarterly*. Vol. 14, No. 3, 1970, pp. 233–309.

HOLSTI, K. (1987). National Role Conceptions in the Study of Foreign Policy. In: *Role Theory and Foreign Policy Analysis*. Durham: Duke University Press, 1987, pp. 5–43.

HOLUB, P. (2017). Trestný čin jménem Čapí hnizdo. In: *ECHO 24*. 11.8.2017. [online]. Available at: goo.gl/6KTo5z. [Accessed 11/5/2018].

Immigrant Naturalization and its Impact on Immigrant Labour Market Performance and Treasury. (2008). In: *The Economics of Citizenship*. Malmo University, 2008.

Immigrants in Regional Markets of Host Nations: Some Evidence from Atlantic Canada. (2012). Springer Science Publishing, 2012.

Immigration New Zealand. (2013). Skilled Migrant Category Expression of Interest Guide INZ 1101 (Government of New Zealand—December, 2013).

INEKO. (2016). *Slovenský pracovný trh protrebuje pružnejšiu imigračnú politiku*. [online]. 2016. Available at: http://www.ineko.sk/projekty/potrebuje-slovensky-pracovny-trh-migraciu. [Accessed 7/10/2018].

INFO.CZ. (2017). Největším strašákem Čechů je podle průzkumu migrace, na životní úroveň si příliš nestěžují. In: *RAZ a ČTK*. 1. 10. 2017. [online]. Available at: goo.gl/sDTK3U. [Accessed 11/5/2018].

INNOCENTI, P. (2015*). Cultural Networks in Migrating Heritage: Intersecting Theories and Practices across Europe*. Farnham: Ashgate Publishing Limited, 2016, p. 166.

Integration of immigrants in the European Union. (2018). [online]. Brussels: European Commission, 2018, 271 p. Available at: http://ec.europa.eu/commfrontoffice/publicopinion/index.cfm/ResultDoc/download/DocumentKy/82537. [Accessed 20/4/2018].

Integration Policy of the Slovak Republic. (2014). [online]. Bratislava: The Ministry of Labour, Social Affairs and Family of the Slovak Republic, 2014, p. 40. Available at: https://www.employment.gov.sk/files/slovensky/ministerstvo/integracia-cudzincov/dokumenty/vlastny-material-integracna-politika-januar-2014.pdf. [Accessed 20/4/2018].

REFERENCES 215

International migrant stock: The 2017 revision. (2017). [online]. New York: United Nations, Department of Economic and Social Affairs, 2017. Available at: http://www.un.org/en/development/desa/population/migration/data/estimates2/data/UN_MigrantStockTotal_2017.xlsx. [Accessed 20/4/2018].

International Migration Report 2017. (2017). [online]. New York: United Nations Department of Economic and Social Affairs, 2017, p. 46. Available at: http://www.un.org/en/development/desa/population/migration/publications/migrationreport/docs/MigrationReport2017.pdf. [Accessed 20/4/2018].

IOM. (2008). *Labour Mobility. A win-win-win model for Trade and Development.* [online]. Geneva: IOM, Available at: http://www.iom.int/jahia/webdav/shared/shared/mainsite/projects/documents/gtdf_flyer_en.pdf. [Accessed 1/6/2018].

IOM. (2012). *Return Migration.* Geneva. *International Organization for Migration.* [online]. Available at: http://www.icm.int/jahia/Jahia/about-migration/ managing-migration/managing-migration-return-migration. [Accessed 30/5/2018].

IOM. (2016). *Referral Guide for Reintegration of Returnees in Armenia.* [online]. Available at: https://publications.iom.int/books/referral-guide-reintegration-returnees-armenia. [Accessed 30/5/2018].

IOM. (2017). *AVRR Statistical Sheet: Returns to Armenia and Georgia, from the EEA / EU 2015-16.* Brussels: IOM, 2017.

IOM. (2018a). *IOM in the World.* [online]. Official site of IOM Slovakia. Available at: https://www.iom.sk/en/iom/iom-in-the-world.html. [Accessed 1/6/2018].

IOM. (2018b). *Assisted Voluntary Return and Reintegration.* [online]. Available at: https://www.icm.int/assisted-voluntary-return-and-reintegration. [Accessed 23/8/2018].

JAKSICSOVÁ, V. (2017). Foreword. In: *"Spirits that I've cited…?" Vladimír Clementis (1902-1952). The political Biography of a Czechoslovak Communist.* Stuttgart, New York: ibidem, Columbia University Press, 2018, XV-XXXI.

JOYCE, S., WOODHOUSE, M. (2013). *Changes to attract more international students to NZ.* [online]. Available at: http://www.beehive.govt.nz/release/changes-attract-more-international-students-nz.

JUDT, T., SNYDER, T. (2012). *Thinking the Twentieth Century*. London: Penguin, 2012, p. 414.

KABÁT, J. (2011). *Psychologie komunismu*. Praha: Práh, 2011, p. 462.

KALM, S. (2010). Liberalizing Movements? The Political Rationality of Global Migration Management. In: *The Politics of International Migration Management*. Hampshire: Pallgrave. Macmillan, 2010, pp. 21-44.

KALOUS, J. (2012). KSČ jako iniciátor a vykonavatel politických čistek a procesů. In: *Český a slovenský komunismus (1921–2011)*. Praha: Ústav pro stadium totalitních režimů, 2012, pp. 87-93.

KAMARA. A. (2013). *International Students and Politics of Growth*. Ph. D. Dissertation. Dalhousie University, 2013.

KAPLAN, K. (1987). *The Short March. The Communist Takeover in Czechoslovakia 1945–1948*. London: Hurst & Co, 1987, 189 p.

KAZHARSKI, A. (2017). The End of 'Central Europe'? The Rise of the Radical Right and the Contestation of Identities in Slovakia and the Visegrad Four. In: *Geopolitics*. [online]. 2017. Available at: https://doi.org/10.1080/146500 45.2017.1389720. [Accessed 6/10/2018].

KDU-ČSL. (2013). *Volební program KDU-ČSL 2013-2017*. [online]. Available at: goo.gl/kAq9Gr. [Accessed 11/5/2018].

KDU-ČSL. (2017). *Zodpovědně pro společný domov. Volební program KDU-ČSL pro Sněmovní volby v roce 2017*. [online]. Available at: goo.gl/VMD7tU. [Accessed 11/5/2018].

KELLER, J. (2017). *Evropské rozpory ve světle migrace*. Praha: Slon, 2017, p. 227.

KISKA, A. (2015). *Vyhlásenie prezidenta Kisku k téme utečencov*. [online]. 2015. Available at: https://www.prezident.sk/article/vyhlasenie-prezidenta-kisku-k-teme-utecencov/. [Accessed 22/9/2015].

KISSOVA, L. (2017). The Production of (Un)deserving and (Un)acceptable: Shifting representations of Migrants within Political Discourse in Slovakia. [online]. In: *East European Politics and Societies and Cultures*. Available at: https://doi.org/10.1177/0888325417745127. [Accessed 6/4/2018].

KLÍMA, I. (2009). *Moje šílené století I*. Praha: Academia, 2009, 370 p.

KLÍMA, M. (2015). *Od totality k defektní demokracii*. Praha: Slon, 2015.

KOCH, A. (2014). The politics and discourse of migrant return: the role of UNHCR and IOM in the governance of return. In: *Journal of Ethnic and Migration Studies*. Vol. 40, No. 6, 2014, pp. 905-923.

KOCHOVÁ, J. (2016). Muslimové zaútočí v Česku. To vám media neřeknou. Policie vyvrací hoaxy, zapojila i nový úřad. In: *Aktuálně.cz*. 3.8.2016. [online]. Available at: goo.gl/vQhfzL. [Accessed 11/5/2018].

KOŁAKOWSKI, L. (2008). The Peasant Marxism of Mao Tse-tung. In: M*ain Currents of Marxism. The Founders. The Golden Age. The Breakdown*. New York, London: W. W. Norton & Company, 2008, pp. 1183-1205.

KOSER, K. (2011). *When is Migration a Security Issue?* [online]. Available at: https://www.brookings.edu/opinions/when-is-migration-a-security-issue/. [Accessed 1/6/2018].

KOSER, K., KUSCHMINDER, K. (2015). *Comparative Research on the Assisted Voluntary Return and Reintegration of Migrants*. Geneva: IOM, 2015.

KOSTLÁN, D. (2014). Kritický pohled na bezpečnostní diskurz migrace. In: *Sociológia*. Vol. 46, No. 4, 2014, pp. 393-411.

KOVÁČ, D. (2007). *Dejiny Slovenska*. Praha: Nakladatelství Lidové Noviny, 2007, p. 246.

KREISI, H. (2013). Introduction—The New Challenges to Democracy. In: *Democracy in the Age of Globalization and Mediatization*. London: Palgrave Macmillan, 2013, p. 250.

KRZYZANOWSKY, M. WODAK, R. (2009). *The Politics of Exclusion: Debating Migration in Austria*. New Jersey: Transaction Publishers, 2009.

KSČM. (2013). *S lidmi pro lidi*. [online]. Available at: goo.gl/NKX3Nh. [Accessed 11/5/2018].

KSČM. (2015). *Přístupy KSČM k problematice a příčinám migrace*. [online]. Available at: goo.gl/hszf29. [Accessed 11/5/2018].

KSČM. (2017). *Aktualizace přístupu KSČM k problematice a příčinám migrace*. Předkladatel: J. Dolejš 14. schůze VV ÚV KSČM ze dne 1.9.2017. Author's Archive.

KSČM. (2017). *Jsme váš hlas! Volební program KSČM pro volby do Poslanecké sněmovny Parlamentu České republiky 2017*. [online]. Available at: goo.gl/zdZDqq. [Accessed 11/5/2018].

KYMLICKA, W. (2007). The New Debate on Minority Rights (and Postscript). In: *Multiculturalism and Political Theory*. Cambridge: Cambridge University Press, 2007.

LASICOVÁ, J. (2006). *Bezpečnosť. Bezpečnostná agenda súčasnosti*. Banská Bystrica: Fakulta politických vied a medzinárodných vzťahov, Univerzita Mateja Bela, 2006, p. 162.

LASICOVÁ, J., UŠIAK, J. (2012). *Bezpečnosť ako kategória*. Bratislava: VEDA, 2012, p. 267.

LEERKES, A., OS, R., BOERSEMA, E. (2017). What drives 'soft deportation'? Understanding the rise in Assisted Voluntary Return among rejected asylum seekers in the Netherlands. In: *Population, Space and Place*. Vol. 23, No. 8, 2017, pp. 1-11.

LEVITT, P. (2001). *The transnational villagers*. Berkeley: University of California Press, 2001.

LEVITT, P. LAMBA-NIEVES, D. (2011). Social Remittances Revisited. In: *Journal of Ethnic and Migration Studies*. Vol. 37, No. 1, 2011, pp. 1-22.

LIĎÁK, J. (2016). Fenomén moslimského prisťahovalectva. In: *Verejná správa a spoločnosť*, Vol. 17, No. 1, 2016. pp. 11-19.

LIETAERT, I., DERLUYN, I., BROEKAERT, E. (2016). The boundaries of transnationalism: the case of assisted voluntary return migrants. In: *Global networks*. Vol. 17, No. 3, 2016, pp. 366-381.

LINZ, J. J. (1975). Totalitarian and Authoritarian Regimes. In: *Handbook of Political Science*. Vol. 3. Reading, MA: Addison-Wesley, 1975, pp. 175-411.

Lista asociațiilor, comunităților și grupurilor de inițiativă ale diasporei Republicii Moldova. [online]. Available at: http://brd.gov.md/ro/content/lista-asocia tiilor-comunitatilor-si-grupurilor-de-initiava-ale-diasporei-republicii-1. [Accessed 30/4/2018].

LOEWENSTEIN, B. (1995). My a ti druzí. In: *Sociologický časopis*. Vol. 31, No. 2, 1995.

LÜBBE, H. (1987). *Politischer Moralismus. Der Triumph der Gesinnung über die Urteilskraft*. Berlin: WJS Corso, 1987, p. 121.

LYNCH, R., OAKFORD, P. (2013). *The Economic Effects of Granting Legal Status and Citizenship to Undocumented Immigrants.* Washington, DC: Center for American Progress, 3/2013. [online]. Available at: http://www.americanprogress.org/wp-content/uploads/2013/03/EconomicEffectsCitizenship-1.pdf.

MAHROUM, S., ELDRIDGE, C., DAAR, A. (2006). Transnational diaspora options: how developing countries could benefit from their emigrant populations. In: *International Journal on Multicultural Societies.* Vol. 8, No. 1, 2006, pp.25-42.

MALÝ, L. (2017). *Projev na demonstraci DSSS v Praze na Můstku 17.11.2017.* [online]. Available at: http://www.facebook.com/groups/295203270559333/permalink/1522518184494496/.

MAREŠ, M. (2003). *Pravicový extremismus a radikalismus v ČR.* Brno: Barrister & Principal, 2003.

MAREŠ, M. et al. (2015). *Ne islámu! Protiislámská politika v České republice.* Brno: CDK, 2015.

MARTIN, P. (2003). Temporary Foreign Worker Programs: US and Global Experiences. In: *Canadian Issues/Themes Canadiens Spring.* 2003, pp. 122-28.

MATĚJNÝ, P. (2015). *Národní obroda—projev.* [online]. 17.11.2015. Available at: https://www.youtube.com/watch?v=jU8IAsH-V3U.

MCGINNITY, F., GROTTI, R., RUSSELL, H., FAHEY, É. (2018). *Attitudes to Diversity in Ireland. Research report.* Dublin: Irish Human Rights and Equality Commission/Economic and Social Research Institute. [online]. 2018. Available at: https://doi.org/10.26504/bkmnext350. [Accessed 5/10/2018].

MCGINNITY, F., KINGSTON, G. (2017). An Irish Welcome? Changing Irish Attitudes to Immigrants and Immigration: The Role of Recession and Immigration. In: *The Economic and Social Review.* Vol. 48, No. 3, 2017, pp. 253-79.

MICHÁLEK, S. (2013). Tri Dakoty—akcia "Erding". In: *Za hranicou Sloboda 1948–1953 (Dakoty 'slobody' a vlak do Selbu).* Bratislava: VEDA, 2013, pp. 149-216.

MICHÁLEK, S. (2013). *Za hranicou Sloboda 1948–1953 (Dakoty 'slobody' a vlak do Selbu).* Bratislava: VEDA, 2013, p. 339.

MICHÁLEK, S., LONDÁK, M. et al (2013). *Gustáv Husák. Moc politiky. Politik moci.* Bratislava: VEDA, 2013, p. 1067.

Migrant Crisis: Macedonia shuts Balkan Route. (2016). [online]. 9.3.2016. Available at: http://www.bbc.com/news/world-europe-35763101. [Accessed 7/6/2016].

Migrant/Migration. (2018). [online]. Available at: http://www.unesco.org/new/en/social-and-human-sciences/themes/international-migration/glossary/migrant/. [Accessed 4/11/2014].

Migration policy of the Slovak Republic: Perspective until the year 2020. (2011). [online] Bratislava: Government of the Slovak Republic, 2011, p. 19. Available at: https://www.minv.sk/?zamer-migracnej-politiky-slovenskej-republiky&subor=153759. [Accessed 20/4/2018].

MIHÁLIK, J. (2017). New-wave political leadership in Slovakia—populism and radicalism in the context of refugees´ crisis. In: *Annual Conference Faculty of Social Sciences UCM Trnava: A Political Science and European Studies.* Trnava: The Faculty of Social Sciences University of Ss. Cyril and Methodius in Trnava. 2017, pp. 159-172.

MILEKIC, S., TOE, R. (2015). Refugees Start Entering Croatia from Bosnia. In: *Balkan Insight.* [online]. 3.11.2015. Available at: http://www.balkaninsight.com/en/article/refugees-starting-to-enter-croatia-from-bosnia-11-03-2015. [Accessed 25/10/2015].

MILLET, R. (2012) Polemic chez gallimard apres la publication d'un eloge. In: *France info radio.* [online]. 27.8.2012. Available at: http://www.franceinfo.fr/societe/polemique-chez-gallimard-apres-la-publication-d-un-eloge-d-anders-breivik-par-719465-2012-08-27.

MINISTRSTVO ZA NOTRANJE ZADEVE REPUBLIKE SLOVENIJE. (2015). *Second Day of Salzburg Ministerial Meeting.* [online]. Available at: http://www.mnz.gov.si/en/media_room/news/article/12137/9258/5cc1f868934d80f0f9729bc78566165f/.

MINISTRSTVO ZA NOTRANJE ZADEVE. (2015). *Vlada sprejela Kontingentni načrt ob povečanem številu prosilcev za mednarodno žaščito.* [online]. 16.7.2015. Available at: http://www.mnz.gov.si/nc/si/novinarsko_sredisce/novica/article//9303/. [Accessed 25/10/2015].

MIPEX. (2015). *Migrant Integration Policy Index 2015. Migration.* [online]. 2015. Available at: http://www.mipex.eu/key-findings. [Accessed 19/7/2018].

MOSNEAGA, V. (2012). *Moldovan Labour Migrants in the European Union: Problems of Integration.* [online]. Available at: http://www.carim-east.eu/media/CARIM-East-2012-RR-41.pdf. [Accessed 30/4/2018].

MOSNEAGA, V. (2017). *Mapping moldovan diaspora in Germany, UK, Israel, Italy, Portugal and Russia.* Chişinău, 2017, p. 212.

MUDDE, C. (2011) Radical Right Parties in Europe: What, Who, Why? In: *Participation.* Vol. 34, 2011, pp. 12-14.

MUDDE, C. (2014). Fighting the System? Populist Radical Right Parties and Party System Change. In: *Party Politics.* Vol. 20, No. 2, 2014, pp. 217-226.

NAVARA, L., ALBRECHT, J. (2010). *Abeceda komunismu.* Brno: HOST, 2010, p. 235.

NEW ZEALAND DEPARTMENT OF LABOUR. (1999). *Migrant Settlement, A Review of the Literature and its Relevance to New Zealand.* 9/1999.

NEWLAND, K. (2017). *The Global Compact for Migration: How Does Development Fit In?.* [online] Washington, D. C.: Migration Policy Institute, 2017, p. 14. Available at: https://www.migrationpolicy.org/sites/default/files/publications/GlobalCompactForMigration-Brief1_FINALWEB.pdf. [Accessed 25/4/2018].

NEYFAKH, L. (2013). The Case for Regional Immigration. In: *The Boston Globe.* 7/7/2013.

NOVOTNÝ, L., ŠÁROVEC, D. (2018). Na vítězné vlně. Analýza úspěchu Alternativy pro Německo ve volbách do Spolkového sněmu 2017. In: *Politické vedy.* Vol. 21, No. 1, 2018, pp. 97-118.

O'REILLY, K. (2012). *International Migration & Social Theory.* London: Palgrave Macmillan, 2014. p. 182.

ODS. (2013). *Volební program. Volím pravici.* [online]. Available at: goo.gl/DT4twG. [Accessed 11/5/2018].

ODS. (2016). *Drsné vystoupení Fialy: Řízená migrace. Západní města, která budou za 20 let muslimská. Brusel má problem a přesunuje je k nám.* [online]. Available at: goo.gl/YJSzur. [Accessed 11/5/2018].

OECD. (2004). Trends. In: *International Migration.* Sopemi 2003 Edition, 2004.

OKAMURA, T. (2015). Jsme cílem invaze vetřelců. In *Právo.* 10.10.2015, p. 9.

OLEJÁROVÁ, B. (2017). Security concerns over the third-countries migration in the Slovak Republic. In: *SGEM 2017: 4th international multidisciplinary scientific conference on social sciences and arts.* Sofia: STEF92, 2017. pp. 983-990.

PALÚŠ, I. (2017) Teoreticko-právne východiská obecnej samosprávy (so zameraním na podmienky Slovenskej republiky. In: *Formy uskutočňovania obecnej samosprávy.* Košice: PJSU in Košice, 2017, pp. 14-27.

PANOSSIAN, R. (2006). *The Armenians: From kings and priests to merchants and commissars.* London: Hurst and Company, 2006.

PASTOR, M., SCOGGINS. J. (2012). *Citizen Gain: The Economic Benefits of Naturalization for Immigrants and the Economy.* Los Angeles: Center for the Study of Immigrant Integration, University of Southern California, 2012.

PAWŁOWSKA, K. (2017). Ethnic return of Armenian Americans: Perspectives. In: *Anthropological Notebooks.* Vol. 23, No. 1, 2017, pp. 93–109.

PIRÁTI. (2013). *Volební program Pirátů pro volby do sněmovny 2013.* [online]. Available at: goo.gl/Pf5MHK. [Accessed 11/5/2018].

PIRÁTI. (2015). *Postoj České pirátské strany k vlně uprchlíků.* 22.10.2015. [online]. Available at: goo.gl/dpZTh2. [Accessed 11/5/2018].

PIRÁTI. (2017). *Volební program. Černé na bílém. Pro volby 2017. Do Poslanecké sněmovny.* [online]. Available at: goo.gl/qgzrBF. [Accessed 11/5/2018].

PISKAČ, M. (2016). Příčiny migrace, multikulturalismu a vliv Židovství. In: *Národní obroda.* [online]. 24. 1. 2016. Available at: http://narodniobroda.cz /úvaha-priciny-migrace-multikulturalismu-a-vliv-zidovstvi.

PIUSSI, Z. (2016). *Czech Allah.* [video]. 91 min.

Po udalostiach v auguste 1968 odišlo z Československa množstvo odborníkov, vedcov a umelcov. (2017). [online] 19.8.2017. Available at: https://www.web noviny.sk/po-udalostiach-v-auguste-1968-odislo-z-ceskoslovenska-mnoz stvo-odbornikov-vedcov-a-umelcov.

POLICIJA REPUBLIKE SLOVENIJE. (2016). *Podatki o številu migrantov, ki so vstopili v Slovenijo do 2. februarja 2016 do 6. ure.* [online]. 2.2.2016. Available at: http://www.policija.si/index.php/component/content/ article/35-sporocila-za-javnost/82801-podatki-o-tevilu-migrantov-ki-so-vstopili-v-slovenijo-do-2-februarja-2016-do-6-ure-.

POROBIĆ, S. (2017). Daring 'life-return projects' to post-Dayton Bosnia and Herzegovina. In: *International Migration*. Vol. 55, No. 5, 2017, pp. 192-204.

Possibilities of Cooperation of Migration Office of Ministry of Interior of the Slovak Republic and ZMOS on integration of persons under international protection. (2016). [online] Bratislava: ZMOS, 2016, 12. Available at: http://www.zmos.sk/download_file_f.php?id=695310. [Accessed 20/4/2018].

PRIECEL, B., BELO-CABAN, V. (2016). *Migration and Asylum in the Conditions of the Slovak Republic*. Bratislava: European Social Fund, 2016, p. 63.

Programma Elettorale Lega: Ecco Le Proposte Di Salvini Per Le Elezioni. (2018). [online]. 2018. Available at: https://www.money.it/programma-elettorale-Lega-Nord-Salvini-elezioni-2018.

RAADSCHERLDER, J. VIGODA-GADOT, E. (2015). *Global Dimensions of Public Administration and Governance: A Comparative Voyage*. New Jersey: John Wiley and Sons, 2015, p. 576.

RATAJ, J. (2003). Český nacionalismus a identita v konceptu současných krajně pravicových hnutí v České republice. In: *Spory o dějiny*. Praha: Masarykův ústav AV ČR, 2003, pp. 44-83.

RATAJ, J. (2009). Národní demokracie jako alternativa zakladatelské koncepce československé demokracie. In: *Karel Kramář (1860-1937). Život a dílo*. Praha: Masarykův ústav AV ČR, Archiv AV ČR, 2009, pp. 509-518.

REALISTÉ. (2017). *33 Realistických kroků vpřed*. [online]. Available at: goo.gl/yucFxZ. [Accessed 11/5/2018].

ROBEJŠEK, P. (2015). Je nesporné, že část migrantů přichází škodit. In: *Právo*. 3. 10. 2015, p. 1.

RODRIGUES, M. J. (2001). The Open Method of Coordination as a New Governance Tool. In: *Journal Europa: Novas Fronteiras*. Special Issue 2-3, 2001, pp. 96-107.

ROY, C. (1980). *Nous*. Paris: Gallimard, 1980, pp. 389-390.

RTV SLOVENIJA. (2015). *Erjavec: kvotam ne bomo nasprotovali; lahko sprejmemo 2000 prebežnikov*. [online]. 4.9.2015 Available at: http://www.rtvslo.si/slovenija/erjavec-kvotam-ne-bomo-nasprotovali-lahko-sprejmemo-2-000-prebeznikov/373224.

RUHS, M. (2002). *Temporary Foreign Worker Programmes: Policies, Adverse Consequences, and the Need to Make Them Work*. Center for Comparative Immigration Studies, Working Paper No. 56. San Diego: University of California, 2002.

RUHS, M., MARTIN, P. (2008). Numbers vs. Rights: Trade-offs and Guest Worker Programs. In: *International Migration Review*. Vol. 42, No. 1, 2008, pp. 249-65.

RUIZ, N. G., WILSON, J. H., CHOUDHURY, S. (2012). *The Search for Skills: Demand for H- 1B Immigrant Workers in U.S. Metropolitan Areas*. The Metropolitan Policy Program at Brookings Institution, Washington D.C., 2012.

RYS, J. (2016). *Hilsneriáda a TGM*. Praha: ABB, 2016.

SAFRAN, W. (1991). Diasporas in modern societies: Myths of homeland and return. In: *Diaspora: A journal of transnational studies*. Vol. 1, No. 1, 1991, pp. 83-99.

SCHAIN, M. A. (2018). *Shifting tides: Radical-right populism and immigration policy in Europe and the United States*. Washington, D.C.: Migration Policy Institute.

SCHOLTEN, P. (2018). Beyond Migrant Integration Policies: Rethinking the Urban Governance of Migration-Related Diversity. In: *Croatian and Comparative Public Administration*. Vol. 18, No. 1, 2018, pp. 7-30.

SHARMA, N. (2007). Freedom to Discriminate: A National State Sovereignty and Temporary Migrant Workers in Canada. In: *Citizenship and Immigrant Incorporation*. New York: Palgrave Macmillan, 2007, pp. 163-68.

SHEFFER, G. (1986). *Modern diasporas in international politics*. London: Taylor and Francis, 1986.

ŠIMÁK, L. (2006). *Manažment rizík*. Žilina: Žilinská univerzita v Žiline, Fakulta špeciálneho inžinierstva, 2006, p. 116.

SINATTI, G., HORST, J. (2015). Migrants as agents of development: Diaspora engagement discourse and practice in Europe. In: *Ethnicities*. Vol. 15, No. 1, 2015, pp. 134-152.

SINGER, P. (2016). *One World Now: The Ethics of Globalization*. New Haven: Yale University Press. 2016, p. 280.

SITEK, P. (2011). (Národní) identita a integrace přistěhovalců do společnosti ve Francii: úroveň diskursů a každodenní žitá realita. In: *Etnické komunity. Integrace. Identita.* Praha: FHS UK, 2011, pp. 29–70.

SLOVAK SPECTATOR. (2010). *Lipšic: multiculturalism doesn't work.* [online]. 9.8.2010. Available at: http://spectator.sme.sk/articles/view/39730/2/lipsic_multiculturalism_doesnt_work.html. [Accessed 8/10/2018].

SME. (2018). *Fico: Krik bratislavských kaviarní ma nezaujíma, komunity moslimov odmietam.* [online]. 26. 1. 2018. Available at: https://domov.sme.sk/c/20747239/fico-krik-bratislavksych-kaviarni-ma-nezaujima-moslimske-komunity-odmietam.html. [Accessed 8/10/2018].

SPD. (2017). *Politický program.* [online]. Available at: http://www.spd.cz/program. [Accessed 11/5/2018].

SPOONLEY, P., BEDFORD, R. (2012). *Welcome to our world? Immigration and the reshaping of New Zealand.* Auckland: Dunmore Publishing, 2012.

SPR-RSC. (2017). *Stručný výtah z programu.* [online]. Available at: goo.gl/QTbXAe. [Accessed 11/5/2018].

STAHL, C., APPLEYARD, R. (1992). International Manpower Flows in Asia: An Overview. In: *Asian and Pacific Migration Journal.* Vol. 1, No. 3–4, 1992, pp. 417-476.

STATE MIGRATION SERVICES. (2017). *2017-2021 Strategy for migration policy of the Republic of Armenia.* [online]. Available at: http://smsmta.am/upload/Migration_Strategy_2017-2021_english.pdf. [Accessed 30/5/2018].

Statistical Overview of Legal and Illegal Migration in the Slovak Republic. (2017). [online] Bratislava Presidium of the Police Force, 2017. Available at: http://www.minv.sk/swift_data/source/policia/hranicna_a_cudzinecka_policia/rocenky/rok_2017/2017-rocenka-UHCP-EN.pdf. [Accessed 2/4/2018].

STATISTICS NEW ZEALAND. (2006). *Quick Stats about Culture and Identity: Birthplace and People born Overseas.* Ottawa, 3/2006. [Accessed 19/11/2013].

STEINMAYR, A. (2018). *Did the Refugee Crisis Contribute to the Recent Rise of Far-Right Parties in Europe?* ifo DICE Report, Vol. 15, No. 4, pp. 24-27.

ŠTEVULOVÁ, Z. (2017). Uncovered Frames of Slovak Migration Policy Responses. In: *Listen to Us, Too! Flight, Migration and Integration from the Perspective of NGOs in the Visegrad Region*. Bratislava: Friedrich Ebert Stiftung, 2017, pp. 16-18.

STURGE G., BILGILI, Ö., SIEGEL, M. (2016). Migrants' capacity as actors of development: do skills matter for economic and social remittances? In: *Global Networks*, Vol. 16, No. 4, 2016, pp. 470-489.

SUMPTION, M., FLAMM, S. (2012). *The Economic Value of Citizenship for Immigrants in the United States*. Migration Policy Institute, 2012. [online]. Available at: http://carnegie.org/fileadmin/Media/Publications/mpi_econ_value_citizenship_01.pdf.

Svetové združenie bývalých československých politických väzňov: Po vpáde armád Varšavského paktu emigrovalo vyše 400.000 občanov. (2015). In: DennikN. [online]. 21.8.2015.

SVOBODNÍ. (2017). *Volební program 2017: Máme na to být svobodnou zemí. Svobodní ve Sněmovně v roce 2017*. [online]. Available at: goo.gl/pG3Lmm. [Accessed 11/5/2018].

TA3. (2015). *V politike: Bezpečnosť Slovenska*. [online]. 15.11.2015. Available at: https://www.ta3.com/clanok/1072856/bezpecnost-slovenska.html. [Accessed 21/4/2018].

TABERY, E. (2017). *Opuštěná společnost. Česká cesta od Masaryka po Babiše*. Praha: Paseka, 2017.

TEJCHMANOVÁ, L. (2017). Populistické či krajně pravicové politické strany ve vybraných státech Evropské unie. In: *Extremismus, radikalismus, populismus a euroskepticismus*. Praha: UJAK, 2017, pp. 179-419.

The Slow Death of Andreas Baader. (2004). [online]. Available at: https://www.marxists.org/reference/archive/sartre/1974/baader.htm. [Accessed 11/4/2017]

THOMSON, C. (2013). Frontiers and Threats: Should Transnational Migration Be Considered a Security Issue? In: *Global Policy*. [online]. Available at: http://www.globalpolicyjournal.com/blog/20/11/2013/frontiers-and-threats-should-transnationalmigration-be-considered-security-issue. [Accessed 1/6/2018].

REFERENCES

Toolkit on International Migration. (2012). [online] New York: United Nations, Department of Economic and Social Affairs, 2012. 15 p. Available at: http://www.un.org/en/development/desa/population/migration/publicatio ns/others/docs/toolkit_DESA_June%202012.pdf. [Accessed 10/4/2018].

TOP 09. (2013). *Volby 2013 do Poslanecké sněmovny.* [online]. Available at: goo.gl/XdpwbH [Accessed 11/5/2018].

TOP 09. (2017). *Volební program.* [online]. Available at: goo.gl/8GFzTP. [Accessed 11/5/2018].

UHLOVÁ, S. (2017). Hrdinové kapitalistické práce. In: *A2larm.* 5.9.2017. [online]. Available at: goo.gl/MbRQhw. [Accessed 11/5/2018].

UN. (2002). *Declaration of the Hague on the Future of Refugee and Migration Policy.* [online]. Hague: OSN. Available at: http://thehagueprocess.org/wordpress/wp-content/uploads/2012/12/Declaration-English.pdf. [Accessed 1/6/2018].

Une solution européenne à la crise des réfugiés. (2018) [online]. Available at: https://en-marche.fr/articles/actualites/crise-migrants-europe.

UNHCR. (2018). *What is a refugee.* [online]. Available at: https://www.unrefu gees.org/refugee-facts/what-is-a-refugee/.

UNITED NATIONS, DEPARTMENT OF ECONOMIC AND SOCIAL AFFAIRS. (2017). *International Migration Report 2017 (Highlights).* [online]. 2017. Available at: http://www.un.org/en/development/desa/population/migration/publications/migrationreport/docs/MigrationReport 2017_Highlights.pdf. [Accessed 15/7/2018].

UNITED NATIONS. (2009). *Trends in International Migrant Stock: The 2008 Revisions.* Department of Economic and Social Affairs, Population Division, 2009.

UPDTO. (2013). *Hnutí Úsvit—Program.* [online]. Available at: goo.gl/9cggX8. [Accessed 11/5/2018].

ÚRAD VLÁDY SLOVENSKEJ REPUBLIKY. (2015). *TB Predsedu vlády SR R. Fica a ministra obrany SR M. Glváča k teroristickým útokom v Paríži.* [online]. 2015. Available at: http://www.vlada.gov.sk/tb-predsedu-vlady-sr-r-fica-a-ministra-obrany-sr-m-glvaca-k-teroristickym-utokom-v-parizi/. [Accessed 7/10/2018].

UŠIAK, J., NEČAS, P. (2011). Societálny a politický sektor v kontexte bezpečnosti štátu. [online]. In: *Politické vedy*. Vol. 14, No. 1, 2011. pp. 30-49. Available at: http://www.fpvmv.umb.sk/userfiles/file/1_2011/USIAK_NECAS.pdf. [Accessed 1/6/2018].

VÁCLAVÍK, L. (2017). Každý desátý Čech je v exekuci. Unikátní mapa vám ukáže,kde dluží nejvíce. In: *enews.cz*. 5. 4. 2017. [online]. Available at: goo.gl/PvWj2R. [Accessed 11/5/2018].

VAN HOUTE, M., DAVIDS, T. (2008). Development and Return Migration: From Policy Panacea to Migrant Perspective Sustainability. In: *Third World Quarterly*. Vol. 29, No. 7, 2008, pp. 1411-1429.

VEJVODOVÁ, P. (2015). Neonacistická vize sjednocené Evropy a její kořeny v nacistické ideologii. In: *Politické vedy*. Vol. 18, No. 3, 2015, pp. 194-213.

VEJVODOVÁ, P., SMOLÍK, J. (2013). Základní ideové zdroje současné krajní pravice v ČR. In: *Slovak Journal of Political Sciences*. Vol. 12, No. 2, pp. 101-115.

VISEGRAD GROUP. (2015). *Joint Statement of the Heads of Government of the Visegrad Countries*. [online]. 2015. Available at: www.visegradgroup/eu/calendar/2015/joint-statement-of-the-150904. [Accessed 8/10/2018].

VOTE LEAVE. (2018). *Why Vote Leave*. [online]. 2018. Available at: http://www.voteleavetakecontrol.org/why_vote_leave.html. [Accessed 12/7/2018.].

Vrahov z augusta 1968 nikto nepotrestal. Okupácia menila osudy ľudí. (2013). In: Sme.sk. [online]. 20.8.2013.

WAISOVÁ, Š., CABADA, L. (2009). *Etika a mezinárodní politika*. Plzeň: Aleš Čeněk, 2009.

WHITE HOUSE. (2013). *Fixing Our Broken Immigration System: The Economics Benefits of Providing a Path to Earned Citizenship*. Washington D.C.: The Executive of the President, 8/2013.

WILSON, H. (2013). *Leaders' Roundtable on Immigration. Australian High Commissioner to Canada*. Power Point Presentation. Ottawa: Conference Board of Canada, 4/12/2013.

WOHLFELD, M. (2014). Is Migration a Security Issue? In: *Migration in the Mediterranean: Human Rights, Security and Development Perspectives.* [online]. University of Malta, 2014. pp. 61-77. Available at: https://www.um.edu.mt/__data/assets/pdf_file/0018/232335/Chapter_6.pdf. [Accessed 1/6/2018].

World Migration Report 2018. (2017). [online] Geneva: International Organization for Migration, 2017, p. 364. Available at: http://publications.iom.int/system/files/pdf/wmr_2018_en.pdf. [Accessed 4/4/2018].

World Public Sector Report 2018. (2018). [online] New York: United Nations, Department of Economic and Social Affairs, 2018, p. 190. Available at: http://workspace.unpan.org/sites/Internet/Documents/UNPAN98152.pdf. [Accessed 20/4/2018].

ŽAKOVÁ, M. BEROVÁ, L. (2014). Public Opinion on Migrants and Their Integration in Slovakia. In: *International Multidisciplinary Scientific Conferences on Social Sciences and Arts.* Albena: SGEM2014 Conference Proceedings, 2014, pp. 697-704.

ZEITLHOFER, H. (2011). Czechia and Slovakia. In: *The Encyclopedia of Migration and Minorities in Europe: From the 17th Century to the Present.* Cambridge: Cambridge University Press, 2011, pp. 152-160.

ZELENÍ. (2017). *Volební program Zelených Pro volební období 2017-2021.* [online]. Available at: goo.gl/XpSgbr. [Accessed 11/5/2018].

ŽOFČINOVÁ, V. (2015). Social Rights and Dignified Work in Labour Law Relations. In: *Ius et Administratio.* Vol. 12, No. 3, 2015, pp. 58-67.

ŽUPOVÁ, E. (2017). Vzdelanie starostov obcí na Slovensku a problematika odbornosti v územnej samospráve. In: *Sociology and Society.* Vol. 2, No. 1, 2017, pp. 24-41.

ŽURNAL 24. (2015) *Begunci v Sloveniji, na Rigoncah največja skupina.* [online]. 22. 10. 2015. Available at: http://www.zurnal24.si/begunci-v-sloveniji-na-rigoncah-najvecja-skupina-doslej-spet-nenapovedana-clanek-258634. [Accessed 30/10/2015].

МОШНЯГА, В. (2000). Население Молдовы и трудовая миграция: состояние и современные формы. Кишинэу: CAPTES. 200 p.

МОШНЯГА, В., ЦУРКАН, В., МОШНЯГА, Г. (2018). Современная миграция молдавского населения: основные причины и мотивы (по результатам социологических исследований в Великобритании, Германии, Израиле, Италии, России и Португалии). In: *MOLDOSCOPIE (Probleme de analiză politică)*. No. 1 (LXXX), 2018, p. 84-99.

Studied corpus contained sources from:

Ministrstvo za notranje zadeve. Available at: http://www.mnz.gov.si/.

Ministrstvo za zunanje zadeve. Available at: http://www.mzz.gov.si.

RTV Slovenija. Available at: http://www.rtvslo.si/begunska-kriza.

Vlada Republike Slovenije. Available at: http://www.vlada.si.

President Republike Slovenije. Available at: http://www.up-rs.si.

Slovenska Policija. Available at: http://www.policija.si.

ABOUT THE AUTHORS

Jarmila ANDROVIČOVÁ
    Faculty of Political Science and International Relations, Matej Bel University in Banská Bystrica, Slovakia,
    e-mail: jarmila.androvicova@umb.sk

Josette BAER HILL
    Faculty of Philosophy, University of Zurich UZH, Switzerland,
    e-mail: baerjose@gmail.com

Martina BOLEČEKOVÁ
    Faculty of Political Science and International Relations, Matej Bel University in Banská Bystrica, Slovakia,
    e-mail: martina.bolecekova@umb.sk

Milan ČÁKY
    Faculty of Social Sciences, University of Ss. Cyril and Methodius in Trnava, Slovakia,
    e-mail: milan.caky@ucm.sk

Ondřej FILIPEC
    Faculty of Social Sciences, University of Ss. Cyril and Methodius in Trnava, Slovakia,
    e-mail: ondrej.filipec@ucm.sk

Karen HENDERSON
    Faculty of Social Sciences, University of Ss. Cyril and Methodius in Trnava, Slovakia,
    e-mail: khenderson@netax.sk

Hana HLAVÁČKOVÁ
    Metropolitan University Prague, Czech Republic,
    e-mail: hana.hlavackova@mup.cz

Sven KRÜGER
(London), PhD-candidate Comenius University (Bratislava), Berlin, Germany
e-mail: nevsberlin@web.de

Lucie MACKOVÁ
Faculty of Science, Palacký University in Olomouc, Czech Republic,
e-mail: lucie.mackova@upol.cz

Ludmila MALIKOVÁ
Faculty of Social Sciences, University of Ss. Cyril and Methodius in Trnava, Slovakia,
e-mail: lmalikova@gmail.com

Jaroslav MIHÁLIK
Faculty of Social Sciences, University of Ss. Cyril and Methodius in Trnava, Slovakia,
e-mail: jaroslav.mihalik@ucm.sk

Ondrej MITAĽ
Faculty of Public Administration, Pavol Jozef Šafárik University in Košice, Slovakia,
e-mail: ondrej.mital@upjs.sk

Gheorghe MOSNEAGA
Laboratory "Sociology of Politics", Moldova State University, Chisinau, Republic of Moldova,
e-mail: gheorghemosneaga@gmail.com

Valeriu MOSNEAGA
Faculty of Social Sciences, University of Ss. Cyril and Methodius in Trnava, Slovakia,
e-mail: vals6412@gmail.com

Jan RATAJ
Faculty of Social Sciences, University of Ss. Cyril and Methodius in Trnava, Slovakia,
e-mail: jan.rataj@ucm.sk

Tatiana TURCO
Faculty of International Relations, Political and Administrative Sciences, Moldova State University, Chisinau, Republic of Moldova,
e-mail: turcotatiana27@gmail.com

ibidem.eu